BIBLE PUZZLERS!

ACROSTICS, CROSSWORDS, CRYPTOSCRIPTURES, WORD SEARCHES, & MORE!

BARBOUR
PUBLISHING

© 2021 by Barbour Publishing, Inc.

ISBN 978-1-63609-031-3

Published by Barbour Publishing, Inc., 1810 Barbour Drive, Uhrichsville, Ohio 44683, www.barbourbooks.com

Our mission is to inspire the world with the life-changing message of the Bible.

Printed in the United States of America.

WELCOME TO
BIBLE PUZZLERS!

So you love the Bible? Enjoy word puzzles? Then this is the book for you!

Scattered throughout the pages of this book are eleven types of fun, challenging, and educational puzzles, all based on the world's greatest Book—the Bible. Exercise your knowledge of scripture and your puzzle-solving abilities as you work your way through the following puzzles:

Drop Twos (see page 5): Remove two letters from each seven-letter word in the left-hand column to create a new five-letter word (you may need to rearrange the remaining letters). Put the two dropped letters into the spaces to the right of the blanks. Then use these letters to spell out a phrase or sentence from the Bible.

Acrostics (see page 6): Read the definition in the left-hand column and write the word it describes in the right-hand column. Then place the coded letters from the right-hand column in the puzzle form following to spell out the verse indicated.

Word Searches (see page 8): Find and circle the search words in the puzzle grid—words may run forward, backward, up, down, and on the diagonal. When a scripture passage is given, find the words highlighted in **bold type**. If a phrase is underlined, those words are found together within the puzzle.

Cryptoscriptures (see page 10): Each of the cryptoscriptures is a Bible verse in substitution code. For example, JEHOVAH might become MPXSTQX if M is substituted for J, P for E, X for H, and so on. One way to break the code is to look for repeated letters: E, T, A, O, N, R, and I are the most often used. A single letter is usually A or I. OF, IT, and IS are common two-letter words. Try THE and AND for a three-letter group. The code is different for each cryptoscripture. (There are two cryptoscriptures per page.)

Bible Sudoku (see page 11): Each 9x9 grid includes "givens," as with traditional sudoku puzzles. In this case, the givens are nine unique letters—which will spell out a biblical word or phrase. The nine-letter word or phrase is determined from the scripture printed below the puzzle. Solving the puzzle involves placing the nine letters in each row, column, and 3x3 minigrid (the white and shaded areas) so that no letter is duplicated in a row, column, or minigrid. Use your skills of deduction!

Crosswords (see page 12): Fill in the puzzle grid by starting answers in the appropriately numbered boxes and continuing either across to the right or down. Capitalized clues have answers that relate to the theme of the puzzle.

Scrambled Circles (see page 18): Unscramble the words from the list provided, placing the corrected words in the blanks corresponding with the numbers. Then use the circled letters to answer the question that follows.

Anagrams (see page 19): Unscramble the letters of the word or phrase given to create another word or phrase from the Bible.

Spotty Headlines (see page 24): Fill in the missing letters of each "headline," which relates to a Bible story. Then unscramble the letters you've added to the headline to form a name, which is the subject of the headline.

Telephone Scrambles (see page 25): Each set of telephone push-buttons contains a hidden Bible word—and you'll need to determine which letter of each combination is part of the word.

Bible Quotations (see page 30): Place the letters in each column into the puzzle grid preceding to form words. The letters may or may not fit into the grid in the same order in which they're given; black spaces indicate the ends of words. When a letter has been used, cross it off and do not use it again. When the grid has been properly filled in, you'll be able to read a Bible verse by scanning the lines of the grid from left to right.

Most clues are direct quotations taken from the King James Version of the Bible, though some newer translations have also been referenced for variety. Puzzle answers begin on page 317.

BORN AGAIN

JOHN 3:1

When others were sleeping, a man came to Jesus, curious as to what it meant for a grown man to be born again. Can you solve this puzzle to determine the name and position of this nighttime caller?

NETBALL	Sheep's cry	_____	1. __ __
ISATINE	Smooth fabric	_____	2. __ __
CHARTED	Detested	_____	3. __ __
PLATOON	Place flowers	_____	4. __ __
FLANGED	Sharp corner	_____	5. __ __
EGALITY	Cheerfully	_____	6. __ __
MARCHED	Followed a curve	_____	7. __ __
EPAULET	Shallow dish	_____	8. __ __
JOBLESS	Tree trunks	_____	9. __ __
EYEBALL	Stomach	_____	10. __ __
WHARVES	Remove beard	_____	11. __ __
STADIUM	Acknowledge	_____	12. __ __

__ __ __ __ __ __ __ __ __ __ __ __

1 2 3 4 5 6 7 8 9 10 11 12

ACROSTIC
by Donna K. Maltese

═══ ASP FOR HEALING ═══

Solve this acrostic to discover how Moses took the bite out of the people's gripping affliction.

What the snakes were described as (Numbers 21:6)

___ ___ ___ ___ ___
40 34 18 4   25

Snakes bit the people because they'd done this
(Numbers 21:5–6)

___ ___ ___ ___ ___ ___ ___ ___ ___ ___
11 23 38 31 19 7   26 3   15 28

Full of poison

___ ___ ___ ___ ___ ___ ___ ___
10 29 17 35 2   39 21 8

Moses was a _____ of Christ

___ ___ ___ ___
30 12 24 6

To die

___ ___ ___ ___ ___ ___
16 5   20 32 37 9

Moses stood _____ God and the people

___ ___ ___ ___ ___ ___ ___
27 36 1   14 22 13 33

7-17-28   38-23-8-15-8   38-7-28-36   7   37-6-20-31-6-17-30

35-40   27-4-7-8-8,   7-3-28   16-21-1   26-1

21-24-39-33   7   16-39-19-29,   7-3-28   26-1   11-7-38-29

1-35   16-7-8-8,   1-9-7-1   32-40   7   37-6-20-31-6-17-30

9-7-28   27-34-1-1-13-33   7-3-12   38-7-3,   14-9-22-33

9-5   27-18-9-18-19-28   1-9-5   37-6-20-31-6-17-30

35-40   27-4-7-8-8,   9-5   19-34-10-5-28.

NUMBERS 21:9

WORD SEARCH
by Marijane G. Troyer

■ SAMSON DEFEATS THE PHILISTINES ■
JUDGES 13–16

ASS	LORD
BARREN	MANOAH
CAMP	NAZARITE
CARCASE	OUT
CHILD	PHILISTINES
DAGON	PILLARS
DAN	RAZOR
DELILAH	RIDDLE
DRINK NOT	ROOF
ENTICE	SAMSON
FIREBRANDS	TAIL
FOXES	THREE HUNDRED
HEAD	TOP
HONEY	UNCLEAN
HOUSE FELL	WIFE
JAWBONE	WINE
LAD	WITH ALL HIS MIGHT
LEAN	WOMAN
LION	

```
N A Z A R I T E N I W H R P T
F I R E B R A N D S M I I H H
O K J D N A E L C N U L F I G
X L A R D L I H C D L D I E I
E L W I H N O S M A S A C R M
S E B N O A L P R E T N A T S
K F O K N T L S N H U Z M P I
E E N N E A E I F O O R P R H
C S E O Y S T D L R K J I T L
I U Y T A S P R P E D D D M L
T O A C I S N O G A D U A N A
N H R L H E T L I L E N I L H
E A I S I F N A E L O L I A T
C H N A M O W S B A R R E N I
P Q D E R D N U H E E R H T W
```

CRYPTOSCRIPTURE
by *Sharon Y. Brown*

▬▬▬▬ IN THE DAYS OF NOAH ▬▬▬▬

A vessel of the Lord's mercy, Noah followed God's instructions to a T. Solve these cryptoscriptures to learn more about God's pre-flood conversation with Noah, a man who was definitely on a learning curve—or, rather, a learning ark.

MEK XLK VMUK BEJL ELMO, JOR REK LA MHH

AHRVO UV FLZR SRALGR ZR; ALG JOR RMGJO

UV AUHHRK TUJO NULHREFR JOGLBXO JORZ;

MEK, SROLHK, U TUHH KRVJGLD JORZ TUJO JOR

RMGJO.

YXS VG WFWZP NEFEXA DCEXA VG YNN

GNWHC, DKV VG WFWZP HVZD HCYND DCVB

UZEXA EXDV DCW YZL, DV LWWT DCWO YNEFW

KEDC DCWW; DCWP HCYNN UW OYNW YXS

GWOYNW.

EHUD'S DEATH

EASY

	A	B	C	D	E	F	G	H	I
1	S					C	L		F
2			O		S			E	
3	L	A	F		E	D	S	C	
4		S		F			E	D	C
5	O	F		C	D				
6			L			E			O
7	E		C		F			A	
8		L		D			C		E
9	T		S	E	C		F		D

Hint: Column I

"And the haft also went in after the blade; and the _____ _____ upon the blade, so that he could not draw the dagger out of his belly; and the dirt came out" (Judges 3:22).

CROSSWORD
by David K. Shortess

■ CLIMBING THE WALLS ■

Instead of climbing the walls—figuratively, of course—spend some time working this crossword. Then let the blessing of Psalm 122:7 sink into your heart and home: *"May there be peace within your walls and security within your citadels"* (NIV).

ACROSS

1 "____ a mocker" (Proverbs 19:25 NIV)
5 "A swelling, ____ or a bright spot" (Leviticus 14:56 NIV) (2 words)
10 "Rehob, toward ____ Hamath" (Numbers 13:21 NIV)
14 "The scarlet ____ in the window" (Joshua 2:21)
15 French river up north
16 "By ____ and living way" (Hebrews 10:20) (2 words)
17 LOCATION OF RAHAB'S HOUSE (Joshua 2:15) (4 words)
20 "Upon the great ____ of his right foot" (Leviticus 8:23)
21 "Have we not all ____ father?" (Malachi 2:10)
22 Formerly Shima Province, Japan, ____ prefecture
23 "And I ____ a vision" (Daniel 8:2) (2 words)
26 Follows *novel-* or *romantic-*
28 "____ younger men as brothers" (1 Timothy 5:1 NIV)
30 WHAT EZEKIEL SAW BY THE DOOR OF THE COURT (Ezekiel 8:7) (5 words)
33 "Were cast into the ____ of fire" (Revelation 20:14)
34 "Behold, I will ____ new thing" (Isaiah 43:19) (2 words)
35 "To him that weareth the ____ clothing" (James 2:3)
36 Lincoln
37 Carnival workers
39 "I am like an ____ of the desert" (Psalm 102:6)
42 Sound from a massage recipient
43 Orthodontist's degree (abbr.)
44 "Am I ____, or a whale" (Job 7:12) (2 words)

45 WHERE THEY PUT THE BODY OF SAUL (1 Samuel 31:10) (3 words)
49 Salsa base
50 Another northern French river
51 "Thou hast asked ____ thing" (2 Kings 2:10) (2 words)
52 Follows *switcher-* and *tab-*
53 G. H. W. Bush was once its director
55 Greek *h*
56 WHERE EZEKIEL SAW CHERUBIMS AND PALM TREES (Ezekiel 41:20) (4 words)
63 "The ants ____ people not strong" (Proverbs 30:25) (2 words)
64 "All of you be on the ____" (Joshua 8:4 NIV)
65 Relative of altitude (abbr.)
66 Hardy heroine
67 "From the tower of ____ shall they fall" (Ezekiel 30:6)
68 "And they shall ____" (Jeremiah 50:36)

DOWN

1 Winter bug
2 "They shoot out the ____" (Psalm 22:7)
3 "Beth Aven, lead ____ Benjamin" (Hosea 5:8 NIV) (2 words)
4 "And also of the ____" (Romans 2:9)
5 "____ that setteth snares" (Jeremiah 5:26) (2 words)
6 "As light of foot as a wild ____" (2 Samuel 2:18)
7 Relative of quantity (abbr.)
8 "And I am a ____ man" (Genesis 27:11)
9 "Was ____ in stone" (Luke 23:53)
10 "Will not do the ____ of thy God" (Ezra 7:26)
11 Cloisonné covering
12 "The children of ____" (2 Chronicles 13:7)

13 Hooting chick
18 "Be with you now and change my _____" (Galatians 4:20 NIV)
19 "With so many the _____ not torn" (John 21:11 NIV) (2 words)
23 "Which was the son of _____" (Luke 3:35)
24 Omri's son (1 Kings 16:28)
25 "Then I _____ up" (Genesis 41:21 NIV)
26 "Took thee _____ naked" (Matthew 25:38) (2 words)
27 "Which say, _____ thyself" (Isaiah 65:5) (2 words)
29 "Without a _____ of brightness?" (Amos 5:20 NIV)
31 Utah neighbor
32 Discharge
37 Multicolored cat
38 July 15, for one
39 Government safety group (abbr.)
40 "Thou wilt surely _____ away" (Exodus 18:18)

41 "Rowed hard to bring it to the _____" (Jonah 1:13)
42 "Hear, _____ ye people" (Micah 1:2)
44 Opposite of proud
45 "And said, _____ those with thee?" (Genesis 33:5) (2 words)
46 Bridal paths
47 Categorically
48 "For either he will _____ the one" (Matthew 6:24)
49 "Every _____ that which is before her" (Amos 4:3) (2 words)
54 "_____ one people speaking the same language" (Genesis 11:6 NIV) (2 words)
55 Suffix meaning "little one"
57 _____ Cruces, NM
58 Haw's TV partner
59 Directional suffix
60 Arafat's group
61 "_____ there be light" (Genesis 1:3)
62 Cain's mother (Genesis 4:1)

ACROSTIC
by Donna K. Maltese

◼◼◼◼◼ SPINNING WHEELS ◼◼◼◼◼

Crack the code to find out what wheels were spinning for Ezekiel when he witnessed this glorious sight!

A supernatural sight

___ ___ ___ ___ ___ ___
27 32 14 9   24 13

Where the Jews were in exile (Ezekiel 17:12)

___ ___ ___ ___ ___ ___ ___
15 2   23 19 31 20 7

Ezekiel's calling (Ezekiel 2:5)

___ ___ ___ ___ ___ ___ ___
26 3   12 21 8   16 1

Each being had four of these (Ezekiel 1:6)

___ ___ ___ ___ ___
34 28 17 4   10

Each being also had four of these appendages (Ezekiel 1:6)

___ ___ ___ ___ ___
6   30 25 11 18

Seeing this sight, Ezekiel must have been struck _____

___ ___ ___ ___
22 5   29 33

14

6-8-4-13   1-8-4   31-32-27-30-7-11   17-3-4-28-1-5-3-4-10

6-16-25-1,   1-8-4   6-8-4-4-31-18   6-16-25-1   23-19

1-8-4-29:   2-7-22   6-8-4-13   1-8-4   31-32-27-30-7-11

17-3-4-28-1-5-3-4-10   6-16-3-16   31-9-34-1-16-22   5-26

34-3-12-29   1-8-4   4-28-3-1-8,   1-8-4   6-8-4-4-31-14

6-16-3-16   31-9-34-1-16-22   5-21.

EZEKIEL 1:19

LADDER TO HEAVEN
GENESIS 28:10–12

And **Jacob** went out **from Beersheba**, and **went toward Haran**. And he **lighted** upon a **certain** place, and **tarried there** all **night**, **because** the sun was set; and he **took** of the **stones** of that place, and put **them** for his **pillows**, and lay **down** in **that place** to **sleep**. And he **dreamed**, and behold a **ladder** set up on the **earth**, and the top of it **reached** to **heaven**: and **behold** the **angels** of God **ascending** and **descending** on it.

```
V H S T A F R M N W O D K C B
B I A J O F W E N T T H B J A
D H B R I U V H Y W T S A P D
T L T E A A A T T R B C U L G
G Q O H E N D R A W O T I A R
O N O H G R U E R B I G P C T
J G I E E I S I R K H S R E A
P E L D F B N H I T O O K M R
E S R G N I D N E C S E D W E
H U M S A E U D D B N E M S D
Z A O T B T C U R E A C H E D
W C R O D P H S W O L L I P A
Z E F N Q D R E A M E D R W L
C B P E E L S I R B Z P O Q H
H S Q S Q N L M M E D T L W V
```

SCRAMBLED CIRCLE
by Ken Save

AH, HINDSIGHT

When we begin to boast and brag, our comeuppance is only a stone's throw away.

1. AGTRE

2. EHOSSR

3. SLJUEOA

4. DTIMS

5. MJEELRAUS

6. TPELMUM

7. SHTOS

He should have ducked. Who was he?

1. ◯ _ _ _ _

2. _ ◯ _ _ _ _

3. _ _ _ ◯ _ _ _

4. _ ◯ _ _ _

5. _ _ _ _ _ ◯ _ _ _

6. _ _ _ _ _ _ ◯

7. ◯ _ _ _ _

Answer: _ _ _ _ _ _ _

IMPORTANT LOCALES

Biblical events happened in biblical places—and these anagrammed locales hosted three of the Bible's greatest stories. Can you figure them out? Hint: The first two are Old Testament stories, the third a New Testament account.

Hen vine

_ _ _ _ _ _ _

A mantra tour

_ _ _ _ _   _ _ _ _ _ _

A sud scam

_ _ _ _ _ _ _ _

CROSSWORD
by Tonya Vilhauer

■ BEAUTY CONTEST ■

It's obvious that the adage "Beauty is only skin deep" did not apply to Esther. Solve this puzzle to discover more about this orphan girl who captured the hearts of her king and her people.

Esther obtained favour in the sight of all them that looked upon her.
ESTHER 2:15

ACROSS

1 ESTHER'S PEOPLE, WHOM HAMAN WANTED TO DESTROY (Esther 3:6)
5 "Thirty milch camels with their colts. . . and ten ____" (Genesis 32:15)
10 Popular cooking spray
13 Iraq's neighbor
14 2:1, for example
15 "I am the LORD, and there is none ____" (Isaiah 45:5)
16 Gambling game
17 A distinct smell
18 "AND THE ____ WAS FAIR AND BEAUTIFUL" (Esther 2:7)
19 Tempo (abbr.)
21 HE WAS ESTHER'S COUSIN (Esther 2:15)
23 "Four days ____ I was fasting until this hour" (Acts 10:30)
26 Dress edge
28 Athletic field
29 Trademark allergy medicine
32 Removes the water (var.)
33 Composer J. S.
34 Indian currency
36 Location
37 Cupid's dart
38 "And he shall pluck away his ____ with his feathers" (Leviticus 1:16)
42 Nothing (Latin)
43 Unsullied
44 ESTHER COULD NOT ENDURE SEEING ____ COME UPON THE JEWS (Esther 8:6)
46 "Who healeth all thy ____" (Psalm 103:3)

49 Malicious burning
51 PART OF ESTHER'S PURIFICATION RITUAL (Esther 2:12)
52 Time zone (abbr.)
53 "Was nothing ____, but rather grew worse" (Mark 5:26)
57 Football association (abbr.)
59 Throb
60 Love intensely
62 Voiced
66 Took to court
67 "____ a right spirit within me" (Psalm 51:10)
68 Electrical current unit
69 "Ye do ____, not knowing the scriptures" (Matthew 22:29)
70 THE WICKED HAMAN WAS ESTHER'S ADVERSARY AND ____ (Esther 7:6)
71 Dutch cheese

DOWN

1 Peanut butter brand
2 Epoch
3 "The children of Ammon made ____ against Israel" (Judges 11:4)
4 Stuck-up person
5 One who contrives evidence against an innocent person
6 "And all that handle the ____, the mariners" (Ezekiel 27:29)
7 Speck
8 Stretched car
9 Glide
10 "I will destroy your high ____" (Leviticus 26:30)

11 A native of the largest continent
12 "THE LADIES OF PERSIA AND ____ " (Esther 1:18)
15 Nail filing board
20 Doctoral degree (abbr.)
22 "None is so fierce that ____ stir him up" (Job 41:10)
23 "Whereby we cry, ____, Father" (Romans 8:15)
24 Cogged wheel
25 "We are sanctified through. . . Jesus Christ ____ for all" (Hebrews 10:10)
27 AN AROMATIC BALM GIVEN TO ESTHER (Esther 2:12) AND JESUS (Mark 15:23)
30 Eureka!
31 Shocking
32 "Who hath begotten the drops of ____?" (Job 38:28)
35 Childhood disease of FDR
37 Pain
38 Accountant (abbr.)
39 Tactic
40 Mined metals
41 Annoyance

42 "Were there not ten cleansed? but where are the ____?" (Luke 17:17)
44 THE KING LOVED HER "ABOVE ALL THE WOMEN" (Esther 2:17)
45 Picked a candidate
47 Stringy
48 Santa's helper
49 "Exalt him that is low, and ____ him that is high" (Ezekiel 21:26)
50 Happen again
54 "It is a ____ thing that the king requireth" (Daniel 2:11)
55 The first garden (Genesis 2:15)
56 THE KING ACCEPTED ESTHER'S REQUEST, AND IT WAS ____ (Esther 9:14)
58 "Thou shalt ____ the LORD thy God" (Deuteronomy 11:1)
61 Phase of sleep (abbr.)
63 "He that spareth his ____ hateth his son" (Proverbs 13:24)
64 In the manner of (Fr.)
65 A mental system for permanently storing and recalling information later (abbr.)

21

ACROSTIC
by Donna K. Maltese

■■■■■ MISCOMMUNICATION ■■■■■

When the sons of Adam set out to build a tower to heaven, God had other ideas. Crack the code to discover how "speaking in tongues" first evolved.

Not apart

___ ___ ___ ___ ___ ___ ___ ___
15   7   36   30   12   26   3   20

Mankind

___ ___ ___ ___ ___ ___
4   23   31   11   16   27

Construct

___ ___ ___ ___ ___
22   10   17   33   2

Dialect

___ ___ ___ ___ ___ ___
28   19   6   13   24   32

Disperse

___ ___ ___ ___ ___ ___ ___
14   29   1   9   21   34   8

Thwart

___ ___ ___ ___
25   35   18   5

15-4-3-8-3-25-7-8-3   17-14   9-4-3   6-1-31-30

7-25   18-12   29-11-5-5-32-2   22-1-22-34-33;

22-30-29-11-10-27-30   9-4-3   33-19-20-2

2-17-2   28-4-3-8-3   29-35-16-25-35-23-16-2

9-4-3   5-1-6-36-24-1-13-32   7-25   11-5-5   9-4-3

34-11-20-21-26.

GENESIS 11:9

━━━━ BATTLE STORIES ━━━━

The Bible is full of exciting military accounts. Can you determine who's behind each of the battle stories in these spotty headlines?

●ERIC●O FALLS TO GENERAL'●
●NORTHODO●X ATT●CK

— — — — — —

D●VID'S ●EAUTIFU● ●ON ●URDERED IN
C●UP ●TTEMPT

— — — — — — —

EGY●TIAN LE●DER'S MIG●TY A●MY
WAS●ED AW●Y, DR●WNED

— — — — — —

TELEPHONE SCRAMBLE
by Nancy Bernhard

CONVERSIONS

We're not talking fractions here but of people who were brought into God's blessed family. Solve this telephone scramble to discover the names of these people who had a change of faith.

| PRS 7 | ABC 2 | TUV 8 | JKL 5 | | | | | |

| PRS 7 | TUV 8 | TUV 8 | GHI 4 | | | | | |

| PRS 7 | ABC 2 | MNO 6 | TUV 8 | DEF 3 | JKL 5 | | | |

| ABC 2 | DEF 3 | MNO 6 | TUV 8 | TUV 8 | PRS 7 | GHI 4 | MNO 6 | MNO 6 |

| PRS 7 | TUV 8 | ABC 2 | JKL 5 | GHI 4 | ABC 2 | ABC 2 | MNO 6 | |

| ABC 2 | ABC 2 | PRS 7 | ABC 2 | GHI 4 | ABC 2 | MNO 6 | | |

| ABC 2 | ABC 2 | MNO 6 | ABC 2 | ABC 2 | MNO 6 | GHI 4 | TUV 8 | DEF 3 |

WORD SEARCH
by Paul Kent

━━ THE ARK OF THE COVENANT ━━

BEZALEEL
CAPTURED
CHERUBIMS
DAVID
EKRON
ELI
EMERODS
FOUR RINGS
GLORY OF THE LORD
GOLD
HOPHNI
MERCY SEAT
MICE

OVERLAID
OXEN
PHILISTINES
PHINEHAS
SACRIFICING
SHEEP
SHITTIM WOOD
SOLOMON
STAVES
TEMPLE
TESTIMONY
WINGS

```
S G N I W P H I N E H A S Z A
L E L E E L A Z E B L T H W Q
A Y N O M I T S E T P I E C M
S M D P R J B R D C S P E N S
P X A Q H Y G A E B M I P T H
T H V S T F O U R R I N G S I
A O I O G V L F U C B O O D T
E P D L X M D P T A U R R O T
S H W O I E E R P H R K U R I
Y N A M X S N Q A M E E M E M
C I R O M N T V C I H L C M W
R T Y N Z W V I E C C P O E O
E E L P M E T O N E P D B R O
M S T A V E S O V E R L A I D
G N I C I F I R C A S W Q N K
```

CROSSWORD
by David K. Shortess

━ NATIONS IN THE PROMISED LAND ━

With God on our side, no foes can stand in our way, no matter how fearsome or tenacious they may be. Solve this puzzle to discover the enemies that God promised to oust if the Israelites remained obedient to Him alone.

I will. . .destroy all the people to whom thou shalt come.
EXODUS 23:27

ACROSS

1. "Now the _____ shall live by faith" (Hebrews 10:38)
5. Book after Micah
10. "And there _____ certain man at Lystra" (Acts 14:8) (2 words)
14. "No _____ will pitch his tent there" (Isaiah 13:20 NIV)
15. Enraged
16. A tenth of an ephah (Exodus 16:36)
17. A NATION ISRAEL ENCOUNTERED IN THE PROMISED LAND (Exodus 23:23)
19. "That nothing be _____" (John 6:12)
20. "_____ woe is past" (Revelation 9:12)
21. _____ Moines, Iowa
22. "Which trieth our _____" (1 Thessalonians 2:4)
24. Wallet fillers
26. "Or if he shall ask an _____" (Luke 11:12)
29. Sprint rival
30. "He _____ to Moses" (Romans 9:15 NIV)
31. Growl
32. Bright tropical fish
35. Rocky hill
37. VIP transport
39. An age
40. "Come again?"
43. ANOTHER NATION FROM EXODUS 23:23
45. "And Jacob _____ pottage" (Genesis 25:29)
46. "It _____; be not afraid" (Matthew 14:27) (2 words)
47. "As if he blessed an _____" (Isaiah 66:3)
48. "He planteth an _____" (Isaiah 44:14)
50. "The apostles and the elders _____ consider this" (Acts 15:6 NIV) (2 words)
52. "I have _____ him to the LORD" (1 Samuel 1:28)
54. Dog's comments
58. KLM rival, once
59. Boston _____ Party
60. "By _____ rebuke I dry up the sea" (Isaiah 50:2 NIV) (2 words)
61. "Our houses to _____" (Lamentations 5:2)
64. Spread hay
66. "The wilderness of _____" (Exodus 16:1)
67. "Record this _____" (Ezekiel 24:2 NIV)
68. ANOTHER NATION FROM EXODUS 23:23
72. Got an A
73. "Behold, _____ was opened" (Revelation 4:1) (2 words)
74. Unit of heredity
75. "A _____ of meat from the king" (2 Samuel 11:8)
76. "The fortified _____ ruin" (Isaiah 25:2 NIV) (2 words)
77. Not evens

DOWN

1. "Now _____ well was there" (John 4:6)
2. Muse of astronomy
3. With rationality
4. Schedule abbreviation
5. "And _____ parts to dwell" (Nehemiah 11:1)
6. "That wicked men have _____ among you" (Deuteronomy 13:13 NIV)
7. Pass the _____ (take a collection)
8. Colorado native
9. "And he wanders into its _____" (Job 18:8 NIV)
10. "Let us _____ ourselves with loves" (Proverbs 7:18)
11. ANOTHER NATION FROM EXODUS 23:23

12 "But ____ the spirits to see" (1 John 4:1 NIV)
13 "Which used curious ____" (Acts 19:19)
18 Commercials
23 Decorate in relief
25 WWII craft (abbr.)
27 "Departed into ____" (Matthew 4:12)
28 Clamp together tightly, as teeth
31 Network
33 "Is there any thing ____ hard for me?" (Jeremiah 32:27)
34 "____ it came to pass" (Luke 2:1)
36 Akron resident
38 "And giveth ____ to her household" (Proverbs 31:15)
40 "For they all saw ____ " (Mark 6:50)
41 "But when ye pray, ____ not vain repetitions" (Matthew 6:7)
42 ANOTHER NATION FROM EXODUS 23:23
44 Unit of electrical potential
49 Canaan's father (Genesis 9:18)

51 Scotch fabrics
53 "O ____ not desired" (Zephaniah 2:1)
55 "And the land ____ from war" (Joshua 11:23)
56 "A ____ loveth at all times" (Proverbs 17:17)
57 "Have their ____ exercised to discern" (Hebrews 5:14)
60 Wood-cutting tool (var.)
61 Enos's grandfather (Luke 3:38)
62 "And thou shalt put it on a blue ____" (Exodus 28:37)
63 "He ____ on the ground" (John 9:6)
65 "And of ____ the priest, the scribe" (Nehemiah 12:26)
69 Former name of Tokyo
70 "And a ____ of new timber" (Ezra 6:4)
71 "Because ____ to the Father" (John 16:16) (2 words)

BIBLE QUOTATION
by Suzanne Stepp

TESTED BY FIRE
Daniel 3:25

When Shadrach, Meshach, and Abednego refused to worship a man-made idol, an enraged king's temperature rose. Solve this puzzle to discover what vision doused the flames of King Nebuchadnezzar's ire.

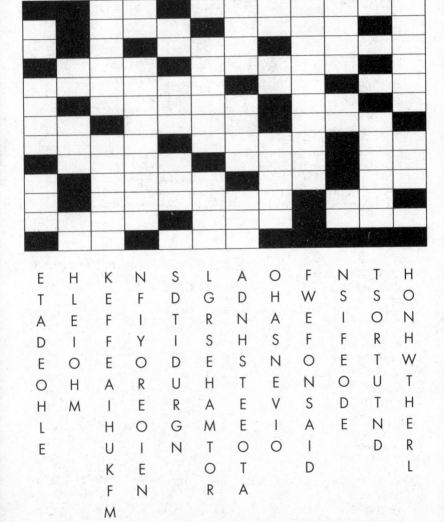

═══ SOWING SEEDS ═══
MATTHEW 13:4

Jesus often spoke in parables. Can you solve this drop two puzzle to uncover part of a parable Jesus planted in the minds of His listeners?

WIDOWER	More open	_____ 1. ____ ____
MATCHED	Performed	_____ 2. ____ ____
ENABLED	Dull	_____ 3. ____ ____
SNARING	Cereal	_____ 4. ____ ____
HOARDER	Devotion	_____ 5. ____ ____
EREMITE	Send money	_____ 6. ____ ____
SCANDAL	Manmade waterway	_____ 7. ____ ____
ONWARDS	Sketched	_____ 8. ____ ____
FROWNED	Male bee	_____ 9. ____ ____
ELEVATE	Male servant	_____ 10. ____ ____
DELIGHT	Octave	_____ 11. ____ ____
SCARLET	Container	_____ 12. ____ ____

__ __ __ __ __ __ __ __ __ __ __ __

1 2 3 4 5 6 7 8 9 10 11 12

STEPHEN'S WITNESS
ACTS 6–7

ASIA
BLASPHEMOUS
BLOOD
CAST OUT
CITY
COUNCIL
DISCIPLES
DISPUTING
EARS
FACE OF AN ANGEL
FALSE WITNESSES
FELL ASLEEP
FULL OF FAITH
GLORY
HEAVENS
HOLY GHOST

JERUSALEM
JESUS
LAMENTATION
LAW
LOUD
MARTYR
MIRACLES
MULTITUDE
RAIMENT
SAUL
SCATTERED
SLEW
STONED
WISDOM
WONDERS
WORD OF GOD

```
S E U M I R A C L E S L E B R
R F A S C A T T E R E D H L F
B A U R T G R Y E T U D O A E
L A I L S O N D R O I I L S L
O M W M L F N I L S J S Y P L
O E O C E O A E P A E C G H A
D L R Y W N F U D W S I H E S
E A D R N L T F I L U P O M L
D S O O T I I T A E S L S O E
U U F L N O N C U I A E T U E
T R G G R E T H N O T S O S P
I E O M S A U L A U T H I P Y
T J D S N E V A E H O S I A T
L L E G N A N A F O E C A F I
U S L A M E N T A T I O N C C
M O D S I W A L E R Y T R A M
```

ACROSTIC
by Donna K. Maltese

━━━━━ NAAMAN'S LUCKY 7 ━━━━━

A servant girl's advice led to a Syrian's healing. Crack the code to discover what Naaman had to do to become whole.

Naaman's military rank (2 Kings 5:1)

—— —— —— —— —— —— ——
38 33 23 7 18 12 5

Naaman's skin disease

—— —— —— —— —— —— ——
11 15 32 27 6 22 36

Prophet of Naaman's time (2 Kings 5:9)

—— —— —— —— —— ——
35 13 30 26 3 20

Another name for an Israelite

—— —— ——
24 2 16

Servant girl (2 Kings 5:2)

—— —— —— ——
17 8 29 1

What Naaman asked for, after his healing (2 Kings 5:18)

—— —— —— —— —— —— —— —— —— —— ——
9 34 31 25 4 19 14 28 10 21 37

7-3-10-28   16-35-28-7   3-10   1-34-16-28,   8-5-1

1-4-23-32-15-1   3-12-17-22-14-11-9   21-2-19-2-5

7-29-17-2-37   30-5   24-6-31-1-33-28,

20-38-38-6-27-1-4-5-25   7-34   7-3-10   26-18-36-4-5-25

34-9   7-3-10   17-8-5   34-9   25-6-1.

2 KINGS 5:14

SUDOKU
by Sara Stoker

JESUS' TRIUMPHAL ENTRY

MEDIUM

	A	B	C	D	E	F	G	H	I
1									Y
2	K	S		Y		O		T	E
3	Y	N							D
4	E	A	Y		D		K		N
5	S		N	E				D	A
6		O	K						T
7	A	D				T	E		
8	N		O					A	K
9			E		Y		D		

Hint: Column E

Jesus _____ on a _____ while people threw down palm leaves before Him (John 12:13–14 NIV).

36

━━ A STORY FOR THE GRANDKIDS ━━

Never forget God's works of wonder, but pass them on as everlasting remembrances.

1. NDSUMCEO

2. CKDMEO

3. MTNOU

4. LOEGRLAY

5. TRSTUO

6. EAFITMSN

7. EYAWR

8. FSLHE

A pile of stones would serve as a way to remember a special event.

1. _ _ _ _ _ ◯ _ _

2. _ _ _ _ ◯ _

3. ◯ _ _ _ _ _

4. _ _ _ _ _ _ ◯ _ _

5. _ _ _ _ ◯ _

6. _ _ _ ◯ _ _ _ _

7. _ _ ◯ _ _

8. _ ◯ _ _ _

Answer: _ _ _ _ _ _ _ _ _

CROSSWORD

by Sarah Lagerquist Simmons

CHARACTERS OF PARABLES AND STORIES

God's Word is full of stories that teach us lessons and aid us in our walk with God. As you solve this puzzle, let the memories of Bible stories you've read and heard roam freely through your mind—in other words, no *tale*-gating!

"Son of man, give this riddle, and tell this story to the people of Israel."
EZEKIEL 17:2 NLT

ACROSS

1 "They practice divination like the Philistines and ____ hands with pagans" (Isaiah 2:6 NIV)
6 THIS TOMB-DWELLER "HAD DEVILS LONG TIME, AND ____ NO CLOTHES" (Luke 8:27)
10 "She dwelleth and abideth. . .upon the ____ of the rock" (Job 39:28)
14 "So the Egyptians made the children of Israel serve with ____" (Exodus 1:13 NKJV)
15 "You own the cosmos—you made everything in it, everything from ____ to archangel" (Psalm 89:11 MSG)
16 Mr. (Ger.)
17 An acid
18 A desert
19 "The ____ is not to the swift" (Ecclesiastes 9:11)
20 "THOU ART THE ____," NATHAN SAID TO DAVID AFTER REVEALING HIS SIN IN A PARABLE (2 Samuel 12:7)
21 "The LORD God caused a ____ sleep to fall upon Adam" (Genesis 2:21)
23 "They put Saul's armor on display. . . and placed his skull as a ____ in the temple of their god" (1 Chronicles 10:9 MSG)
25 THE PRODIGAL SON WAS EMPLOYED BY FEEDING THESE
26 Male turkey
27 An overbearing woman
30 HE EARNED HIS MASTER'S PRAISE BY MANAGING HIS MONEY WISELY (Luke 16)
34 Car model
35 THIS ____ WIDOW GAVE ALL SHE HAD (Mark 12:43)
36 Harridan

38 "These dreamers. . .revile and ____ and scoff at [heavenly] glories" (Jude 1:8 AMP)
39 Pull
40 Friend (Sp.)
42 Unsaturated carbon compound (suffix)
43 "Five gold tumors and five gold ____" (1 Samuel 6:4 NIV)
44 Part of a mortise joint
45 Trollish
48 SAMSON WAS VERY ____
49 Female army corps (abbr.)
50 The Queen of Sheba told Solomon, "It was a ____ report that I heard. . .of thy acts and of thy wisdom" (1 Kings 10:6)
51 To stop the flow of blood
54 "It is a scabby sore of the head or ____" (Leviticus 13:30 NLT)
55 One millionth gram (abbr.)
58 English General in Revolutionary War
59 Republic in West Africa
61 U.S. state
63 Gelatin derived from algae
64 Related
65 JOSHUA'S TWO SPIES "CAME INTO A HARLOT'S HOUSE, ____ RAHAB" (Joshua 2:1)
66 SAMUEL'S "SONS WALKED NOT IN HIS ____, BUT TURNED ASIDE AFTER LUCRE" (1 Samuel 8:3)
67 Back of neck
68 ONE OF JOB'S WOES: "NIGHT ____ AT MY BONES; THE PAIN NEVER LETS UP" (Job 30:16 MSG)

DOWN

1 Stuff
2 Bean
3 Opposed to (var.)

4 THE ELDEST _____ WAS JEALOUS (Luke 15)
5 RUNAWAY SON WHO LEFT HOME (Luke 15)
6 A DISPUTE ABOUT _____ WAS PART OF ONE PARABLE JESUS TOLD (Matthew 20)
7 Upon
8 THIEVES DID _____ A MAN IN THIS PARABLE (Luke 10)
9 Sender
10 Purity of a color
11 "I _____ where I sowed not" (Matthew 25:26)
12 Missouri's Gateway _____
13 Color of the Southern Confederates (var.)
22 Self-image
24 "The men did their best to _____ back to land" (Jonah 1:13 NIV)
25 "She shall shave her head, and _____ her nails" (Deuteronomy 21:12)
27 "The _____ of Siddim was full of slime pits" (Genesis 14:10)
28 Frosting
29 Male first name (var.)
30 "Abraham journeyed. . .toward the _____ country" (Genesis 20:1)

31 Garments
32 Herbivore (abbr.)
33 This idol fell before the Ark of the Covenant (1 Samuel 5:3)
35 Groups of parents and instructors (abbr.)
37 Bell
40 Adjusting
41 "You have made my days a _____ handbreadth" (Psalm 39:5 NIV)
43 HE BEGGED A DROP OF WATER FROM LAZARUS (Luke 16) (2 words)
46 ONE SLAVE GIRL EARNED MONEY FOR HER _____ BY FORTUNE-TELLING (Acts 16:16 NIV)
47 Computer (abbr.)
48 Title of respect in India
50 "Not my will, but _____" (Luke 22:42)
51 Band leader Artie
52 Roman apparel
53 "They sent him _____" (Genesis 12:20)
54 Fast pace
55 Mother's nickname
56 "Ye shall not eat of them that _____ the cud" (Deuteronomy 14:7)
57 "Ye shall be as _____" (Genesis 3:5)
60 Known also as (abbr.)
62 Jacob's son

WORD SEARCH
by Conover Swofford

GOD IS FAITHFUL IN THE OLD TESTAMENT

ACHOR
AJALON
BERACHAH
CHARASHIM
CRAFTSMEN
DECISION
ELAH
ESCHOL
GERAR
GIANTS
GIBEON
HAMONGOG
HEBRON
HINNOM
JERICHO
JEZREEL

JIPHTHAHEL
KEZIZ
KINGS
MEGIDDO
MIZPEH
MOUNTAINS
PASSENGERS
SALT
SHITTIM
SLAUGHTER
SOREK
VISION
ZARED
ZEBOIM
ZEPHATHAH

```
O H P Z H E P Z I M I O B E Z
H H I N N O M Z O D D I G E M
Z P C S R E G N E S S A P N O
J J M I T T I H S J S H O S U
Z H E B R O N P H A A L G J N
H H S O R E K J L T A N R Z T
A D E R A Z J T H J I J L L A
M M M R O H C A A K J K Z L I
O M H A L E H A H T H P I J N
N E M S T F A R C Z I Z E K S
G Z R E T H G U A L S L L T J
O P E M I H S A R A H C N Z K
G H N O I S I C E D R A R E G
M I L O H C S E B V I S I O N
J J E Z R E E L J G I B E O N
```

TELEPHONE SCRAMBLE
by Connie Troyer

▬▬▬ THANKS FOR YOUR HELP ▬▬▬

Wouldn't the world be great if everyone lived by the Golden Rule? Decipher the clues below to uncover the names of people who aided and abetted in a good way.

TUV 8	WXY 9	PRS 7	ABC 2	MNO 6	MNO 6	TUV 8	PRS 7	

PRS 7	ABC 2	MNO 6	ABC 2	PRS 7	GHI 4	TUV 8	ABC 2	MNO 6

ABC 2	WXY 9	PRS 7	TUV 8	PRS 7

JKL 5	MNO 6	MNO 6	ABC 2	TUV 8	GHI 4	ABC 2	MNO 6

MNO 6	ABC 2	ABC 2	DEF 3	GHI 4	ABC 2	GHI 4

PRS 7	GHI 4	MNO 6	ABC 2	GHI 4

ABC 2	ABC 2	GHI 4	MNO 6	ABC 2	DEF 3	ABC 2	ABC 2

━━ BEFORE THE THRONE ━━

Earthly rulers may die, but our King who reigns in heaven lives forever! Here's a prophet who saw God in all His glory. Can you crack the cryptoscripture codes to discover this humble man's heavenly vision?

WJ VAT GTML VAMV OWJF XCCWMA NWTN W

PMQ MSPB VAT SBLN PWVVWJF XEBJ M VALBJT,

AWFA MJN SWIVTN XE, MJN AWP VLMWJ

IWSSTN VAT VTYEST.

ABTC EGDR D, IHT DE QT! ZHW D GQ NCRHCT;

KTMGNET D GQ G QGC HZ NCMVTGC VDSE,

GCR D RITVV DC ABT QDREA HZ G STHSVT HZ

NCMVTGC VDSE: ZHW QDCT TJTE BGOT ETTC

ABT UDCY, ABT VHWR HZ BHEAE.

CROSSWORD
by David K. Shortess

━━ WINDOWS OF OPPORTUNITY ━━

Take this opportunity to see what these windows reveal to you.

Prove me now herewith, saith the LORD of hosts, if I will not open you the windows of heaven, and pour you out a blessing.
MALACHI 3:10

ACROSS

1 Victor's companion
4 Gun (the engine)
7 Volga feeder
10 "Much learning doth make thee ____" (Acts 26:24)
13 Swiss river (var.)
14 Of aircraft electrical systems
16 "But I am slow of speech, and ____ slow tongue" (Exodus 4:10) (2 words)
17 "And ____ them about thy neck" (Proverbs 6:21)
18 WHERE JEZEBEL WAS THROWN FROM A WINDOW AND DIED (2 Kings 9:30–33)
19 October follower (abbr.)
20 "Whether he be a sinner ____, I know not" (John 9:25) (2 words)
22 "God: ____ me according to thy mercy" (Psalm 109:26) (2 words)
23 Meaning three (comb. form)
24 WHERE A RAVEN AND A DOVE WERE RELEASED FROM A WINDOW (Genesis 8:6–8) (2 words)
27 Responded vocally to a tongue depressor
29 Baseball great Ott
30 Rockies and Cascades (abbr.)
32 "And ____ did that which was right in the eyes of the LORD" (1 Kings 15:11)
35 Click beetle
38 "Take thee a ____, and lay it before thee" (Ezekiel 4:1)
42 THE DIRECTION DANIEL'S WINDOWS FACED (Daniel 6:10) (2 words)
45 Part of CEO (abbr.)
46 "She gave me some fruit from the tree, and ____" (Genesis 3:12 NIV) (3 words)
47 "Your lightning ____ up the world" (Psalm 77:18 NIV)
48 ____-do-well (slang)
50 "Unto us a ____ is given" (Isaiah 9:6)

52 "And took a ____, and girded himself" (John 13:4)
55 WHERE PAUL ESCAPED THROUGH A WINDOW (2 Corinthians 11:32–33)
60 "For ye tithe mint and ____ and all" (Luke 11:42)
61 Muslim women's garments
64 "His children, their ____ is the sword" (Job 27:14 NIV)
65 Similar to OCS (abbr.)
66 WHERE RAHAB TIED A THREAD IN A WINDOW (Joshua 2:1–21)
69 "He maketh me to ____ down in green pastures" (Psalm 23:2)
70 "As though I shot ____ mark" (1 Samuel 20:20) (2 words)
71 "Therefore I said, Surely these ____" (Jeremiah 5:4) (2 words)
72 Shimei's father (1 Kings 4:18 NIV)
73 "They that ____ in tears shall reap in joy" (Psalm 126:5)
74 "And ____ him in the sand" (Exodus 2:12)
75 Oolong or mint
76 "In the Valley of ____ Hinnom" (2 Kings 23:10 NIV)

DOWN

1 Betray (2 words, slang)
2 Capital on the Nile
3 "Men condemned to die in the ____" (1 Corinthians 4:9 NIV)
4 British rule in India
5 Grandmother of Enos (Genesis 4:25–26)
6 Eyeshade (var.)
7 "To every ____ loaf of bread" (1 Chronicles 16:3) (2 words)
8 Capital of Ukraine
9 "Create in me ____ heart, O God" (Psalm 51:10) (2 words)
10 "Which is the ____ Adar" (Esther 8:12)

11 "As I wrote ____ in few words" (Ephesians 3:3)
12 WHO MICHAL LET DOWN FROM A WINDOW (1 Samuel 19:12)
15 Russian city on the Ural River
21 Bit of electrical resistance
25 Soothsayer or clairvoyant
26 "For as in Adam ____ " (1 Corinthians 15:22) (2 words)
28 Nick and Nora Charles's cinematic pup
30 "Are you not ____ men" (1 Corinthians 3:4 NIV)
31 Self-evident verity
32 "And ____ the sacrifices of the dead" (Psalm 106:28)
33 Red or white in baseball
34 "Stand in ____, and sin not" (Psalm 4:4)
36 "Go into the city, and a man carrying ____ of water will meet you" (Mark 14:13 NIV) (2 words)
37 Vietnamese holiday
39 "Wherefore dealt ye so ____ with me" (Genesis 43:6)
40 Island garland
41 911 responder (abbr.)
43 Teen bane

44 Greek portico
49 He slew 450 prophets of Baal (1 Kings 18:40)
51 It may cause a check to bounce (abbr.)
52 WHERE EUTYCHUS WENT TO SLEEP AND FELL FROM A WINDOW (Acts 20:6–9)
53 "And led him ____ crucify him" (Mark 15:20) (2 words)
54 "And there ____ the giants, the sons of Anak" (Numbers 13:33) (2 words)
55 "The mountains will ____ new wine" (Joel 3:18 NIV)
56 It's a tie
57 One of the twelve spies (Numbers 13:6)
58 Useful
59 "And thou shalt ____ enemy in my habitation" (1 Samuel 2:32) (2 words)
62 A son of Jeduthun (1 Chronicles 25:3)
63 "That they bring thee ____ heifer" (Numbers 19:2) (2 words)
67 "Once cultivated by the ____" (Isaiah 7:25 NIV)
68 "Or athirst, ____ stranger" (Matthew 25:44) (2 words)

ACROSTIC
by Donna K. Maltese

— A GATED COMMUNITY —

Decipher this puzzle to discover John's description of the gated community of New Jerusalem. Sounds priceless!

John was one of twelve

___ ___ ___ ___ ___ ___ ___ ___
2 14 28 19 37 10 3 6

A revelation

___ ___ ___ ___ ___ ___
20 39 31 5 11 18

Precious stones ___ the new city's walls (Revelation 21:19)

___ ___ ___ ___ ___ ___ ___ ___ ___
43 36 7 16 23 1 32 8 29

A translucent variety of quartz (Revelation 21:19)

___ ___ ___ ___ ___ ___ ___ ___ ___ ___
17 25 42 38 24 12 46 40 35 21

The words John wrote were true and ___ (Revelation 21:5)

___ ___ ___ ___ ___ ___ ___ ___
26 13 47 44 33 4 22 30

Number of tribes of Israel

___ ___ ___ ___ ___ ___
9 45 15 41 34 27

9-33-8   44-45-3-10-20-3   43-13-37-12-6   45-8-7-8

44-45-3-10-20-3   14-27-42-7-38-31:   3-34-3-7-21

31-3-34-3-7-36-41   43-13-37-12   45-2-1   11-4   40-18-15

14-27-42-7-38:   2-16-29   9-33-8   31-9-7-3-3-9   11-26

9-32-8   17-5-9-21   45-2-1   14-22-7-12   43-28-30-46,

2-1   39-9   45-8-7-8   9-7-36-35-19-14-36-7-15-35-9

43-10-36-6-6.

REVELATION 21:21

AN EVEN EXCHANGE
GENESIS 22:13

God is always there for us, but we must be watchful to see where He's working. Solve this puzzle to discover how God provided for a faithful man just in the nick of time.

N		I		D		F		H		F		R		D		T		S		E		A
E		N		C		E		H		O		F		M		A		I		R		G
M		O		I		F		A		H		D		S		T		B		N		A
A		U		B		A		B		R		A		E		A		H		O		A
D		N		T		E		I		N		I		D		R		A		N		D
I		T		P		H		U		R		E		T		A		O		B		K
R		N		F		S		O		H		H		R		S		I		N		W
		D		H		A		T		R		A		E		N		M		I		Y
		H		T				F		C		E		H				S		B		H
				O				E		I		M						T		E		N
				T						O		L								O		U
				N						G		K										M
												O										

▬▬ GOVERNMENT INTRIGUE ▬▬

"The bureaucracy" may not seem like an exciting place, but these biblical officials experienced some real government intrigue. These spotty headlines relate to the stories of three widely differing rulers. Can you solve each one?

●ULER SLAUG●TERE● ALL MALE BABIES IN H●PE OF ●LIMINATING FUTURE KING

__ __ __ __ __

MAN HO●ELESSLY ●RI●S TO ER●SE B●AME W●TH HAND WASHING

__ __ __ __ __ __

GOV●RNMENT OFF●CI●L SPEN●S ●IGHT WITH ●IONS

__ __ __ __ __ __

GOD IS FAITHFUL
IN THE NEW TESTAMENT

ANANIAS
BARNABAS
CORNELIUS
DORCAS
ELISABETH
EUNICE
JOSEPH [OF
    ARIMATHAEA]
LAZARUS
LOIS
LYDIA
MARTHA
MARY
NICANOR
NICODEMUS

NICOLAS
ONESIMUS
PARMENAS
PAUL
PHEBE
PHILIP
PROCHORUS
SILAS
STEPHEN
TABITHA
TIMON
TIMOTHEUS
TITUS
WITNESS
ZACCHAEUS

```
T  I  M  O  T  H  E  U  S  A  I  D  Y  L  O
I  A  P  I  L  I  H  P  R  O  N  A  C  I  N
M  H  B  P  A  R  M  E  N  A  S  O  M  I  E
O  T  S  I  M  N  E  H  P  E  T  S  C  M  S
N  R  A  O  T  A  C  H  O  S  A  O  O  A  I
I  A  B  E  J  H  T  H  I  L  D  A  M  R  M
C  M  A  C  M  O  A  L  S  E  M  A  K  Y  U
O  I  N  I  S  E  A  U  M  D  O  R  C  A  S
L  P  R  N  T  S  E  U  K  L  U  A  P  J  U
A  S  A  U  H  A  S  S  E  N  T  I  W  O  R
S  E  B  E  H  P  R  O  C  H  O  R  U  S  A
S  H  M  C  O  H  T  E  B  A  S  I  L  E  Z
H  M  C  X  O  S  L  O  I  S  W  S  S  P  A
S  A  N  A  N  I  A  S  U  T  I  T  W  H  L
Z  T  O  L  T  S  S  U  I  L  E  N  R  O  C
```

■ ANIMAL STORIES ■

God made animals that serve, sustain, and challenge us. Solve this puzzle to uncover some amazing and memorable stories of the creatures with which God has blessed us and this earth.

God made the wild animals according to their kinds, the livestock according to their kinds, and all the creatures that move along the ground according to their kinds. And God saw that it was good.

GENESIS 1:25 NIV

ACROSS

1   Pulpy residue left after pressing grapes
5   Group of three feathers in a bird's wing
10   Sandwich (abbr.)
13   Toad species
14   Highland musician
15   Knife
16   Carol: "The First ____"
17   Form of oxygen
18   "COME THOU. . .____ THE ARK" (Genesis 7:1)
19   Money group (abbr.)
21   MOST FAMOUS BIBLE ANIMAL STORY (2 words)
23   Tunisian Cape
26   Legume seed
28   Jots
29   Terse maxim
32   Mountain in Sicily
33   Suitor
34   "A SHEPHERD DIVIDETH HIS SHEEP FROM THE ____" (Matthew 25:32)
36   Pain
37   Persona non ____
38   Move
42   "DANIEL IN THE ____ DEN" IS ANOTHER WELL-KNOWN BIBLE ANIMAL STORY
43   Michigan's neighbor
44   THE ____ FELL FOR 40 DAYS DURING THE FLOOD
46   Withdrawing
49   Mission in Texas
51   Summer month (abbr.)

52   Organization linking parents and schools
53   "Soldiers likewise ____ of him" (Luke 3:14)
57   Unit of weight
59   Propellers
60   Smells
62   Humorist Bombeck
66   Siblings (abbr.)
67   Bestow
68   "The ____ out of the wood doth waste it" (Psalm 80:13)
69   AT THE ____ OF A STORY ABOUT A MAN AND HIS SHEEP, DAVID REPENTED
70   "Twelve lions stood. . .upon the six ____" (1 Kings 10:20)
71   German Roman Catholic theologian Johann

DOWN

1   IF IT HAD NOT BEEN FOR HIS DONKEY, BALAAM WOULD HAVE BEEN A DEAD ____
2   "Four days ____ I was fasting" (Acts 10:30)
3   Repent
4   THIS ANIMAL WAS KILLED FOR A FEAST (Luke 15:23)
5   Pinnacle
6   Girl's name, for short
7   JESUS CAME RIDING INTO JERUSALEM, SITTING ____ A DONKEY
8   Type of weave
9   Region

10 Music for one or two solo instruments
11 Excessive
12 "Many. . .brought their ____ together, and burned them" (Acts 19:19)
15 Once roamed the northern plains of the US
20 Speedometer reading (abbr.)
22 Visits to a Web site
23 Leavened cake
24 Oil cartel (abbr.)
25 HE SPENT UP TO 100 YEARS BUILDING A BOAT FOR HIS FAMILY AND ANIMALS
27 Violent behavior
30 Day of the week (abbr., var.)
31 Groans
32 Seventh letter of Greek alphabet
35 On the ocean (2 words)
37 Snare
38 Home-building material for pioneers
39 "A ____ for the horse, a bridle for the ass" (Proverbs 26:3)
40 Uneducated speech includes this word for "am not"

41 Exercise
42 WHAT SAMSON KILLED WITH HIS BARE HANDS
44 Used for cleaning a muzzle
45 Accumulate
47 "He ____ off every branch. . .that bears no fruit" (John 15:2 NIV)
48 Conceit
49 Sun-dried brick of clay
50 STORIES IN THE BIBLE ARE TOLD SO THAT WE CAN ____ A LESSON
54 ELIJAH PROPHESIED THAT ____ WOULD EAT WICKED QUEEN JEZEBEL (2 Kings 9:36)
55 Revise
56 BIRD SENT FROM THE ARK
58 Cornhusker State (abbr.)
61 Salesman (abbr.)
63 "Ashahel was as light of foot as a wild ____" (2 Samuel 2:18)
64 Raincoat (abbr.)
65 WHAT SAVED NOAH'S FAMILY AND THE ANIMALS

ACROSTIC
by Connie Troyer

■ A STORY, A STORY ■

God's Word was written to be read. Solve this puzzle to uncover its purpose and how it can change our mindset.

Displaced queen (Esther 1:19)

‾‾8‾‾ ‾‾18‾‾ ‾‾33‾‾ ‾‾26‾‾ ‾‾1‾‾ ‾‾36‾‾

Six safe places in Palestine (Numbers 35:9–11; Joshua 20:7–9)

‾‾9‾‾ ‾‾59‾‾ ‾‾20‾‾ ‾‾52‾‾ ‾‾47‾‾ ‾‾13‾‾ ‾‾28‾‾ ‾‾57‾‾

‾‾15‾‾ ‾‾53‾‾ ‾‾29‾‾ ‾‾35‾‾ ‾‾23‾‾ ‾‾51‾‾

Samson was set apart as this (Judges 13:5, 24)

‾‾12‾‾ ‾‾38‾‾ ‾‾14‾‾ ‾‾48‾‾ ‾‾3‾‾ ‾‾55‾‾ ‾‾32‾‾ ‾‾25‾‾

Jonathan's crippled son (2 Samuel 4:4)

‾‾6‾‾ ‾‾41‾‾ ‾‾16‾‾ ‾‾46‾‾ ‾‾58‾‾ ‾‾24‾‾ ‾‾2‾‾ ‾‾54‾‾ ‾‾56‾‾ ‾‾17‾‾ ‾‾22‾‾ ‾‾40‾‾

The last plague (Exodus 11:1, 5)

‾‾10‾‾ ‾‾27‾‾ ‾‾49‾‾ ‾‾39‾‾ ‾‾50‾‾ ‾‾30‾‾ ‾‾2‾‾ ‾‾44‾‾ ‾‾21‾‾

A well appeared here for Hagar (Genesis 21:14–21)

‾‾31‾‾ ‾‾7‾‾ ‾‾5‾‾ ‾‾11‾‾ ‾‾43‾‾ ‾‾34‾‾ ‾‾37‾‾ ‾‾4‾‾ ‾‾19‾‾ ‾‾45‾‾

10-2-15   31-26-48-1-39-28-17-8-47-44

32-46-7-21-23-19   31-25-44-4   31-49-55-32-50-25-37

18-10-2-44-53-32-36-6-51   31-51-15-41

31-34-27-50-20-47-21   10-28-49   28-35-15

5-51-48-44-12-59-21-23,   50-40-18-22   31-17

32-46-3-2-35-23-40   16-38-32-58-53-12-9-43

48-37-11   9-42-6-29-42-3-20   28-57   20-40-4

13-9-3-55-16-22-35-34-4-54   6-52-23-46-22   26-38-8-17

26-2-16-25.

ROMANS 15:4

ANAGRAM
by Paul Kent

━━━ MORE IMPORTANT LOCALES ━━━

As we've already noted, biblical events happened in biblical places—and these anagrammed spots hosted three more of the Bible's greatest stories. Can you figure them out? Hint: The first two are from Old Testament stories, the third from a New Testament account.

Need of danger

_ _ _ _ _ _   _ _   _ _ _ _ _

Rich Joe

_ _ _ _ _ _ _

O lost movie fun

_ _ _ _ _   _ _   _ _ _ _ _ _

WATER PROVIDED
SEE EXODUS 17:6

You can't get water from a stone. . .or can you? Solve this puzzle to find out what God told Moses to do in order to quench the thirst of His people.

SCALENE	Not dirty	_____	1. ____ ____
MIDMOST	Surrounded by	_____	2. ____ ____
PIANIST	Discolor	_____	3. ____ ____
TACKLER	Squeak	_____	4. ____ ____
EYEHOLE	Full of holes	_____	5. ____ ____
MOBSTER	Judge's garments	_____	6. ____ ____
HEADMAN	Described	_____	7. ____ ____
ENDWAYS	Batons	_____	8. ____ ____
RAMBLED	Accuse	_____	9. ____ ____
RAZORED	Demolished	_____	10. ____ ____
TITANIC	Corrupt	_____	11. ____ ____
KNITTER	Hackneyed	_____	12. ____ ____
PRICKET	An instant	_____	13. ____ ____

— — — — — — — — — — — — —

__ __ __ __ __ __ __ __ __ __ __ __ __
1 2 3 4 5 6 7 8 9 10 11 12 13

WORD SEARCH
by David Austin

━━━ JOSEPH AND MARY ━━━
Luke 1–2

ANGEL	GLORY
APPEAR	JESUS
APPEARED	JOSEPH
AUGUSTUS	MARY
BETHLEHEM	MESSIAH
BIRTH	NAZARETH
CAESAR	PEACE
DREAM	PROPHECY
ELIZABETH	PROPHET
EMMANUEL	SHEPHERDS
GABRIEL	ZECHARIAH

```
A  J  T  M  V  N  H  E  E  S  S  G  C
U  D  T  S  E  B  A  L  T  M  H  L  E
G  A  E  B  I  S  I  Z  R  M  E  O  D
U  K  P  R  E  Z  S  A  A  A  P  R  P
S  L  T  P  A  T  S  I  W  R  H  Y  R
T  H  K  B  E  E  H  E  A  Y  E  E  O
U  G  E  E  A  A  P  L  H  H  R  T  P
S  T  O  C  C  J  R  P  E  U  D  Q  H
H  Z  E  C  H  A  R  I  A  H  S  J  E
E  M  M  A  N  U  E  L  F  N  E  B  C
Z  H  P  E  S  O  J  P  F  Q  G  M  Y
L  E  I  R  B  A  G  A  S  U  S  E  J
T  E  H  P  O  R  P  D  R  E  A  M  L
```

CROSSWORD

by David K. Shortess

■ THREE MONETARY LESSONS ■

The three theme answers are possible titles for the three lessons cited, all dealing with coins.

Sell all that thou hast, and distribute unto the poor,
and thou shalt have treasure in heaven.
LUKE 18:22

ACROSS

1 "An ____ pleasing to the LORD" (Leviticus 1:9 NIV)
6 Transcript data (abbr.)
9 "Crying, ____, Father" (Galatians 4:6)
13 Largest Philippine island
14 "Eat not of it ____, nor sodden" (Exodus 12:9)
15 Chunk of earth
16 LESSON 1: WHEN A SINNER REPENTS (Luke 15:8–10 NIV) (4 words)
19 *Daily Planet* reporter
20 "He ____ and worshipped him" (Mark 5:6)
21 "Men condemned to die in the ____" (1 Corinthians 4:9 NIV)
22 "How long will it be ____ they believe me" (Numbers 14:11)
23 Valley of ____ Hinnom (Joshua 18:16 NIV)
24 "Walking after their ____ lusts" (Jude 1:16)
25 Links gadget
26 Sure competitor
27 ____ Mahal
30 Get soaked
33 Obtain
34 Woody's son
35 LESSON 2: ON THE PAYING OF TAXES (Matthew 17:27 NIV) (5 words)
38 "From the lions' ____" (Song of Solomon 4:8)
39 "You may know the hope to which he ____ called you" (Ephesians 1:18 NIV)
40 Philistines' god (Judges 16:23)
41 112° 30' from N
42 "Their conscience seared with a ____ iron" (1 Timothy 4:2)
43 "____ it is written" (Matthew 4:6)
44 "And the ____ of Carmel shall wither" (Amos 1:2)
45 Push hard
46 Mineral spring
49 "And ____ Aaron of his garments" (Numbers 20:26)
52 "A wise ____ maketh a glad father" (Proverbs 10:1)
53 ____ Street
54 LESSON 3: TRUE SACRIFICE (Mark 12:41–44) (3 words)
57 "They ____ perverse and crooked generation" (Deuteronomy 32:5) (2 words)
58 "____ no man any thing" (Romans 13:8)
59 Esso competitor
60 Signs of spring
61 "For our ____ is come" (Lamentations 4:18)
62 "She maketh fine ____" (Proverbs 31:24)

DOWN

1 "Cast alive into ____ of fire" (Revelation 19:20) (2 words)
2 "I will make thee ____ over many things" (Matthew 25:21)
3 Earth's natural UV blocking layer
4 "It is ____ holy unto the LORD" (Exodus 30:10)
5 "Go to the ____" (Proverbs 6:6)
6 "For in this we ____" (2 Corinthians 5:2)
7 "The ____ as of a woman in travail" (Jeremiah 22:23)
8 Rye bristle
9 Sign of fall

10 "And he made a vail of _____" (Exodus 36:35)
11 Former capital of West Germany
12 "Then he shall _____ fifth part" (Leviticus 27:13) (2 words)
17 Manitoba tribe
18 Forest youngster
23 _____ there, done that
24 "And again he denied with an _____" (Matthew 26:72)
25 "Give us _____ day our daily bread" (Matthew 6:11)
26 All _____ are off
27 Math branch (abbr.)
28 "Sweeter _____ than honey" (Psalm 19:10)
29 Zebedee's son (Matthew 10:2)
30 Said (arch.)
31 Hits a hole-in-one
32 Musical sound
33 Pest
34 "So is good news from _____ country" (Proverbs 25:25) (2 words)
36 Where "pancake" is understood (abbr.)
37 Esau's land
42 Arizona tribe
43 "Who _____ the coals into flame" (Isaiah 54:16 NIV)
44 Natives of northern New Mexico
45 "Nevertheless the men _____ hard" (Jonah 1:13)
46 "And _____ the right hand of God" (Mark 16:19) (2 words)
47 _____ work (such as sewing)
48 "Happy Days" actor Williams
49 Pierce
50 "No _____ Street"
51 "A _____ shaken with the wind" (Matthew 11:7)
52 "That which was _____ in his heart" (Matthew 13:19)
53 "La Boheme" role
55 "A loving _____, a graceful deer" (Proverbs 5:19 NIV)
56 Last OT book

SCRAMBLED CIRCLE

by Suzanne Stepp

— WOULD *YOU* WANT THIS JOB? —

By the simplest, humblest acts of service, we can show our greatest love.

1. LOTEW	5. ESDIA	9. DDRIEG
2. SGATMRNE	6. ARTWE	10. SFATE
3. NDAH	7. RUOH	11. UPRSPE
4. HDEA	8. IWEP	12. ATRP

Jesus acted as His disciples' servant.

1. _ _ Ο _ _
2. _ Ο _ _ _ _ _ Ο
3. Ο _ _ _
4. _ Ο _ _
5. _ _ _ Ο _
6. _ _ Ο _ _
7. Ο _ _ _
8. _ _ _ Ο
9. _ Ο Ο _ _ _
10. Ο Ο _ _ _
11. _ _ _ _ Ο _
12. _ _ _ Ο

Answer: _ _ _ _ _ _   _ _ _ _ _   _ _ _ _

TELEPHONE SCRAMBLE
by Connie Troyer

SOUND THE TRUMPETS

The word *trumpet* is mentioned sixty-six times in the Bible. Solve this puzzle to find out how this blaringly evident instrument has been used.

PRS 7	PRS 7	ABC 2	GHI 4	PRS 7	DEF 3

JKL 5	DEF 3	PRS 7	GHI 4	ABC 2	GHI 4	MNO 6

WXY 9	ABC 2	PRS 7	MNO 6	GHI 4	MNO 6	GHI 4

QZ 0	GHI 4	MNO 6	MNO 6

ABC 2	MNO 6	GHI 4	DEF 3	JKL 5	PRS 7

JKL 5	TUV 8	ABC 2	GHI 4	JKL 5	DEF 3	DEF 3

DEF 3	PRS 7	GHI 4	PRS 7	ABC 2	GHI 4	MNO 6

GHI 4	ABC 2	TUV 8	GHI 4	DEF 3	PRS 7

ACROSTIC
by Donna K. Maltese

━━ A SIGN OF THINGS TO COME ━━

With God's help via the prophet Isaiah, an ailing Hezekiah was given a sign of his imminent healing. Crack the code with 2 Chronicles 32 to learn more about this good king who, after regaining his health, spent his remaining years in prosperity.

Hezekiah was _____ of Judah

___ ___ ___ ___
26 9   1   17

Isaiah's father

___ ___ ___ ___
6   12 18 24

Hezekiah and his city were delivered from the king of this country

___ ___ ___ ___ ___ ___ ___
15 23 8   38 33 29 2

To have regained health

___ ___ ___ ___ ___ ___ ___ ___ ___
27 14 36 30 19 10 22 34 7

Aid

___ ___ ___ ___
4   13 21 32

Hezekiah rerouted the _____ of Gihon

___ ___ ___ ___ ___ ___ ___ ___ ___ ___ ___
16 28 5   35 25 37 11 20 39 31 3

29-1   5-4-18-31-14   7-15-38-23   4-3-24-3-26-9-28-4

16-2-23   8-9-37-26   5-30   5-4-10   7-13-28-5-4,   6-1-7

32-22-2-38-35-7   20-1-5-11   5-4-10   21-18-33-7:   6-1-7

4-34   8-32-15-26-35   20-1-5-11   4-29-12,   6-1-7   4-34

17-15-19-35   4-29-12   6   8-9-17-1.

2 CHRONICLES 32:24

■ THE PHILISTINES AND THE ARK ■

MEDIUM

	A	B	C	D	E	F	G	H	I
1		H				W		N	
2			O			G	W	H	T
3	N		G	I					
4	H			W	E			G	
5			T	H	G			I	
6			L					E	W
7	L		I		W		E	T	
8		N	W		I			L	O
9	O			G			N		

Hint: Row 1

_____ _____ kine carried the captured ark back to Israel (1 Samuel 6:12).

DON'T LOOK BACK!
Genesis 19:26

A woman's "need to know" can sometimes spice up her life a little *too* much.
Work this puzzle to discover a verse about a woman whose curiosity cost her
a lot.

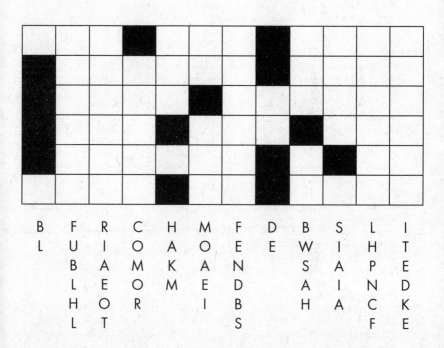

B	F	R	C	H	M	F	D	B	S	L	I
L	U	I	O	A	O	E	E	W	I	H	T
B	A	M	A	O	E	N		S	A	P	E
L	E	O	K	A	A	D		A	I	N	D
H	O	R	M	E	D	B		A	N	C	K
L	T		M	I		S		H	C		E
									F		

CROSSWORD

by Sarah Lagerquist Simmons

■■■ GOOD GUYS AND VILLAINS ■■■

Isn't it great to know that good always reigns over evil? Solve this puzzle to uncover just some of the many "good guys" mentioned in the Bible, as well as the villains they came up against.

Bad guys have it in for the good guys, obsessed with doing them in. But God isn't losing any sleep; to him they're a joke with no punch line.
PSALM 37:12 MSG

ACROSS

1 American astronomer Sagan
5 "I will ____ off from the top" (Ezekiel 17:22)
9 "David took an ____, and played with his hand" (1 Samuel 16:23)
13 Healing plant included in Nicodemus's mixture (John 19:39)
14 Pundit
15 "I will even appoint over you terror, consumption, and the burning ____" (Leviticus 26:16)
16 Alpaca (var.)
17 Armor plate over the nose
18 Football six-pointer (abbr.)
19 Art technique
21 VILLAIN IN THE STORY OF MOSES
24 "Moab shall ____ over Nebo" (Isaiah 15:2)
26 "You own the cosmos. . .everything from ____ to archangel" (Psalm 89:11 MSG)
27 UN agency formed to defeat world-wide hunger (abbr.)
30 DAVID CUT OFF THE VILLAIN GOLIATH'S ____
32 "No decree or ____ that the king issues can be changed" (Daniel 6:15 NIV)
35 Constrained (abbr.)
36 Writer Poe
38 DAVID CUT A PIECE OF FABRIC FROM THE ____ OF A VILLAINOUS KING
40 Straighten
42 End of the day
43 VILLAIN WHO HAD JOHN THE BAPTIST KILLED

44 VILLAIN TURNED GOOD GUY
45 Ransack
47 Opposite of south-southwest (abbr.)
48 Sneer
51 Academic administrator
52 Want
53 "I have not done them of mine own ____" (Numbers 16:28)
55 Bark
57 City in northern Japan
60 VILLAINOUS RULER TO WHOM TAXES WERE DUE (Mark 12:14)
64 Girls, slang
65 Dried coconut meat
67 Weapon of war
68 "His soul shall dwell at ____" (Psalm 25:13)
69 "Let us ____ before the LORD our maker" (Psalm 95:6)
70 Gawk
71 "I ____ them like dirt in the streets" (2 Samuel 22:43 NKJV)
72 "He shall ____ his angel before thee" (Genesis 24:7)
73 VILLAIN TO DAVID'S GOOD GUY

DOWN

1 The Israelites made a golden ____ to worship
2 Composed of wings
3 "Claudius had commanded all Jews to depart from ____" (Acts 18:2)
4 "Can you make a pet of him. . .or put him on a ____. . . ?" (Job 41:5 NIV)
5 Women's organization (abbr.)
6 Scrape
7 City in Nebraska

8 ALLOWED JESUS TO BE PUT TO DEATH
9 Exclamation
10 Farming (abbr.)
11 BOAZ WAS HER GOOD GUY
12 Foot (suffix)
14 Hoodwinked
20 Jewish surname from Hebrew word for priest
22 GOD USED MOSES' _____ TO PERFORM WONDERS IN FRONT OF A VILLAINOUS RULER
23 Whereupon (Hung.)
25 Camp defended by wagons forming a circle (var.)
27 "Stand at the tent _____" (Judges 4:20 MSG)
28 Collection of maps
29 Abhorrence
31 _____ HAD TO FLEE FOR HIS LIFE FROM SAUL
33 Trite
34 Type of steak
37 "I _____ to those whose sin does not lead to death" (1 John 5:16 NIV)
39 PARADISE WHERE THE SERPENT BEGUILED EVE

41 Glanced
43 "My lover is to me a cluster of _____ blossoms" (Song of Solomon 1:14 NIV)
46 Secular
49 "They will tear me like a lion and _____ me to pieces" (Psalm 7:2 NIV)
50 "Everyone who _____, has the door opened to him" (Matthew 7:8 NLV)
54 Male honeybee
56 Exhibitions (abbr.)
57 River in France
58 SAMSON WAS _____ A GOOD GUY
59 "A man shall _____ a pit. . .and not cover it" (Exodus 21:33)
61 Chronicle
62 US organization that defends individual rights (abbr.)
63 "The earth shall _____ to and fro" (Isaiah 24:20)
64 "_____ thee into the land of Moriah" (Genesis 22:2)
66 THE _____ SEA WAS THE SITE OF A VILLAINOUS EGYPTIAN RULER'S DESTRUCTION

NATHAN'S PARABLE
2 SAMUEL 12–14

And the **LORD** sent **Nathan** unto **David**. And he came unto him, and **said** unto him, There were **two men** in **one city**; the one **rich**, and the **other poor**. The rich man had **exceeding many flocks** and **herds**: But the poor man had **nothing**, save one **little ewe lamb**, which he had **bought** and **nourished** up: and it **grew** up **together** with him, and with his **children**; it did eat of his own **meat**, and **drank** of his own **cup**, and lay in his bosom, and was unto him as a **daughter**. And there came a **traveller** unto the rich man, and he **spared** to take of his own flock and of his own herd, to **dress** for the **wayfaring** man that was come unto him; but took the poor man's lamb, and dressed it for the man that was come to him.

```
D  I  V  A  D  R  I  C  H  E  X  R  T  J  D
E  A  O  T  E  J  D  Q  L  J  P  O  N  E  A
R  O  U  H  E  R  D  S  I  P  G  O  K  L  F
A  C  T  G  A  X  R  E  T  E  O  P  N  L  N
P  O  Z  N  H  Z  O  E  T  H  G  U  O  B  T
S  M  K  I  O  T  L  H  L  H  L  C  P  R  D
S  U  E  R  L  U  E  T  E  W  K  O  A  Y  A
E  Y  N  A  M  R  R  R  O  S  W  V  N  O  U
R  Z  M  F  T  G  N  I  D  E  E  C  X  E  G
D  B  E  Y  S  N  R  L  S  L  C  I  T  Y  H
E  L  N  A  E  I  R  E  L  H  A  X  E  W  T
N  X  I  W  M  H  A  E  W  L  E  M  H  L  O
T  D  C  C  A  T  R  C  H  I  L  D  R  E  N
D  C  H  I  L  O  E  L  L  I  T  T  W  E  A
J  A  I  Q  A  N  A  H  T  A  N  E  U  A  J
```

CRYPTOSCRIPTURE
by Donna K. Maltese

═══ THE PROPHET AND THE HARLOT ═══

At the Lord's prompting, a prophet took to wife a harlot, an act that reflected God's displeasure with Israel's adulterous behavior. Can you break the code to discover the name of the prophet, his bride, and their firstborn son?

BJN USQ KHXN WBYN UH SHWQB, ZH,

UBIQ PJUH USQQ B GYVQ HV GSHXQNHLW

BJN FSYKNXQJ HV GSHXQNHLW: VHX USQ

KBJN SBUS FHLLYUUQN ZXQBU GSHXQNHL,

NQTBXUYJZ VXHL USQ KHXN.

IF BP EPQR DQZ RFFV YFUPN RBP ZDGYBRPN FX

ZMSADMU; EBMWB WFQWPMOPZ, DQZ SDNP

BMU D IFQ. DQZ RBP AFNZ IDMZ GQRF BMU,

WDAA BMI QDUP TPJNPPA.

THEY MET JESUS

Of the billions of people who've lived on earth, only a handful actually met Jesus in the flesh. Can you solve these spotty headlines telling the stories of three men who had the great opportunity of meeting the Lord?

D●VOUT MAN REC●G●IZES BABY AS
PRO●I●ED MESS●AH

— — — — — —

S●ORT T●X ●OLLE●TOR H●S ●ESTFULLY
RET●RNED ●TOL●N FUNDS

— — — — — — — —

●URI●US PHAR●S●E SEEKS TO●GH
AN●WERS IN ●ID●LE OF ●IGHT

— — — — — — — —

ACROSTIC
by Donna K. Maltese

━━━ A HOT TOPIC ━━━

Crack the code to discover the request of the rich man who found himself facing the heat "down under."

Jesus' short stories

$\overline{35}$ $\overline{11}$ $\overline{27}$ $\overline{1}$ $\overline{31}$ $\overline{10}$ $\overline{22}$ $\overline{19}$

Hades

$\overline{5}$ $\overline{28}$ $\overline{15}$ $\overline{3}$ $\overline{21}$ $\overline{34}$ $\overline{41}$ $\overline{13}$ $\overline{30}$ $\overline{24}$ $\overline{18}$

Small fragment of bread

$\overline{39}$ $\overline{32}$ $\overline{20}$ $\overline{9}$ $\overline{14}$

Give witness

$\overline{8}$ $\overline{40}$ $\overline{36}$ $\overline{23}$ $\overline{4}$ $\overline{12}$ $\overline{29}$

What beggars have

$\overline{37}$ $\overline{26}$ $\overline{17}$ $\overline{6}$

Lament

$\overline{25}$ $\overline{7}$ $\overline{16}$ $\overline{2}$ $\overline{33}$ $\overline{38}$

74

12-1-15-3-2-7   1-14-30-1-3-1-9,   3-1-33-22

9-28-17-39-29   6-5   9-28,   11-5-18   19-21-5-18

10-1-37-1-34-20-36,   8-3-11-8   3-2   9-1-29   18-4-35

8-3-2   23-4-35   6-12   3-4-36   12-16-5-25-38-27   4-5

41-1-8-26-32,   11-5-18   39-6-6-24   9-29

8-13-5-25-20-40.

LUKE 16:24

CROSSWORD
by David K. Shortess

━━ ALPHA-NUMERIC MIX-UP ━━

Here's a puzzle that has words and numbers mixed up in the answers to its theme clues. So get your thinking cap on, sharpen your pencils, flex your digits, and begin!

*For where two or three are gathered together in my name,
there am I in the midst of them.*
MATTHEW 18:20

ACROSS

1 Jehoshaphat's dad (1 Kings 15:24)
4 "Neither do they ____" (Matthew 6:28)
8 Between-meal treats
14 One Bobbsey twin
15 Ambience
16 Beach shelter
17 "He will silence her noisy ____" (Jeremiah 51:55 NIV)
18 "How we may ____ one another" (Hebrews 10:24 NIV)
19 Thomas Alva ____
20 JONAH'S STAY IN THE FISH (Jonah 1:17) (3 words, 2 numerals)
23 "Mine ____ is consumed with grief" (Psalm 31:9)
24 "____ the ramparts we watched"
25 Dewy
28 "____, give me this water" (John 4:15)
30 "As ____ in heaven" (Matthew 6:10) (2 words)
34 "There ____ lad here" (John 6:9) (2 words)
35 Thursday was named after him
37 "And ____ and mourning shall flee away" (Isaiah 51:11)
39 "THE FATHER, THE WORD, AND THE HOLY GHOST: ____" (1 John 5:7) (4 words, 1 numeral)
42 "Howbeit there is a kinsman ____ than I" (Ruth 3:12)
43 "And ____ it in a book" (Isaiah 30:8)
44 Contend
45 "Then came I with an ____" (Acts 23:27)
46 NUMBER OF VIRGINS WHO WENT TO MEET THE BRIDEGROOM (Matthew 25:1)

47 "A shadow from the ____" (Isaiah 25:4)
48 "Let us make ____ name" (Genesis 11:4) (2 words)
50 "As for all the hills once cultivated by the ____" (Isaiah 7:25 NIV)
52 IN WHICH THE LEAVEN WAS HIDDEN (Matthew 13:33) (3 words, 1 numeral)
61 Band leader Glenn
62 "The same shall be ____ of all" (Mark 9:35)
63 Attorneys' organization (abbr.)
64 Regal fur
65 Away from the wind and weather
66 "So a ____ tongue brings angry looks" (Proverbs 25:23 NIV)
67 Wise old man of Greek mythology
68 "Saying, What ____ these stones" (Joshua 4:21)
69 "____, of the Gentiles also" (Romans 3:29)

DOWN

1 "HE HAD ALSO SEVEN SONS ____ DAUGHTERS" (Job 42:13) (1 word, 1 numeral)
2 "And God ____, Let there be light" (Genesis 1:3)
3 "And there was one ____, a prophetess" (Luke 2:36)
4 Impudent
5 Between caterpillars and butterflies
6 "____ in the path of your commands" (Psalm 119:32 NIV) (2 words)
7 "Then Mary took about a pint of pure ____" (John 12:3 NIV)
8 "A crowd was running to the ____" (Mark 9:25 NIV)

76

9 Opposite the zenith

10 "He rolled _____ stone in front of the entrance" (Matthew 27:60 NIV) (2 words)

11 Country singer Johnny

12 Nautical mile per hour

13 *Lacking* or *without* (Fr.)

21 Quick affirmative

22 "THAT WHEN JEHUDI HAD READ _____ FOUR LEAVES" (Jeremiah 36:23) (1 word, 1 numeral)

25 Ephesian goddess (Acts 19:34)

26 Lou Grant: Ed _____

27 Polite address

28 Call for help

29 "Good night" girl

30 Anger

31 Word with *treasure*

32 Greek region where Ephesus was located

33 "Eat the fat, and drink the _____" (Nehemiah 8:10)

35 "_____ LORD is my shepherd" (Psalm 23:1)

36 "And all _____ paths are peace" (Proverbs 3:17)

37 "And _____ upon the bed" (Genesis 48:2)

38 "For _____ in the blackest darkness" (Job 28:3 NIV)

40 "But _____ the spirits whether" (1 John 4:1)

41 "AND _____ THAT SIDE" (Ezekiel 40:10) (1 word, 1 numeral)

46 "And _____ for mortar" (Genesis 11:3 NIV)

47 "And touched the _____ of his garment" (Matthew 9:20)

48 "_____ HOOKS!" (crate marking; 2 words)

49 More certain

50 Son of Beeri (Hosea 1:1)

51 "For as _____ as ye eat this bread" (1 Corinthians 11:26)

52 "BEHOLD, _____ SEEK THEE" (Acts 10:19) (1 word, 1 numeral)

53 "I sink in deep _____" (Psalm 69:2)

54 "Under oaks and poplars and _____" (Hosea 4:13)

55 Stepped down, as from a carriage

56 Shem's son (Genesis 10:22)

57 "Then let him count the years of the _____ thereof" (Leviticus 25:27)

58 "For my yoke is _____, and my burden is light" (Matthew 11:30)

59 "They say unto him, We are _____" (Matthew 20:22)

60 "The good shepherd _____ down his life for the sheep" (John 10:11 NIV)

THE VOYAGE BEGINS
ACTS 27:9–13

Now when much **time** was spent, and when **sailing** was now **dangerous**, because the **fast** was now **already past**, Paul **admonished** them, and said unto them, **Sirs**, I **perceive** that this **voyage** will be with **hurt** and **much damage**, not **only** of the lading and **ship**, but also of our **lives**. **Nevertheless** the **centurion believed** the **master** and the **owner** of the ship, more than those things which were **spoken** by **Paul**. And because the haven was not commodious to winter in, the more part advised to **depart** thence also, if by any **means** they might **attain** to **Phenice**, and there to winter; which is an **haven** of **Crete**, and **lieth toward** the **south west** and **north** west. And when the south wind **blew** softly, **supposing** that they had obtained their **purpose**, loosing thence, they sailed close by Crete.

```
H C U M A E S O P R U P I H S
T G N I S O P P U S N H S S Y
D F A Y C E G A Y O V E I A I
E V I E C R E P I N G N R D D
V H O N L Y E R S E D I S M A
E T I M E A U T L V R C A O N
I R L H T T S U E E A E I N G
L O W T N E A E Q R W H L I E
E N A E V P G L E T O U I S R
B I C I S A O T R H T R N H O
N W L L M T S W D E T T G E U
N E V A H A F D N L A U S D S
C L D F M S P O K E N D O A K
B B M E A N S A F S R X Y S P
R J A D E P A R T S A F C M X
```

ACROSTIC
by Donna K. Maltese

━━━ REDEEMING LOVE ━━━

God loves us as Boaz loved Ruth. Solve this puzzle to discover the offer Ruth didn't refuse from her kinsman-redeemer.

Corn

$\overline{25}$ $\overline{31}$ $\overline{5}$ $\overline{23}$ $\overline{15}$

As much as one can grasp

$\overline{16}$ $\overline{20}$ $\overline{6}$ $\overline{28}$ $\overline{10}$ $\overline{1}$ $\overline{24}$

Harvest

$\overline{33}$ $\overline{26}$ $\overline{8}$ $\overline{4}$ $\overline{19}$ $\overline{13}$

Grain used for feed, malt, and cereal (Ruth 2:17)

$\overline{11}$ $\overline{18}$ $\overline{22}$ $\overline{32}$ $\overline{3}$ $\overline{29}$

Boaz was from the _____ of Elimelech (Ruth 2:1)

$\overline{9}$ $\overline{14}$ $\overline{2}$ $\overline{30}$

Works

$\overline{27}$ $\overline{34}$ $\overline{12}$ $\overline{7}$ $\overline{21}$ $\overline{17}$

17-20-5-28   11-7-26-23   1-6-8-7   13-1-8-4,

16-3-31-21-3-17-8   8-4-7-1   6-7-8,   25-29

28-34-1-33-4-8-15-22?   33-7   6-7-8   8-7   33-27-3-18-30

5-30   2-30-7-8-4-19-13   10-5-3-32-28,   30-3-5-8-4-3-13

33-7   10-13-7-25   16-3-6-9-3,   12-1-8   20-11-5-28-19

16-3-21-3   10-2-17-8   12-29   25-29   25-2-5-28-3-6-17.

RUTH 2:8

ANAGRAM
by Paul Kent

— SCENES FROM THE EXODUS —

The Bible's second book is packed with memorable stories. Can you unscramble these three events from Exodus? Note: None of these exact terms is found in the King James Version, but you'll definitely recognize each one.

Go label up food

_ _ _ _ _ _   _ _

_ _ _ _ _

Throne of fat birds

_ _ _ _ _   _ _

_ _ _ _ _ _ _ _ _

Trade a spring foe

_ _ _ _ _ _ _   _ _

_ _ _ _ _ _

THE BEST BIRTHDAY EVER

LUKE 2:11

Solve this Bible quotation puzzle to discover the most joyous birth ever to arrive on this unstable earth.

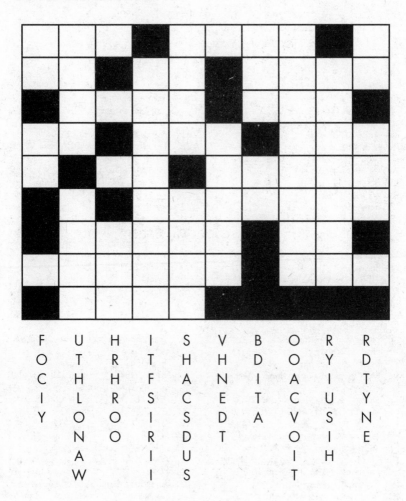

CROSSWORD
by Tonya Vilhauer

ON TRIAL

To save us from sin, Jesus, an innocent man, was tried, found guilty, and condemned to die. Oh, what a Savior! As you work this puzzle, remember what He suffered for our sakes and raise up a prayer of joyful thanksgiving!

But he was wounded for our transgressions, he was bruised for our iniquities: the chastisement of our peace was upon him; and with his stripes we are healed.
ISAIAH 53:5

ACROSS

1 Cobblers (Brit.)
6 In Joseph's lineage, the son of Eliezer (Luke 3:29)
10 "Every head was made ____, and every shoulder was peeled" (Ezekiel 29:18)
14 Diamond weight unit
15 Black (var.)
16 A dueling sword
17 Impersonation
18 A SOLDIER PIERCED JESUS' ____ (John 19:34)
19 Praise
20 Plateau
21 Prompt
22 "The vessel that he made of clay was ____" (Jeremiah 18:4)
24 Slant
26 HE SAID, "I FIND NO FAULT IN THIS MAN" (Luke 23:4)
27 Loose
30 Flow out slowly
31 Relating to hearing
32 "A ____ word stirs up anger" (Proverbs 15:1 NIV)
33 Radio frequency band (abbr.)
36 "SAVE THYSELF, AND COME DOWN FROM THE ____" (Mark 15:30)
37 "They would have repented long ____ in sackcloth and ashes" (Matthew 11:21)
38 "Thou shalt not ____ carnally with thy neighbour's wife" (Leviticus 18:20)
39 Compass point (abbr.)
40 "Ye blind guides, which strain at a ____, and swallow a camel" (Matthew 23:24)
41 Moisten meat
43 Cowboy apparel

44 "Thou shalt utterly ____ it, and thou shalt utterly abhor it" (Deuteronomy 7:26)
45 Stomach muscles (abbr.)
48 "For God ____ love" (1 John 4:8)
49 Invoke
50 Raise higher
51 "It shall be seven days under the ____" (Leviticus 22:27)
52 "For there shall be no ____ of any man's life" (Acts 27:22)
56 "Expose these things for the ____ they are" (Ephesians 5:11 MSG)
57 Private school (abbr.)
59 Church part
60 Antic
61 "The greater light to ____ the day" (Genesis 1:16)
62 "You are from ____; I am from above" (John 8:23 NIV)
63 "Is this house, which is called by my name, become ____ of robbers?" (Jeremiah 7:11) (2 words)
64 "AND THEY ____ UPON HIM. . .AND SMOTE HIM" (Matthew 27:30)
65 THEY PUT A ____ OF THORNS ON JESUS' HEAD (Matthew 27:29)

DOWN

1 "I worked an elaborate ____? Where's the evidence?" (2 Corinthians 12:16–17 MSG)
2 "She took the goatskins and covered. . . the smooth ____ of his neck" (Genesis 27:15 MSG)
3 Minerals
4 "WHOM WILL YE THAT I RELEASE UNTO YOU? ____, OR JESUS. . . ?" (Matthew 27:17)

5 Pigpen
6 "BUT ____ HELD HIS PEACE" (Matthew 26:63)
7 Off-Broadway award
8 "And Jacob ____ pottage" (Genesis 25:29)
9 "Love your ____, do good to them which hate you" (Luke 6:27)
10 Baseball player Yogi
11 "Wherefore lay ____ all filthiness" (James 1:21)
12 Embankment
13 "If we. . .be examined of the good ____ done" (Acts 4:9)
21 Key
23 A to Z
25 "They are not plagued by human ____" (Psalm 73:5 NIV)
26 Philanthropist and former presidential contender
27 Women's branch of US Army in World War II (abbr.)
28 "Let us kill him, that the inheritance may be ____" (Luke 20:14)
29 "Led him unto the ____ of the hill" (Luke 4:29)
30 Epics
32 "PILATE. . .WASHED HIS ____ BEFORE THE MULTITUDE" (Matthew 27:24)

33 "Thy life be for his life, or ____ thou shalt pay a talent of silver" (1 Kings 20:39)
34 "The sword that ____ him cannot cut" (Job 41:26 NLV)
35 "BEHOLD MY HANDS AND MY ____" (Luke 24:39)
40 Acoustical or electric stringed instruments
42 Artist's studio
44 "Now the eyes of Israel were ____ for age" (Genesis 48:10)
45 Ladybug fare
46 "First the ____, then the ear, after that the full corn" (Mark 4:28)
47 HE CARRIED JESUS' CROSS (Matthew 27:32)
49 Plebe
50 Beef graders (abbr.)
51 Surrealist Spanish painter
53 Scandinavian national capital
54 "The LORD is. . .____ to anger" (Psalm 103:8)
55 Stitched together
58 "LET THIS ____ PASS FROM ME" (Matthew 26:39)
59 TV network (abbr.)

━━━ NO LONGER DOUBTING ━━━
JOHN 20:26–28

And **after eight days again** his **disciples** were **within**, and **Thomas** with **them**: then **came Jesus**, the **doors being shut**, and **stood** in the **midst**, and said, **Peace** be unto you. **Then saith** he to Thomas, Reach hither thy **finger**, and **behold** my **hands**; and **reach hither** thy hand, and **thrust** it into my **side**: and be not **faithless**, but **believing**. And Thomas **answered** and said unto him, My **Lord** and my God.

```
S  A  M  O  H  T  L  U  D  B  D  A  Y  S  H
E  S  I  D  E  H  P  H  L  E  Z  O  K  L  A
L  M  E  H  T  K  C  K  O  O  C  H  O  O  N
P  A  Q  L  P  F  A  A  H  B  C  A  K  R  D
I  Q  N  J  H  F  G  N  E  H  T  B  E  D  S
C  G  W  S  A  T  A  L  B  R  H  G  C  P  F
S  W  I  K  W  E  I  G  H  T  N  S  O  W  A
I  F  T  T  B  E  N  A  H  I  T  H  E  R  U
D  M  H  E  V  W  R  T  F  O  S  S  R  S  E
T  J  I  I  Y  Y  I  E  O  C  U  R  Y  O  M
P  N  N  D  V  A  V  D  D  S  R  E  T  F  A
G  G  Q  N  S  H  C  H  E  R  H  C  U  G  C
W  F  V  H  U  T  E  J  G  F  T  Y  H  I  Y
M  N  C  E  A  F  U  E  N  I  E  B  S  N  M
E  S  D  G  H  A  E  T  A  V  T  L  E  Q  D
```

DROP TWO
by Dorothy Pryse

▬▬▬ PETER JAILED ▬▬▬
SEE ACTS 12:5

Herod hated people who worshipped Jesus. Work this drop two puzzle to discover what this king did to sabotage Peter's influence on his people.

STRANGE	Bestow	_____	1. ____ ____
OCTOPUS	Boy or girl	_____	2. ____ ____
PETRIFY	Torridly hot	_____	3. ____ ____
EROSIVE	Wanders	_____	4. ____ ____
TRODDEN	More peculiar	_____	5. ____ ____
POWDERY	Bride's offering	_____	6. ____ ____
SPARRED	Shovel	_____	7. ____ ____
WARSHIP	Key signature	_____	8. ____ ____
SESTINA	Beer mug	_____	9. ____ ____
SEAPORT	Talk idly	_____	10. ____ ____
NORFOLK	Level surface	_____	11. ____ ____

— — — — — — — — — — —

‾1‾ ‾2‾ ‾3‾ ‾4‾ ‾5‾ ‾6‾ ‾7‾ ‾8‾ ‾9‾ ‾10‾ ‾11‾

88

■ TO SHOW THE WAY ■

God has always been a beacon for followers of the Light. Decode these cryptoscriptures to find verses highlighting His guidance and His presence, from the Old Testament to the New.

KYZ WCR UQBZ NRYW XRAQBR WCRI XV ZKV

MY K JMUUKB QA K EUQDZ, WQ URKZ WCRI

WCR NKV; KYZ XV YMTCW MY K JMUUKB QA

AMBR, WQ TMSR WCRI UMTCW; WQ TQ XV

ZKV KYZ YMTCW.

HGK AIB AIHEE UZVGY OTZPI H ATG, HGK PITJ

AIHEP SHEE IVA GHQB MBAJA: OTZ IB AIHEE

AHWB IVA LBTLEB OZTQ PIBVZ AVGA.

ACROSTIC
by Donna K. Maltese

A BEWITCHING TALE

Solve the puzzle to discover the tale of a man who dabbled in magic and, for a spell, developed quite a following.

He converted an Ethiopian eunuch (Acts 8:26–38)

$\overline{22}$ $\overline{8}$ $\overline{31}$ $\overline{26}$ $\overline{2}$ $\overline{15}$

Caster of spells

$\overline{13}$ $\overline{27}$ $\overline{7}$ $\overline{3}$ $\overline{20}$

Skill in deceiving to gain something

$\overline{23}$ $\overline{9}$ $\overline{1}$ $\overline{17}$ $\overline{12}$

Satan's henchmen

$\overline{18}$ $\overline{11}$ $\overline{28}$ $\overline{30}$ $\overline{21}$ $\overline{5}$

Make confused

$\overline{14}$ $\overline{29}$ $\overline{6}$ $\overline{25}$ $\overline{19}$ $\overline{4}$

Clever

$\overline{16}$ $\overline{10}$ $\overline{24}$

7-8-4-9-4 13-1-5 1 23-29-9-12-1-27-21 28-1-21,

23-1-10-10-29-18 19-31-28-30-21, 13-20-2-3-20

14-11-17-30-9-11-12-2-6-11 2-21 7-8-4 16-1-6-29

23-2-12-24 25-5-29-18 19-30-9-3-29-9-24, 1-21-18

14-11-13-2-12-3-20-11-18 7-8-4 15-11-30-22-26-11

30-17 16-1-6-1-9-2-1.

ACTS 8:9

CROSSWORD
by *David K. Shortess*

━━ BIBLICAL BIG BOYS ━━

Because the Lord is with us, we need not fear anything—no matter how gigantic. Solve this puzzle to uncover verses dealing with biblical big boys who lived in days of yore.

And there we saw the giants. . .and we were in our own sight as grasshoppers, and so we were in their sight.
NUMBERS 13:33

ACROSS

1 Its capital has been Agana
5 "In ____ also is his tabernacle" (Psalm 76:2)
10 "And he ____ the sin of many" (Isaiah 53:12)
14 Taj Mahal city
15 North Florida city
16 Son of Seth (Genesis 4:26)
17 "____ IN THE EARTH IN THOSE DAYS" (Genesis 6:4) (3 words)
20 Help a felon
21 *Dead*, in Paris
22 "Surely in vain the ____ is spread" (Proverbs 1:17)
25 "And they filled them up to the ____" (John 2:7)
27 In abundance
31 "And ____ of oil" (Leviticus 14:21) (2 words)
33 Company head
35 "Able was I ____ saw Elba" (2 words)
36 Slightest
39 Former home of the Mets
42 Japanese volcano
43 "THERE WENT OUT A CHAMPION. . . NAMED ____, WHOSE HEIGHT WAS SIX CUBITS AND A SPAN" (1 Samuel 17:4) (3 words)
46 Pale
47 Malayan sailboat (var.)
48 Treble clef guys
50 "The ____ are a people not strong" (Proverbs 30:25)
52 Swift boat from Vietnam War (abbr.)
54 Three in Thüringen
55 Put away

58 Kind of hoop
61 1,760 equal 1 mile (abbr.)
62 "He. . .measured the ____ all around" (Ezekiel 42:15 NIV)
64 "How much ____ shall I answer him" (Job 9:14)
66 "WITH ALL BASHAN, WHICH WAS CALLED ____" (Deuteronomy 3:13) (4 words)
73 "Wherein I ____ erred" (Job 6:24)
74 Tapeworm (var.)
75 "____ certain man was sick" (John 11:1) (2 words)
76 "And Abraham lifted up his ____" (Genesis 22:13)
77 Fishhook leader
78 "The nations are as a ____ of a bucket" (Isaiah 40:15)

DOWN

1 "And Moses ____ him into the camp" (Numbers 11:30)
2 Cry of disgust
3 "____ not my days few" (Job 10:20)
4 "Call me not Naomi, call me ____" (Ruth 1:20)
5 "Hear ye therefore the parable of the ____" (Matthew 13:18)
6 Acid found in vinegar
7 Roman household god or spirit
8 Primary school (abbr.)
9 "And I will send a fire on ____" (Ezekiel 39:6)
10 George Harrison was one
11 New England Cape
12 "But the name of the wicked shall ____" (Proverbs 10:7)

13 Ogee shape
18 "As their lives ____ away in their mothers' arms" (Lamentations 2:12 NIV)
19 "Was ____ the son of Ikkesh" (1 Chronicles 27:9)
22 Viet ____
23 Appealing to refined taste
24 Blue Jays' home
26 Furnace survivor (Daniel 3:26)
28 Public speaking
29 Tear up again
30 Old MacDonald's refrain ending
32 Hair goop
34 Expression of discovery
37 A little drink
38 "Now the Valley of Siddim was full of ____ pits" (Genesis 14:10 NIV)
40 Newt
41 "He is of ____; ask him" (John 9:23)
44 "From the ____ of the rocks I see him" (Numbers 23:9)
45 "____ the Word was made flesh" (John 1:14)
46 "There ____ a man sent from God" (John 1:6)
49 Bro's sib

51 Marshlands
53 "I am not come to destroy, but to ____" (Matthew 5:17)
56 Baseball stat
57 Fender blemishes
59 "It must be settled in a ____ assembly" (Acts 19:39 NIV)
60 "As many ____ love, I rebuke and chasten" (Revelation 3:19) (2 words)
63 "Ye have made it ____ of thieves" (Luke 19:46) (2 words)
65 "I shall multiply my days as the ____" (Job 29:18)
66 "____ LORD is my light" (Psalm 27:1)
67 "The ____ is withered away" (Isaiah 15:6)
68 "Adam was. . .formed, then ____" (1 Timothy 2:13)
69 "I am ____ that bear witness of myself" (John 8:18)
70 "Fight neither with small ____ great" (1 Kings 22:31)
71 "No man can serve ____ masters" (Matthew 6:24)
72 "The trees. . .are full of ____" (Psalm 104:16)

93

TELEPHONE SCRAMBLE

by Nancy Bernhard and Connie Troyer

CURSED

Here are things, places, people, and objects that were the opposite of blessed, some through no fault of their own. Can you solve the puzzle to figure them out?

ABC 2	ABC 2	GHI 4	MNO 6

ABC 2	ABC 2	MNO 6	ABC 2	ABC 2	MNO 6

GHI 4	PRS 7	MNO 6	TUV 8	MNO 6	DEF 3

MNO 6	ABC 2	TUV 8	TUV 8	PRS 7	DEF 3

PRS 7	DEF 3	PRS 7	PRS 7	DEF 3	MNO 6	TUV 8

JKL 5	TUV 8	DEF 3	ABC 2	GHI 4

JEZEBEL'S DEATH

MEDIUM

	A	B	C	D	E	F	G	H	I
1			W				O		H
2		S		A		O			R
3	A		O	W				S	
4	R							T	S
5			H		S	W			
6		A	I			H	R	O	
7	I			S	D		A		
8									T
9	T	O	A			R	S		D

Hint: Row 6

"And he _____, _____ her down. So they threw her down: and some of her blood was sprinkled on the wall, and on the horses: and he trode her under foot" (2 Kings 9:33).

■ SODOM AND GOMORRAH ■
GENESIS 19:24–28

Then the **Lord rained** upon **Sodom** and upon **Gomorrah brimstone** and **fire** from the Lord out of **heaven**; and he **overthrew** those **cities**, and all the **plain**, and all the **inhabitants** of the cities, and that which **grew** upon the **ground**. But his **wife looked back** from **behind** him, and she **became** a **pillar** of **salt**. And **Abraham** gat up **early** in the **morning** to the **place** where he **stood** before the Lord: And he looked toward Sodom and Gomorrah, and toward all the **land** of the plain, and beheld, and, lo, the **smoke** of the **country** went up as the smoke of a **furnace**.

```
B X B R A I N E D O O T S A P
I T L A N D R G R O U N D J N
Q J P L C I A N B V W I F E P
K L C L F K Y X H E N N V P Z
Z G N I N R O M W R C A H L L
W U E P T S W O Y T E A L A W
L S T N A T I B A H N I M C B
L L U L O O K E D R P Z W E L
E O T X R T L A S E Q L Y S B
C R R G E U S M B W N L A E R
A H A D G G O M O R R A H I K
N Y L T R K F O I A A I C T N
R D R U E R S D E R N H E I D
U B N W W U E O E D B A A C J
F A I Q A U U S M Z P P G M A
```

ACROSTIC
by Donna K. Maltese

ONE GREAT CATCH

When we listen to Jesus, we reap great benefits. Solve this puzzle to discover how some fishermen were blessed with bounty after heeding Jesus' advice.

The sea on which this story takes place (John 21:1)

___ ___ ___ ___ ___ ___ ___ ___
21 36 15   3 41 11 28 33

Simon and Andrew's initial livelihood (Matthew 4:18)

___ ___ ___ ___ ___ ___ ___ ___ ___
8   14 22 40 34 27   2 19 12

The disciples followed Jesus' ____ (John 21:6)

___ ___ ___ ___ ___ ___ ___ ___ ___
1   23 10 29 35   7 13 20 31

The apostle who took a dive (John 21:7)

___ ___ ___ ___ ___
16 42 30 24 18

The night before, the disciples ____ naught (John 21:3)

___ ___ ___ ___ ___ ___
39   4 25 17   5 37

If we ____ depend on Jesus, we will have more than enough

___ ___ ___ ___ ___ ___
43 38   6 32   9 26

ACROSTIC
by Donna K. Maltese
(continued)

35-4-22-7   7-5-3   12-3-30   6-12   7-5-3   18-23-17-5-37

33-14-1-3   6-8   7-5-3   33-5-36-16,   4-31-1   26-42

33-40-28-9-9   8-11-12-1.   7-5-3-26   39-4-22-7

7-5-3-10-3-8-20-10-3,   4-31-1   12-6-43   7-5-3-26

43-24-41-24   12-6-21   28-15-9-34   7-6   1-27-4-43

13-7   8-20-10   7-5-3   2-25-32-7-13-7-25-1-29   20-8

8-11-22-38-19-22.

JOHN 21:6

by Paul Kent and Sara Stoker

━━━━━ RUINED LIVES ━━━━━

"Choose life," God commanded His people through Moses. But not everyone chooses wisely. These spotty headlines relate to the stories of three men who blew it, big-time. Can you solve them?

●EBREW SL●IN FOR SN●TCHING
JERI●HO PLU●DER

— — — — —

DECEPTIO● COME● B●CK TO H●UNT
CHR●STI●N BE●EFACTOR

— — — — — —

UN●UST ●INFUL MAN COMMITS S●ICI●E
RATHER THAN ●SK FORGIVENESS

— — — — —

— A BIG FISH TALE —

When God calls us to perform a duty, we would be wise to stop treading water and swim in His will.

1. SUSJE
2. RWOSD
3. HNREET
4. ELTNMA
5. AHHPROA

6. TWDLE
7. TTLHWFE
8. NLAIS
9. EANLFL
10. TUDETMLIU

Jesus made reference to this slimy story.

1. ◯ _ _ _ _
2. _ _ ◯ _ _
3. ◯ _ _ _ _ _
4. _ ◯ _ _ _ _
5. _ _ _ _ _ ◯

6. _ ◯ _ _ _
7. _ _ _ _ _ _ _ ◯
8. _ _ ◯ _ _
9. _ _ _ ◯ _ _
10. _ _ _ _ _ _ _ _ ◯

Answer: _ _ _ _ _ and the _ _ _ _ _

CROSSWORD
by Tonya Vilhauer

A DOUBLE PORTION

Sometimes good things come in twos, as in the case of the godly men revealed in this puzzle. Pay "pair-ticular" attention to the clues when teaming up these faithful and honorable duos. . . .

Let the elders that rule well be counted worthy of double honour.
1 TIMOTHY 5:17

ACROSS

1 Whipped dairy food
6 Madagascar franc (abbr.)
9 RED-HAIRED TWIN (Genesis 25:25)
13 Shampoo brand
14 To suffer illness
15 "Ahasuerus laid a tribute. . .upon the _____ of the sea" (Esther 10:1)
16 Colder
17 One (Sp.)
18 "They look and _____ upon me" (Psalm 22:17)
19 _____ vu
20 "THE SPIRIT OF ELIJAH DOTH REST ON _____" (2 Kings 2:15)
22 Up-to-date (abbr.)
23 Amendment proposed to guarantee equal rights regardless of sex (abbr.)
24 Time zone (abbr.)
25 "The coat was without _____" (John 19:23)
27 "Take thee a _____ knife" (Ezekiel 5:1)
29 Spanish fortress commander
33 Outlaw
34 "I have broken the _____ of Pharaoh" (Ezekiel 30:21)
35 Christmas carol
36 HEEL-HOLDING TWIN (Genesis 25:26)
39 Swollen spot on the eyelid
40 "His spear _____ in the ground" (1 Samuel 26:7)
41 Seaweed substance
42 Roberto's "Yes!"
43 "They were _____ filled with the Holy Ghost" (Acts 2:4)
44 "JACOB GAVE ESAU BREAD AND _____" (Genesis 25:34)
46 "Your own _____ have said" (Acts 17:28)
49 Father
50 Compass point (abbr.)
51 "Given to hospitality, _____ to teach" (1 Timothy 3:2)
53 Crow's cry
56 Assign
58 Soft cheese
59 Red pigment (var.)
61 Native or resident of (suffix)
62 Fish tank dweller
63 "The first day of the feast of unleavened _____ the disciples came to Jesus" (Matthew 26:17)
64 Pastor (abbr.)
65 Step
66 "Let the archer _____ his bow" (Jeremiah 51:3)
67 Compass point (abbr.)
68 Celebration

DOWN

1 "He will not always _____: neither. . . keep his anger" (Psalm 103:9)
2 Speed contestants
3 ELISHA BECAME HIS SERVANT (1 Kings 19:21)
4 Adrift
5 "After this manner will I _____ the pride of Judah" (Jeremiah 13:9)
6 Pilate said he found no _____ in this man (Luke 23:4)

7 Brief
8 List of definitions
9 Suffix denoting the most
10 Close the door hard
11 Air (prefix)
12 "The ox hath _____ to push in time past" (Exodus 21:36)
15 JACOB AND ESAU'S FATHER (Genesis 25:26)
20 Cable sports channel
21 Great ships can be turned by a very small _____ (James 3:4)
24 *The Little Mermaid*'s Sebastian
26 ELISHA TOOK ELIJAH'S _____ (2 Kings 2:13)
28 Terminates
30 Note of debt
31 Last month of year (abbr.)
32 Deer relative
34 Snacked
36 Native of Nippon (abbr.)
37 "I knew a man in Christ above fourteen years _____" (2 Corinthians 12:2)

38 Kitty
39 Dozers
40 "The Cretians are alway liars, evil beasts, _____ bellies" (Titus 1:12)
42 Giant
43 Church part
45 Helped
47 What dentists remove
48 ELISHA ASKED FOR A DOUBLE PORTION OF ELIJAH'S _____ (2 Kings 2:9)
50 Actor Martin
52 Watery
53 Baseball player Ty
54 "As it were a half _____ of land" (1 Samuel 14:14)
55 "And _____ the day of Pentecost was fully come" (Acts 2:1)
57 "Learn to maintain good works for necessary _____" (Titus 3:14)
58 Second letter of the Greek alphabet
60 Radiation dose (abbr.)
62 Cooking measurement (abbr.)

WORD SEARCH
by Conover Swofford

THE PROMISED LAND

ABRAHAM
ACHAN
ALTAR
ARK
CANAAN
GIANTS
GIBEON
GRAPES
HONEY
ISRAEL
JORDAN
JOSHUA

MIGHTY MEN
MILK
MOSES
POMEGRANATES
PRIEST
RAHAB
SPY
STONES
TRIBES
VALOR
WAR

```
G T J U L O P A Q X Z Y T T R
G J O Q C A N A A N P H R S N
I P P X Z B H T S T O N E S S
B R R S P R I E S T M S R R R
E C L B J A W C S R E H R A R
O Y E N O H A R T I G L T V L
N B Y B R A R K N B R L X A S
I A Y Y D M E E A E A Y Y L T
T U R P A E M R D S N H A O N
E H T T N Y P N N N A M A R A
S S R S T R S R E S T R S R I
K O G H G R R S C S E P A R G
L J G A C H A N S Z S E Y P S
I I S R A E L X E Z E C C R G
M O S E S T T X D A H A R R G
```

ACROSTIC
by Donna K. Maltese

━━ TALK ABOUT JOB LOSS! ━━

When bereft of all his worldly goods, Job still maintained a good attitude.
Solve this puzzle to find out his exact frame of mind.

Job was God's _____ (Job 1:8)

 ___ ___ ___ ___ ___ ___ ___
 13 34 28 23 1   18 9

God's protection (Job 1:10)

 ___ ___ ___ ___ ___
 24 17 5   31 12

Calamity

 ___ ___ ___ ___ ___ ___ ___ ___ ___ ___
 11 26 2   19 8   22 29 4   32 36

Dismal

 ___ ___ ___ ___ ___
 6   20 14 33 27

God let Satan have his _____ with Job

 ___ ___ ___
 30 15 3

In all his suffering, Job never _____ God

 ___ ___ ___ ___ ___ ___
 35 25 10 21 7   16

18-33-27-17-16   35-15-11-34   26   8-25-29   8-19

11-3   11-8-29-24-7-28-2   30-8-11-6,   1-32-5

18-33-27-17-16   13-24-15-20-20   26   22-36-29-4-22-18

9-24-26-9-24-7-10:   9-24-7   20-8-10-5   31-15-23-14,

1-32-5   9-24-7   20-8-10-5   24-15-9-24   9-15-27-7-18

1-30-1-3;   6-20-12-21-21-12-16   6-12   9-24-7

18-33-11-17   8-19   9-24-7   20-8-10-5.

Job 1:21

by Paul Kent

JESUS WAS HERE

Stories of Jesus are the best stories imaginable. Can you unscramble these three events in the Lord's life? Note: None of these exact terms is found in the King James Version, but you'll definitely know them and their stories.

Puts pearls

___ ___ ___ ___   ___ ___ ___ ___ ___ ___

Fast rain touring

___ ___ ___ ___ ___ ___ ___ ___ ___ ___ ___ ___ ___

As in cones

___ ___ ___ ___ ___ ___ ___ ___

═ ZECHARIAH'S SEVENTH VISION ═

This prophet wasn't horsing around when he experienced his seventh vision. Can you break the cryptoscripture codes to discover the vehicles seen and what they represented?

YCR H OQKCPR, YCR BHNOPR QG AHCP

PVPM, YCR BEEDPR, YCR, ZPJEBR, OJPKP TYAP

NEQK TJYKHEOM EQO NKEA ZPOXPPC OXE

AEQCOYHCM; YCR OJP AEQCOYHCM XPKP

AEQCOYHCM EN ZKYMM.

DAQ UYC DARCP DAXBCZCQ DAQ XDTQ OAUH

LC, UYCXC DZC UYC GHOZ XNTZTUX HG UYC

YCDMCAX, BYTJY RH GHZUY GZHL XUDAQTAR

FCGHZC UYC PHZQ HG DPP UYC CDZUY.

CROSSWORD
by David K. Shortess

━━ SOWING THE WORD ━━

To reap a bountiful harvest for Christ, we must not only be grounded in the Word, but obey, serve, and persist in the Way, keeping our eyes on Jesus. Field these scriptural clues to find a crop of "sow-ful" answers scattered throughout this puzzle.

> *Hearken; Behold, there went out a sower to sow:*
> *And it came to pass, as he sowed. . .*
> MARK 4:3–4

ACROSS

1 "Who ____ thou?" (Genesis 27:32)
4 "____ a watch, O LORD" (Psalm 141:3)
7 "How right they are to ____ you!" (Song of Solomon 1:4 NIV)
12 Constrictors
14 Japheth's father (Genesis 5:32)
15 "No mention shall be made of ____" (Job 28:18)
16 Ambience
17 "There is none ____" (Deuteronomy 4:39)
18 Short news pieces
19 "SOME FELL ____" (Mark 4:4) (4 words)
22 One who stores fodder on a farm
23 Lots of ounces (abbr.)
24 Its agents work underground (abbr.)
27 Repeat in music
28 Used in posting a letter to oneself
29 "And it became ____ in his hand" (Exodus 4:4) (2 words)
30 Naval initials
33 "AND SOME FELL ON ____ " (Mark 4:5) (2 words)
36 Indian princess or rajah's wife
38 "Have gone into exile, captive before the ____" (Lamentations 1:5 NIV)
39 It may be a golden one
40 "AND SOME FELL ____ " (Mark 4:7) (2 words)
43 "Doth not the ____ try words?" (Job 12:11)
44 "And cried with a ____ voice" (Mark 5:7)
45 "To ____, Jerusalem" (Jeremiah 25:18)

46 "Which strain ____ gnat" (Matthew 23:24) (2 words)
48 "And it ____ upon each of them" (Acts 2:3)
49 Brother's sibling (abbr.)
50 "Even on the ____ laid a very heavy yoke" (Isaiah 47:6 NIV) (2 words)
54 "AND OTHER FELL ____" (Mark 4:8) (3 words)
56 "Let me ____" (Deuteronomy 9:14)
59 "But thou art ____" (Daniel 4:18)
60 Son of Boaz (Ruth 4:21)
61 Sweet, musically (Ital.)
62 Homophone for land amphibian
63 "And mules, a ____ year by year" (2 Chronicles 9:24)
64 More strange
65 "And the moon shall not give ____ light" (Ezekiel 32:7)
66 "Let them not feed, ____ drink water" (Jonah 3:7)

DOWN

1 "For he is ____ " (Hebrews 5:13) (2 words)
2 City in southwest Quebec
3 Small pies
4 Free energy
5 "For my yoke is ____" (Matthew 11:30)
6 "Then shall ____ return" (Joshua 20:6) (2 words)
7 Sulfuric and nitric
8 "And they shall ____" (Jeremiah 50:36)
9 "And my people the ____" (Jeremiah 6:27 NIV)

10 "And a _____ on every altar" (Numbers 23:30)
11 Golfer Ernie
13 Indian honorific
14 Latest
20 Pillar in Wales
21 "_____ you, don't torture me!" (Luke 8:28 NIV) (2 words)
24 Indecorous
25 Western Turkey, at one time
26 "By the way, an _____ in the path" (Genesis 49:17)
28 Snob
29 Popular ISP (abbr.)
30 They separate Asia from Europe
31 Apia location
32 "As a jewel of gold in a swine's _____" (Proverbs 11:22)
34 "Abraham, and _____ unto Isaac" (1 Chronicles 16:16) (3 words)
35 List of names
37 "Nor _____ of life" (Hebrews 7:3)
41 "Away like a _____ on the surface of the waters" (Hosea 10:7 NIV)

42 Griped and whined
47 "I had digged in the wall, behold _____ " (Ezekiel 8:8) (2 words)
49 "At whom do you _____ and stick out your tongue?" (Isaiah 57:4 NIV)
50 Psychiatrist who rejected Freud
51 Coffee type
52 "Every _____ his brother" (Jeremiah 34:17) (2 words)
53 Milk faucet
54 "Saying, Come up this _____" (Judges 16:18)
55 Bassoon relative
56 "Why make ye this _____, and weep?" (Mark 5:39)
57 "The children of _____" (Nehemiah 7:37)
58 "I am an _____ man" (Luke 1:18)

WORD SEARCH
by David Austin

━━━ THE BETRAYER ━━━

BETRAY
CHIEF PRIESTS
CONDEMNED
CONSPIRE
COVENANTED
DELIVER
DISCIPLE
ELDERS
GETHSEMANE
HANGED
ISCARIOT
JUDAS
KISS
MASTER
MULTITUDE

OPPORTUNITY
PHARISEES
PIECES
REPENTED
SCRIBES
SIGN
SILVER
SIMON'S SON
SINNED
THIEF
THIRTY
TORCHES
TRAITOR
TRANSGRESSION
WEAPONS

```
B E T R A Y S I N N E D B X A
P P I E C E S E L P I C S I D
I I W T T H A N G E D O J Q E
S E E S I R A H P E P V J E L
C C A A T P A K N P N E T D I
A O P M P S I M O K L N O U V
R N O I S S E R G S N A R T E
I S N C S D T I I X H N C I R
O P S N N U E M R E N T H T E
T I Z O N Z O T T P L E E L V
N R C I W N H L N H F D S U L
G E T H S E M A N E I E E M I
I Y W S E B I R C S P R I R S
S R O T I A R T J D A E T H S
Y N J U D A S T H I E F R Y C
```

BIBLE QUOTATION
by Suzanne Stepp

ANSWERED PRAYER
1 SAMUEL 1:20

If we pray in faith, we will receive in faith. Solve this puzzle to discover the woman who got what she asked for and then gave it back.

S	W	C	B	D	E	T	V	A	C	E
T	L	H	S	M	V	A	I	T	D	A
E	I	O	R	D	M	U	H	R	H	E
T	E	N	H	A	E	O	C	O	A	A
Y	L	H	I	O	W	H	E	S	D	M
M	L	A	E	S	E	E	T	A	F	I
D	I	M	S	C	N	U	S	L	H	E
A	S	T	A	N	E	H	A	B	E	C
H	A	O	N	A	U	E	O	A	T	A
R	C	H	E	O	N	A	F	E	S	T
	I	L	W	M	H	N		N	U	E
			G	H	B	F				D
			A	R						E
			E							

═══ ALLEGORIES ═══

Some things are used as a symbolic representation of a hidden truth. Can you solve this puzzle to uncover some of these allegorical people, animals, places, and things?

GHI	ABC	GHI	ABC	PRS
4	2	4	2	7

JKL	GHI	MNO	MNO	DEF	PRS	PRS
5	4	6	6	3	7	7

PRS	ABC	PRS	ABC	GHI
7	2	7	2	4

TUV	GHI	MNO	DEF
8	4	6	3

TUV	GHI	MNO	DEF	WXY	ABC	PRS	DEF
8	4	6	3	9	2	7	3

GHI	MNO	MNO	DEF	PRS
4	6	6	3	7

by Donna K. Maltese

■ A HAIR-RAZING TALE ■

Crack the code to discover the ploy a calculating woman used to cut down a mighty Nazarite.

Delilah was hired by lords of the _____ (Judges 16:5)

___ ___ ___ ___ ___ ___ ___ ___ ___ ___ ___
15   3   12   24   5   21   34   31   9   28   8

Delilah wove Samson's locks with this (Judges 16:13)

___ ___ ___
29   2   17

Samson's father (Judges 13:20–24)

___ ___ ___ ___ ___ ___
16   33   19   11   1   22

To calculate

___ ___ ___ ___ ___ ___
23   4   30   10   18   27

How often Delilah nagged Samson (Judges 16:16)

___ ___ ___ ___ ___
32   26   13   7   20

To shear

___ ___ ___
25   14   6

32-27-24-5-24-33-22   21-26-12-32   34-11

8-1-16-8-11-19,   34-2-7-7   16-2,   5   15-18-1-20

6-3-2-2,   29-3-2-18-2-31-19   6-3-20   30-18-28-1-34

21-34-18-27-9-30-34-22   7-13-28-34-22,   1-9-32

29-3-2-18-2-29-4-6-3   6-3-11-14   16-4-30-3-6-27-8-6

17-2   17-11-10-19-32   34-11   1-23-23-7-4-25-34

6-3-2-2.

JUDGES 16:6

CROSSWORD
by Tonya Vilhauer

■ OVERCOMERS ■

When God is with us, we can overcome any obstacles that cross our paths. Work this puzzle to discover biblical men who, with help from above, lived victorious lives.

Ye are of God, little children, and have overcome them:
because greater is he that is in you, than he that is in the world.
1 JOHN 4:4

ACROSS

1   Agency charged with protecting the environment (abbr.)
4   "I'll. . .____ your bones in the valleys" (Ezekiel 32:5 MSG)
9   "And none ____ stay his hand" (Daniel 4:35)
12   "Till they ____ the stone from the well's mouth" (Genesis 29:8)
14   Speak in public
15   "He that findeth his life shall ____ it" (Matthew 10:39)
16   WHERE PAUL WAS HELD PRISONER IN ACTS 28:16
17   Helmet's nosepiece
18   Colored part of eye
19   OTHERWISE KNOWN AS HANANIAH (Daniel 1:7)
21   Behold (2 words)
23   Wrath
24   ____ Francisco
25   On the foot of cat or dog
28   DANIEL'S "FRIENDLY" HOME (Daniel 6:16)
31   Invitation abbreviation
34   ROYAL ADVISOR TO NEBUCHADNEZZAR, BELSHAZZAR, AND DARIUS
36   Teachers' labor union (abbr.)
38   French "yes"
40   "The Pharisees began to ____ him vehemently" (Luke 11:53)
41   To incorporate
43   Tenor (var.)
44   Stretch to make do
45   African antelope
46   Time periods

48   "And shall ____ carry captives into Egypt" (Daniel 11:8)
51   "That I may ____ Christ" (Philippians 3:8)
53   "That they might not ____ thy voice" (Daniel 9:11)
54   Hertz (abbr.)
56   "The king of the south. . .shall return into his ____ land" (Daniel 11:9)
58   Detective
61   OTHERWISE KNOWN AS AZARIAH (Daniel 1:7)
66   Title of peerage
67   "Thou art a stranger, and also an ____" (2 Samuel 15:19)
69   "The king of Babylon will stop. . .to seek an ____" (Ezekiel 21:21 NIV)
70   "They ____ not, neither do they spin" (Matthew 6:28)
71   "The men. . .which ____ him in the killing of his brethren" (Judges 9:24)
72   "Then Samuel took a ____ of oil" (1 Samuel 10:1)
73   Compass point (abbr.)
74   DANIEL'S FRIENDS WERE CAST INTO THIS TYPE OF FURNACE (Daniel 3:21)
75   "Some of them of understanding shall fall, to ____ them, and to purge" (Daniel 11:35)

DOWN

1   Makes mistakes
2   Fictional bear
3   ____ mater
4   Echolocation
5   Trailed

6 "Be not _____ with thy mouth" (Ecclesiastes 5:2)
7 Terminal abbreviation
8 "These are _____ without water" (2 Peter 2:17)
9 Wine bottle cap
10 Paul and Timothy weren't to preach the word here (Acts 16:6)
11 "As a bird that wandereth from her _____" (Proverbs 27:8)
13 "I have _____ thee in right paths" (Proverbs 4:11)
15 DANIEL WAS DELIVERED FROM THEM
20 "They shall _____ from the dead" (Mark 12:25)
22 Rowing aid
25 Heavy coat
26 GOD SENT THIS TO SHUT THE LIONS' MOUTHS (Daniel 6:22)
27 "I shall not _____, but live, and declare the works of the LORD" (Psalm 118:17)
29 Boredom
30 Formerly known as
32 "I will sacrifice unto thee with the _____ of thanksgiving" (Jonah 2:9)
33 Aggressively determined

34 "Give unto the LORD the glory _____ unto his name" (Psalm 96:8)
35 To dawdle
37 "The _____ head fell into the water" (2 Kings 6:5)
39 "That which groweth of _____ own accord of thy harvest" (Leviticus 25:5)
42 Compass point (abbr.)
43 BIBLICAL CHARACTER KNOWN FOR HIS ADVERSITIES
47 Small lake
49 Row
50 Choose
52 More dignified
55 "They take away the _____ from the hungry" (Job 24:10)
57 Overgrown
58 Divisions of a tennis match
59 Country in SE Asia
60 _____ Canal
61 Assistant
62 Winter month (abbr.)
63 Discharge
64 Tackle
65 JOB'S SERVANT WAS THE _____ ONE TO ESCAPE THE CHALDEANS (Job 1:17)
68 Roman dozen

119

WORD SEARCH
by Ruth Graether

━━━ AARON'S GOLDEN CALF ━━━
Exodus 32

AARON	GRAVING TOOL
ALTAR	HAND
BRAKE	ISRAEL
BREAK	LAND
BURNT OFFERINGS	LORD
CONSECRATE	MOSES
CORRUPTED	PEACE
DANCING	PEOPLE
DRINK	PLAY
EARRINGS	REPENTED
EGYPT	SACRIFICED
FEAST	SEED
FIRE	SELF
FORGIVE	SIN
GAVE	STARS
GODS	WAR
GOLD	WRATH

```
D R M O D W E S D N C W S G S
Q A S O R N O G L S O W A R G
E D N A S F K N O T N R F B N
K K T C C E I I G A S L A C I
A H N M I R S R V R E N O A R
R D V I A N I E E S C R L F R
B T R T R E G F I G R V A O A
G S L O X D I F I U A O L R E
A A Z Y L V P O P C T M T G G
V E R E P E N T E D E S T I O
E F H Z O P E N S I N D E V D
E G Y P T D P R P E A C E E S
J P L A Y K U U K A E R B B D
M E D N A H Y B L E A R S I A
G R A V I N G T O O L D N A L
```

SUDOKU
by Sara Stoker

PREPARING MOSES

DIFFICULT

	A	B	C	D	E	F	G	H	I
1	O					A		U	H
2	G		H	T			D		
3		U		O			G		
4	U				R		H		A
5			C	A		T			
6		T				G		C	
7			A				C		
8	C	O	G	R				A		U
9			U		A	C	O		

Hint: Column B

"And he put forth his hand, and _____ it, and [the serpent] became a _____ in his hand" (Exodus 4:4).

THE BIRTH OF JESUS

See Luke 2:16

Sometimes by following our star, we come across amazing things. Work this drop two puzzle to find out what some lowly shepherds discovered in a Bethlehem shed.

FRAILTY	Pathway	_____	1. ____ ____
OPALINE	Jail Punishment	_____	2. ____ ____
UNSTRAP	Portions	_____	3. ____ ____
GRINDER	Equestrian	_____	4. ____ ____
DIBASIC	Fundamental	_____	5. ____ ____
TWANGED	Fought	_____	6. ____ ____
HEATHER	Anesthetic	_____	7. ____ ____
EMERGED	Excessive desire	_____	8. ____ ____
ABALONE	Solitary	_____	9. ____ ____
ALCORAN	Reef	_____	10. ____ ____
BRACING	Mound of stones	_____	11. ____ ____
EASTERN	Mountain lakes	_____	12. ____ ____
LIGHTER	Octave	_____	13. ____ ____

___ ___ ___ ___ ___ ___ ___ ___ ___ ___ ___ ___ ___

1　2　3　4　5　6　7　8　9　10　11　12　13

ACROSTIC
by Donna K. Maltese

━━━ ONE, TWO, THREE, TESTING ━━━

Sometimes we need confirmation of our godly commission. Solve this puzzle to discover how Gideon requested God's assurance via "sign language."

God called Gideon a "mighty man of ____." (Judges 6:12)

19	39	32	27	14	8

Enemies of Israel (Judges 6:6)

20	9	33	41	38	30	15	7	1	26

Bearing sheep's fur

36	22	5	18	11

Tribe of Israel (Judges 6:35)

10	21	16	2	29	34	42	25

Removing doubt

31	40	35	28	17	6	37	23	4	12

Foreign god (Judges 6:25)

13	43	24	3

3-1-29   20-1   16-8-40-19-1,   41   16-8-39-11   7-2-1-1,

13-14-7   7-2-9-26   27-35-31-1   36-25-7-2   7-2-1

28-18-1-1-31-1;   3-1-29   15-7   10-5-36   13-1   33-6-11

27-30-32-11   14-16-22-4   7-2-1   28-18-1-1-31-1,

21-4-33   14-16-22-4   24-42-42   7-2-1   12-6-5-14-4-33

3-1-29   7-2-1-6-1   13-1   33-1-36.

JUDGES 6:39

CROSSWORD
by *David K. Shortess*

━━━━ A SNAKE IN THE GRASS ━━━━

The theme answer is a long, familiar Bible quote that snakes up and down
and back and forth and across the grid, even jumping across black squares.
Follow the arrows and stay within the shaded squares.

Thou art cursed above all cattle, and above every beast of the field;
upon thy belly shalt thou go.
GENESIS 3:14

ACROSS

1 START OF QUOTE FROM GENESIS 3 (see note above)
5 PART OF QUOTE
9 PART OF QUOTE
14 "And ____ bare Jabal" (Genesis 4:20)
15 "_____ abhor me" (Job 30:10)
16 Wealthy or powerful person
17 "Or clothe his neck with a flowing ____?" (Job 39:19 NIV)
18 Negative replies
19 Recover metal by heating ore
20 "The LORD shall judge the ____ of the earth" (1 Samuel 2:10)
21 Charlotte Brontë's Jane and family
23 Asian inland sea
24 PART OF QUOTE
25 Oklahoma town
27 Avenue crossers (abbr.)
30 "____ to your faith virtue" (2 Peter 1:5)
32 PART OF QUOTE
36 "Round about the ____ thereof" (Exodus 28:33)
37 "I know it ____ of a truth" (Job 9:2) (2 words)
39 "For whether is ____" (Matthew 9:5)
40 Ecology watchdog group (abbr.)
41 PART OF QUOTE
43 "They ____ the ship aground" (Acts 27:41)
44 "Now learn this ____ from the fig tree" (Matthew 24:32 NIV)
46 "Ye shall find a colt ____" (Mark 11:2)
47 "We ____ many" (Mark 5:9)
48 PART OF QUOTE
49 "Jerusalem, ____, she is broken" (Ezekiel 26:2)
50 Manuscripts (abbr.)

51 "As it had been the face ____ angel" (Acts 6:15) (2 words)
53 PART OF QUOTE
55 "____ do all things through Christ" (Philippians 4:13) (2 words)
58 "Who will ____ us?" (Isaiah 6:8) (2 words)
61 Expression of annoyance
65 Natives of northern Ohio, once
67 Friskies rival
68 "Why should ____ with thee?" (2 Samuel 13:26) (2 words)
69 "Get a new ____ on life" or start over
70 Afrikaans, language of South Africa
71 Swiss river
72 PART OF QUOTE
73 PART OF QUOTE
74 PART OF QUOTE

DOWN

1 "He shall have no ____ in the street" (Job 18:17)
2 "Thy god, ____, liveth" (Amos 8:14) (2 words)
3 Baton
4 PART OF QUOTE
5 PART OF QUOTE
6 Nautical greeting
7 "O thou ____, go, flee thee away" (Amos 7:12)
8 "That thou wilt not cut off ____ after me" (1 Samuel 24:21) (2 words)
9 ____ and offs
10 Southwestern covered porches
11 Salah's son (Genesis 10:24)
12 Alone (Sp.)
13 PART OF QUOTE
22 Tin in Chemistry 101

26 "Shall go ____ out" (John 10:9) (2 words)
27 Off-the-____ (not custom-made)
28 Conical abode
29 "____ her jugs" (Jeremiah 48:12 NIV)
30 Abijam's son (1 Kings 15:8)
31 "This man ____ many miracles" (John 11:47)
33 "Solomon sent to ____, saying" (1 Kings 5:2)
34 "They that sow in ____ shall reap in joy" (Psalm 126:5)
35 Sea eagles
37 "Let them break ____" (Exodus 32:24) (2 words)
38 Nine-digit ID (abbr.)
39 "Mine ____ is consumed because of grief" (Psalm 6:7)
42 US Native American agency
45 "Over these ____ have buried here" (Jeremiah 43:10 NIV) (2 words)
49 "As he that feareth ____" (Ecclesiastes 9:2) (2 words)
52 Ashcroft, e.g. (abbr.)
53 PART OF QUOTE

54 PART OF QUOTE
55 PART OF QUOTE
56 "Immediately the cock ____" (Matthew 26:74)
57 Rizpah's mother, Saul's concubine (2 Samuel 3:7)
59 "The wall of the city shall fall down ____" (Joshua 6:5)
60 Colorful tropical fish
62 Quantity of paper
63 Taj Mahal site
64 Having pedal digits
66 "In just a ____" (very shortly)

SCRAMBLED CIRCLE
by Ken Save

━━━ SLAVE LABOR ━━━

Although our situations may go from bad to worse, God is with us through them all.

1. RNMIOF

2. SIHFNI

3. TDYSEOR

4. LBTIU

5. TSLDEEAO

6. NONOATMBIIA

7. TIYMGH

8. IATAGSN

9. ESEAL

10. NVSOII

Who sold Joseph to Potiphar in Egypt?

1. _ _ _ _ _ ◯

2. _ ◯ _ _ _ _

3. ◯ _ _ _ _ _ _

4. _ _ ◯ _ _

5. _ _ _ _ _ ◯ _ _

6. _ _ _ _ _ ◯ _ _ _ _ _

7. _ ◯ _ _ _ _

8. _ _ _ _ _ _ ◯

9. _ _ _ _ ◯

10. _ _ ◯ _ _ _

Answer: The _ _ _ _ _ _ _ _ _ _

128

■ STORIES OF THE MIRACULOUS ■

Everyone loves a good miracle story. Can you solve these spotty headlines to find three New Testament men who experienced something beyond the realm of normal, everyday reality?

MAN B●INDED WHILE TR●VELING TO PER●EC●TE CHRISTIANS

— — — —

●LIND B●GG●R ●AN ●H●ILLED BY JE●●S' HE●L●NG

— — — — — — — —

INNOCEN● MAN FR●ED FROM CHAINS AND P●ISON BY ANSW●RED ●RAYER

— — — — —

━━ ARMY OF ONE ━━
1 Samuel 17:37, 42

David said **moreover**, The Lord **that delivered** me out of the paw of the **lion**, and out of the paw of the **bear**, he **will** deliver me out of the **hand** of **this** Philistine. And **Saul said unto** David, Go, and the Lord be **with thee**. . . . And **when** the **Philistine looked about**, and saw **David**, he **disdained** him: for he was but a **youth**, and **ruddy**, and of a **fair countenance**.

```
P T Z O G U P E O O E F A X Q
O H R S U W T V W J A F L U Y
B E I F I N D L R M D L X P Q
S E D L Y H T I M Z E M M W N
X B L E I A T O A B F Y X O I
D F A I R S R N F S H L W D C
E C N A E T N U O C R U A E
N H T U O Y V I W S S S G D M
I J H V K B E I N Z D H O C E
A Q E V P F T T L E B Q X K S
D R S L T H A T K E K M D T J
S D W A I W B O Y D D U R D I
I N Q I U Q O P Q G G A O N K
D A V I D L U C X Q E T L F Q
W H E N A I T M L B J R D M Z
```

ACROSTIC
by Donna K. Maltese

━━━ MAKING WAVES ━━━

Sometimes we have trouble recognizing God. Crack the code to find out how Jesus' appearance made waves for a boatload of frightened followers.

Seagoing vessel

$\overline{7}$ $\overline{23}$ $\overline{4}$ $\overline{15}$

Tasteless liquid

$\overline{10}$ $\overline{16}$ $\overline{21}$ $\overline{33}$ $\overline{6}$

Unbelief

$\overline{34}$ $\overline{28}$ $\overline{22}$ $\overline{14}$ $\overline{8}$

Trouble

$\overline{29}$ $\overline{17}$ $\overline{20}$ $\overline{1}$ $\overline{32}$ $\overline{36}$ $\overline{26}$ $\overline{11}$

Cognizance

$\overline{12}$ $\overline{5}$ $\overline{9}$ $\overline{24}$ $\overline{31}$ $\overline{2}$ $\overline{19}$ $\overline{27}$ $\overline{35}$

In some situations, Peter showed little of this

$\overline{25}$ $\overline{13}$ $\overline{18}$ $\overline{30}$ $\overline{3}$

1-5-34   10-3-2-5   8-3-2   19-36-7-29-36-15-20-35-7

7-13-10   3-36-32   24-16-31-12-36-5-27   9-5   8-3-2

7-2-17,   8-3-2-11   24-2-6-2   26-6-28-22-14-20-35-19,

7-13-11-36-5-27,   4-21   4-7   17   7-15-4-6-4-30;   1-5-34

8-3-2-11   29-6-18-33-19   28-22-30   25-9-6   25-33-13-6.
MATTHEW 14:26

MOSES' STORY

From babyhood on, Moses lived a pretty amazing life. Here are three important things from Moses' story in the book of Exodus. . . . Can you unscramble the letters to solve these anagrams?

No main suit

— — — — —   — — — — —

Cold flange

— — — — — —   — — — —

Uh bring buns

— — — — — —   — — — —

━━━ IN THE LAND OF PHARAOH ━━━

Egypt was ruled by a man with a heart of stone. Crack the telephone codes to dig up more information about this land, out of which the Jews once made a mass exodus.

| MNO 6 | GHI 4 | JKL 5 | DEF 3 |

| DEF 3 | ABC 2 | MNO 6 | GHI 4 | MNO 6 | DEF 3 |

| PRS 7 | DEF 3 | DEF 3 | | PRS 7 | DEF 3 | ABC 2 |

| PRS 7 | JKL 5 | ABC 2 | TUV 8 | DEF 3 | PRS 7 | WXY 9 |

| PRS 7 | ABC 2 | PRS 7 | ABC 2 | GHI 4 |

| JKL 5 | MNO 6 | PRS 7 | DEF 3 | PRS 7 | GHI 4 |

| MNO 6 | GHI 4 | PRS 7 | GHI 4 | ABC 2 | MNO 6 |

| DEF 3 | PRS 7 | DEF 3 | ABC 2 | MNO 6 | PRS 7 |

CROSSWORD
by Sarah Lagerquist Simmons

━━━ STORIES WITH A PURPOSE ━━━

Jesus and other wise men told stories to guide and teach their listeners. As you work this crossword, may you return to these notable biblical tales and allow their hidden meaning to increase your understanding.

Let the wise listen and add to their learning, and let the discerning get guidance for understanding proverbs and parables, the sayings and riddles of the wise.
PROVERBS 1:5–6

ACROSS
1 "The waters called he ____" (Genesis 1:10)
5 Crooked
10 JESUS TOLD A PARABLE ABOUT A SOWER WHO WENT OUT TO ____ SEEDS
13 Spin
15 French river
16 The very first woman
17 "Wild animals will like it just fine, filling the vacant houses with ____ night sounds" (Isaiah 13:21 MSG)
18 "Who hath. . .____ out heaven with the span" (Isaiah 40:12)
19 "Deliver thyself as a ____ from the hand of the hunter" (Proverbs 6:5)
20 "____ them loose from the grip of Egypt" (Exodus 3:8 MSG)
21 JESUS SAID HE IS THE ____ SHEPHERD
23 NATHAN TOLD A STORY TO MAKE ____ SEE HIS SIN
25 Buzz
26 Easels
28 "They take counsel together. . .they ____ to take away my life" (Psalm 31:13 NKJV)
31 "Ye shall not make any cuttings in your flesh. . .nor ____ any marks upon you" (Leviticus 19:28)
32 "Let the living bird ____ into the open field" (Leviticus 14:7)
33 "I will ____ unto the LORD" (Exodus 15:1)
34 Freedom (abbr.)
37 Margarine
38 "My beloved is like a gazelle or a young ____" (Song of Solomon 2:9 NASB)
40 Rage
41 "Their lungs breathe out poison ____" (Psalm 5:9 MSG)

42 "A banana ____ lands them flat on their faces" (Psalm 37:14 MSG)
43 Unit for measuring precious gems
45 "These Gadites were the ____ of the crop" (1 Chronicles 12:14 MSG)
46 Capital of Albania
47 Legume husks (2 words)
50 THE PRODIGAL SON WAS TREATED TO THIS FOR DINNER
51 "Her husband may confirm it or. . . ____ it" (Numbers 30:13 NASB)
52 JESUS TOLD ABOUT A MAN WHO WAS FORGIVEN OF A DEBT OF 10,000 TALENTS BUT PUT A MAN IN ____ WHO OWED HIM 100 PENCE
53 "He doesn't endlessly ____ and scold" (Psalm 103:9 MSG)
56 Restricted (abbr.)
57 "One cake of ____ bread" (Exodus 29:23)
60 Crumble
62 "Do ye not therefore ____, because ye know not the scriptures. . . ?" (Mark 12:24)
63 "The ____ of them that sing do I hear" (Exodus 32:18)
64 Large couch
65 Color
66 A WEDDING ____ WITHOUT THE PROPER GARMENT WAS CAST OUT OF THE WEDDING IN THIS STORY
67 "The One. . .has founded His vaulted ____ over the earth" (Amos 9:6 NASB)

DOWN
1 "There is but a ____ between me and death" (1 Samuel 20:3)
2 Pitcher
3 Breezy
4 ____ Lanka

136

5 PAUL WROTE THAT CHRISTIANS NEED TO PUT ON THE WHOLE _____ OF GOD, IN ORDER TO STAND AGAINST THE DEVIL
6 "Their feet are swift to _____ blood" (Romans 3:15)
7 Gear
8 Unsaturated carbon compound (suffix)
9 GUESTS INVITED TO A _____ WOULD NOT COME, SO THEY INVITED ANYONE THEY COULD FIND IN THIS STORY
10 Control system (abbr.)
11 Egg-shaped
12 "The _____ were wrapped about my head" (Jonah 2:5)
14 Bean
22 "I have made you a tester of metals and my people the _____" (Jeremiah 6:27 NIV)
24 "Men of might. . .were strong and _____ for war" (2 Kings 24:16)
25 Mexican coin
26 Neat
27 Japanese money
28 Toil
29 Pop
30 "The charge was two-thirds of a shekel for the plowshares. . .and to fix the _____" (1 Samuel 13:21 NASB)
31 "David delivered first this _____ to thank the LORD" (1 Chronicles 16:7)

34 Turkish money
35 Iraq's neighbor
36 Second letter of Greek alphabet
38 JESUS TOLD A STORY ABOUT _____ THAT WAS CAST INTO STONY PLACES
39 Drinks
42 "Keep therefore his statutes. . .that thou mayest _____ thy days upon the earth" (Deuteronomy 4:40)
43 DAVID HAD BATHSHEBA'S HUSBAND _____
44 Noise a dog makes
45 Computer (abbr.)
46 Siamese
47 Blanched
48 IN PROVERBS, IT TELLS US THAT WISDOM CRIES OUT AT THE _____ OF THE CITY (Proverbs 8:3)
49 Benedict Arnold's coconspirator
50 Trainee
52 Strap used in falconry
53 Recent (Portuguese)
54 The first man
55 Basic unit of heredity
58 Debt
59 "If a soul sin. . .and _____ unto his neighbor" (Leviticus 6:2)
61 "I will _____ you out of their bondage" (Exodus 6:6)

137

SHIPWRECKED
Acts 27:41–44

And falling into a place where two **seas** met, they ran the **ship aground**; and the **forepart stuck fast**, and **remained unmovable**, but the **hinder** part was **broken** with the **violence** of the **waves**. And the **soldiers' counsel** was to **kill** the **prisoners**, lest any of them should **swim** out, and escape. But the **centurion**, **willing** to **save Paul**, kept them from their **purpose**; and **commanded** that they which could swim should **cast themselves** first into the sea, and get to **land**: And the **rest**, some on **boards**, and some on broken **pieces** of the ship. And so it came to pass, that they **escaped** all **safe** to land.

```
Z H E S O P R U P W A P I D P
Q J C P U A S N I A S W I M U
K L N O N S A F E V U I C B R
H N E N M Z V Z C E K L W R C
H L L W O M E U E S C L W O O
Y L O W V L A B S C U I U K C
L Z I C A S T N S A T N S E E
D D V L B R S R D P S G R N N
X J N L L S E V L E S M E H T
Q F A U E N R M L D D D I G U
E U A F O R E P A R T N D N R
S E A S D R A O B I R A L H I
H A I K T Y G L T F N L O C O
I R E D N I H A D R I E S U N
P R S E F B N W U K E E D A I
```

CRYPTOSCRIPTURE
by Sharon Y. Brown

━━━ THE FINAL MOMENTS ━━━

Jesus came to earth to show us the way to God. Solve these cryptoscriptures to discover details of Jesus' final moments on the cross as He made the ultimate sacrifice.

KSR VJDKLB UHCLB K LJLDB, KSR VAL JL CS LGB

MHCQQ. KSR LGB UHJLJST UKQ, OBQAQ CW

SKIKHBLG LGB XJST CW LGB OBUQ.

VYC QAOY UOBZB AVC TPEOC QEJA V XGZC

FGETO, AO BVEC, HVJAOP, EYJG JAN AVYCB E

TGWWOYC WN BSEPEJ: VYC AVFEYR BVEC JAZB,

AO RVFO ZS JAO RAGBJ.

THE PHILISTINES AND GOD'S JUDGMENT

MEDIUM

	A	B	C	D	E	F	G	H	I
1	H	O	N				K	A	E
2			E		O	N			H
3			T				R		N
4	O	R	G		T		A		
5	E	H					N		
6	T	N	K		A		G		
7					G		O		
8	N				H			T	A
9		E	R			T	H	K	G

Hint: Row 3

Two of the five Philistine capital cities under God's judgment were
_____ and _____ (1 Samuel 5:8–10).

ACROSTIC
by Donna K. Maltese

━━━━ IT'S A FAMILY AFFAIR ━━━━

Decipher this puzzle to find out which son of David's was literally lovesick.

Tamar's dad (1 Chronicles 3:9)

$\overline{20}$ $\overline{4}$ $\overline{13}$ $\overline{33}$ $\quad$ $\overline{10}$ $\overline{19}$ $\overline{30}$ $\overline{24}$ $\overline{16}$

Jonadab to Amnon (2 Samuel 13:3)

$\overline{31}$ $\overline{6}$ $\overline{29}$ $\overline{8}$ $\overline{23}$ $\overline{15}$

To grow in intensity

$\overline{25}$ $\overline{2}$ $\overline{35}$

David to Amnon (2 Samuel 3:2)

$\overline{28}$ $\overline{17}$ $\overline{9}$ $\overline{1}$ $\overline{21}$ $\overline{7}$

What Amnon resorted to

$\overline{32}$ $\overline{26}$ $\overline{12}$ $\overline{5}$ $\overline{22}$

Sullen

$\overline{11}$ $\overline{18}$ $\overline{27}$ $\overline{14}$ $\overline{34}$ $\overline{3}$

19-11-13-18-13   25-17-8   34-14   30-21-35-21-16,

9-1-2-9   1-21   28-21-32-32   34-24-31-20   28-6-27

1-24-34   8-4-8-9-3-7   9-17-11-17-7;   28-6-27   8-1-3

25-17-8   2   30-12-7-33-12-15;   2-5-10   19-11-13-18-13

9-1-6-29-22-1-9   23-9   1-2-7-16   28-6-27   1-24-11   9-14

10-14   2-5-26-9-1-23-5-22   9-14   1-3-7.

2 Samuel 13:2

CROSSWORD
by David K. Shortess

━━ BETHLEHEM'S VISITORS ━━

From near and far, people came to see the Christ child born in Bethlehem.
Can you solve this puzzle to find the names or descriptions of those who
made the manger pilgrimage?

And thou Bethlehem. . .out of thee shall come a Governor,
that shall rule my people Israel.
MATTHEW 2:6

ACROSS

1 Brig occupant
5 "Who passing through the valley of ____ make it a well" (Psalm 84:6)
9 "If he arrives ____ will come with him to see you" (Hebrews 13:23 NIV) (2 words)
14 Puerto ____
15 Maj. Hoople's favorite expression
16 "But the ____ are the children of the wicked one" (Matthew 13:38)
17 US island occupied by Japan during WWII
18 Goulash
19 Bathsheba's first husband (2 Samuel 11:3)
20 VISITORS (Luke 2:15) (2 words)
23 "Yet we did ____ him stricken" (Isaiah 53:4)
24 Mr. Charles
25 OT book (abbr.)
28 Scale notes
29 Deteriorate
32 "Praise thy ____ Zion" (Psalm 147:12) (2 words)
33 City from which David took "exceeding much brass" (2 Samuel 8:8)
34 Corolla component
35 MORE VISITORS (Luke 2:4–7) (3 words)
40 "You are worried and ____ about many things" (Luke 10:41 NIV)
41 "The Philistines gathered ____ Dammim" (2 Samuel 23:9 NIV) (2 words)
42 Mend, as a sock
43 Open, as a flag
45 Weasel
48 Golfer Ernie
49 Menlo Park monogram
50 Electrical unit
52 MORE VISITORS (Matthew 2:1–11) (3 words)
55 Stockpile
58 Mariner who discovered Cape of Good Hope
59 Bye-bye
60 "Whom shall ____?" (Psalm 27:1) (2 words)
61 Sea eagle
62 Land west of Nod (Genesis 4:16)
63 In accord (2 words)
64 "But in ____ and in truth" (1 John 3:18)
65 "And Jacob ____ his clothes" (Genesis 37:34)

DOWN

1 Top drawer
2 "Compassed about ____ great a cloud of witnesses" (Hebrews 12:1) (2 words)
3 Musical groups
4 Despicable person
5 "Behold now ____, which I made with thee" (Job 40:15)
6 "I had rebuilt the wall and not ____ was left in it" (Nehemiah 6:1 NIV) (2 words)
7 Not "plastic"
8 Stick like glue
9 "____ to show thyself approved unto God" (2 Timothy 2:15)
10 "Wherein shall go no galley with ____" (Isaiah 33:21)
11 "Give light to my eyes, ____ will sleep in death" (Psalm 13:3 NIV) (2 words)
12 Education assn. (abbr.)
13 Like (suffix)

21 What Jesus did at Lazarus's tomb (2 words)
22 "They ____ the ship aground" (Acts 27:41)
25 "But he answered her ____ word" (Matthew 15:23) (2 words)
26 "The twelfth month, which is the month ____" (Esther 3:13)
27 "Sacrifice, ____, acceptable unto God" (Romans 12:1)
30 British rule in India
31 Quiverful
32 Rubies, for example
33 Has ____, kin of also ran
34 "In ____ and hymns and spiritual songs" (Colossians 3:16)
35 Revelation preceder
36 Iridescent gem
37 Belonging to Lithuania and Estonia, once (abbr.)
38 Former cabinet secretary Udall, to his friends
39 "His hand is still ____" (Isaiah 10:4 NIV)
43 Egypt and Syria, once (abbr.)
44 Required

45 Created again
46 "The ten horns which thou sawest ____ kings" (Revelation 17:12) (2 words)
47 Apartment dweller
49 "And God said, Let ____ be light" (Genesis 1:3)
51 Andrew's brother
52 Comparison word
53 Ireland, formerly
54 "And your moon will ____ no more" (Isaiah 60:20 NIV)
55 Mole's milieu? (abbr.)
56 Exchange student organization (abbr.)
57 Company bigwig (abbr.)

PAUL'S JOURNEYS

SEE ACTS 27:15

Oftentimes Paul journeyed into troubled waters. Fortunately, he knew Jesus would keep him afloat. Solve this puzzle to find out how Paul's boat was faring off the shores of Crete.

Word	Clue		
TRADING	Empty	_____	1. ___ ___
HUSHING	Employing	_____	2. ___ ___
EMITTED	Speed recorded	_____	3. ___ ___
UNASKED	Nude	_____	4. ___ ___
HAPLESS	Price cuts	_____	5. ___ ___
IONIZED	Area coded	_____	6. ___ ___
PLANTER	Not now	_____	7. ___ ___
WROUGHT	Coarse	_____	8. ___ ___
ADENOID	Ate	_____	9. ___ ___
WHISKED	Walked	_____	10. ___ ___
INSCAPE	Windows	_____	11. ___ ___
NAMABLE	Stroll	_____	12. ___ ___
USHERED	Transparent	_____	13. ___ ___

__ __ __ __ __ __ __ __ __ __ __ __ __

__ __ __ __ __ __ __ __ __ __ __ __ __
1 2 3 4 5 6 7 8 9 10 11 12 13

A MEMORABLE MEAL
LUKE 22:19–20

Work this Bible quotation puzzle to decode a memorable meal the disciples could not pass over.

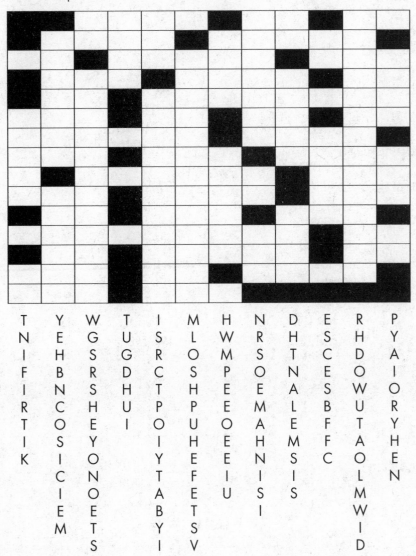

WORD SEARCH
by Connie Troyer

BRINGING UP THE AXE

2 KINGS 6:1–7

ALAS	PLACE
AXE HEAD	PROPHETS
BEAM	PUT
BORROWED	SERVANTS
CAST	SHEWED
CONTENT	SONS
CRIED	STICK
CUT DOWN	SWIM
ELISHA	TAKE
FELLING	THEE
HAND	THITHER
IRON	TOOK
JORDAN	WATER
MAN OF GOD	WHERE
MASTER	WOOD

```
T O K A E K A T H I T H E R A
D O R E C A L P R O U I L T U
E T A D U X O J E N O R I R T
W B N A L C U T D O W N S E N
E A E R N K A E T P L O H T E
H R S O A O W S A U N B A A T
S P W E D O K O T S D A L W N
F O I O R T H N O V A T I H O
E P M R O V R T A D E U R E C
L H O E J E A S T E H P O R P
L B W A T B E N O N E R K E D
I E J S R O B S T Y X I C E I
N X A P T H E E F S A M I L K
G M O R S S A L A U S R T E T
A L D O G F O N A M C A S O C
```

ACROSTIC
by Donna K. Maltese

━━━ TROUBLED WATERS ━━━

Jesus is our bridge over troubled waters. Decipher this puzzle to uncover a certain man's plea for Jesus' help at Bethesda.

Day of rest

___ ___ ___ ___ ___ ___ ___
19   8   14   29 34   1   25

Free of defect

___ ___ ___ ___ ___
24   6   11   35   17

Feast of the Jews (John 2:13)

___ ___ ___ ___ ___ ___ ___ ___
10   20   13   31   2   18   7   26

Crippled

___ ___ ___ ___
32   21   4   15

Length of time something lasts

___ ___ ___ ___ ___ ___ ___ ___
16   28   9   33   30   27   22   3

Recline

___ ___ ___
23   5   12

1-25-17   27-4-10-11-30-12-3-30   4-21-3

33-3-19-24-7-9-7-16   6-5-4,   31-5-26,   27   6-34-18-15

3-22   4-21-3,   24-6-7-3   1-25-17   24-20-30-7-26   5-13

30-9-22-28-14-32-7-16,   1-22   10-28-30   4-7   5-3-1-22

1-25-17   10-2-2-23.

JOHN 5:7

CROSSWORD

By David K. Shortess

■ SOME PARABLES OF JESUS ■

Everyone loves a good story, and Jesus' listeners were no exception. Can you solve this parable-filled puzzle to uncover four story topics told by Jesus?

And with many such parables spake he the word unto them,
as they were able to hear it.
MARK 4:33

ACROSS

1 "Beau ____"
6 Part of centerpiece
10 Belonging to good king of Judah
14 Top story
15 Smidgen
16 Where Jesus met the Samaritan woman
17 "So that a bow of ____ is broken" (2 Samuel 22:35)
18 Care facility workers (abbr.)
19 ____ bellum
20 PARABLE (Luke 18:2–8) (2 words)
23 Architect I. M. ____
24 "For ____ stiffnecked people" (Exodus 34:9) (3 words)
25 PARABLE (Luke 10:30–37) (2 words)
32 Money, biblically
33 Radio host Limbaugh
34 Test for some seniors (abbr.)
37 Tolkien's bad guys
38 Queen of ____, Solomon's guest
40 "And fashioned it with a graving ____" (Exodus 32:4)
41 "Be prepared" organization (abbr.)
42 Chow ____
43 "How ____ that day will be" (Jeremiah 30:7 NIV)
44 PARABLE (Matthew 25:31–46) (3 words)
48 "____ sending you out like lambs" (Luke 10:3 NIV) (3 words)
50 Keats product
51 START OF PARABLE (Matthew 13:3–9) (4 words)
59 Left ____, in Paris
60 Despise
61 "How right they are to ____ you" (Song of Solomon 1:4 NIV)

62 S-shaped molding
63 Sea eagle
64 "That the aged men be ____" (Titus 2:2)
65 Comedian Foxx
66 "As ____ man who casteth firebrands" (Proverbs 26:18) (2 words)
67 Cornered

DOWN

1 "I cry out, I ____ and pant" (Isaiah 42:14 NIV)
2 Major-ending
3 Follower of *young* or *old* alike
4 Bow and ascot
5 Solar, for one
6 "Then you will become their ____" (Habakkuk 2:7 NIV)
7 Top drawer
8 Funny man Laurel, familiarly
9 "On the ____ of Eden" (Genesis 4:16)
10 "And we eagerly ____ Savior" (Philippians 3:20 NIV) (2 words)
11 "Is the ____ message by the hand of a fool" (Proverbs 26:6 NIV) (3 words)
12 Choir members
13 "And they ____ bullock" (1 Samuel 1:25) (2 words)
21 Salt ____, biblical body
22 Away or back (comb. form)
25 Shapeless mass
26 Belonging to you and me
27 "I have ____ the death of all the persons of thy father's house" (1 Samuel 22:22)
28 Doctors (abbr.)
29 "Condemned to die in the ____" (1 Corinthians 4:9 NIV)
30 "There's the ____"

31 OT book (abbr.)
35 Lopsided win
36 Building additions
38 Understand
39 With it
40 "And she threw in ____ mites" (Mark 12:42)
42 Same, in Strasbourg
43 Get older rapidly (2 words)
45 Peddled
46 "I have ____ of you" (1 Corinthians 12:21 NKJV) (2 words)
47 Banned insecticide (abbr.)
48 Eva of "Green Acres"
49 Missouri river
52 Flightless bird
53 Cozy
54 Sicilian spewer
55 "By this time there is a bad ____" (John 11:39 NIV)
56 "And put on him a scarlet ____" (Matthew 27:28)
57 "Hast thou eaten of the ____" (Genesis 3:11)

58 "Into the ____ of swine" (Matthew 8:31)

by Paul Kent and Sara Stoker

━━━━ HUSBANDS AND WIVES ━━━━

You'll find more men than women on the pages of scripture, but the fairer sex is there, too—sometimes in the stories of married couples. Try to solve these spotty headlines relating to memorable wives and the men they married.

●U●T MAN T● WED ●IS
●REGNANT FIANC●E

— — — — — —

RU●ER'S W●F● S●EAKS UP FOR
MAN ●CCUSED OF ●REASON

— — — — — —

MAN'S WIFE BEC●MES SA●T S●ATUE

— — —

LOST AND FOUND

If we seek Christ, we will find Him.

1. GSTUOH

2. FTAES

3. ZAEDMA

4. MAPCOYN

5. KFISNOKL

6. NSISBSEU

A young boy was found here.

1. _ _ _ _ _ ◯

2. _ ◯ _ _ _

3. _ ◯ _ _ _ _

4. _ _ _ ◯ _ _ _

5. _ _ _ _ _ _ ◯ _

6. _ _ _ _ _ ◯ _ _

Answer: _ _ _ _ _ _ _

━━ ARK OF BULRUSHES ━━
EXODUS 2:2–3; HEBREWS 11:23

The **woman conceived**, and **bare** a son: and when she saw him that he was a **goodly child**, she hid him **three months**. And when she **could** not **longer hide** him, she **took** for him an ark of **bulrushes**, and **daubed** it with **slime** and with **pitch**, and put the child **therein**; and she **laid** it in the **flags** by the **river's brink**. . . .

By **faith Moses**, **when** he was **born**, was hid three months of his **parents**, **because** they saw he was a **proper** child; and **they were** not **afraid** of the **king's commandment**.

```
R  G  M  Y  E  D  I  H  V  F  C  Y  G  S  B
E  T  C  R  S  H  T  N  C  O  W  F  Y  U  O
P  N  E  O  I  L  A  H  M  T  J  S  L  W  R
O  W  X  C  U  M  I  M  E  A  I  R  D  F  N
R  E  G  N  O  L  A  M  W  Y  U  P  O  L  H
P  O  E  W  D  N  S  E  S  O  M  O  A  W
N  U  P  R  D  A  C  B  H  T  S  C  G  G  Q
U  I  U  M  H  Q  D  E  B  U  A  D  H  S  A
U  A  E  Q  U  T  S  C  I  I  I  C  T  K  F
A  N  B  R  I  N  K  A  A  V  B  N  I  O  S
T  R  I  V  E  R  S  U  F  A  E  N  A  O  B
Z  M  O  N  T  H  S  S  R  R  G  D  F  T  U
P  X  E  Q  D  W  T  E  A  S  Y  U  L  I  W
Y  H  M  T  Q  L  W  P  I  Y  A  Y  V  X  M
W  L  W  J  V  L  A  I  D  V  G  R  G  J  P
```

ACROSTIC
by Donna K. Maltese

▬▬▬ WAKING THE DEAD ▬▬▬

Jesus always takes care of those He loves. Solve this puzzle to find out who He helped get a "raise."

Town near Jerusalem (John 11:1)

$\overline{12}$ $\overline{35}$ $\overline{28}$ $\overline{3}$ $\overline{21}$ $\overline{8}$ $\overline{16}$

Astonish

$\overline{10}$ $\overline{19}$ $\overline{2}$ $\overline{25}$ $\overline{33}$

What Thomas's fellow disciples called him (John 11:16)

$\overline{9}$ $\overline{13}$ $\overline{22}$ $\overline{37}$ $\overline{32}$ $\overline{18}$ $\overline{7}$

Jesus performed this miracle so that God would be ____
(John 11:4)

$\overline{26}$ $\overline{17}$ $\overline{6}$ $\overline{23}$ $\overline{1}$ $\overline{29}$ $\overline{34}$ $\overline{20}$ $\overline{11}$

When Jesus witnessed His friends' grief, He did this (John 11:35)

$\overline{24}$ $\overline{4}$ $\overline{30}$ $\overline{15}$

Smell

$\overline{31}$ $\overline{5}$ $\overline{14}$ $\overline{36}$ $\overline{27}$

5-3-4-7-4   5-3-1-36-26-31   31-2-13-9   3-4:

2-8-11   2-29-15-35-23   5-3-2-5   3-4   31-2-13-5-3

18-36-28-6   5-3-4-19,   6-18-23   29-23-14-35-8-22

17-10-25-10-23-18-7   7-17-20-20-30-4-5-3;   12-18-28   1

26-6,   5-3-2-5   1   32-2-16   21-24-21-27-33   3-34-32

6-18-28   6-29   7-17-20-20-30.

JOHN 11:11

— A BUDDING ENTERPRISE —

God gives us signs to assure us of our calling. Solve this puzzle to discover how God helped a priest keep his divine appointment.

The number of tribes of Israel

—	—	—	—	—	—
10	28	32	3	16	24

Aaron's relationship to Moses

—	—	—	—	—	—	—
7	15	36	23	4	18	11

Complaining (Numbers 17:10)

—	—	—	—	—	—	—	—	—
2	17	9	21	30	5	35	25	13

Another word for *rod*

—	—	—	—	—
20	33	12	29	1

To be discovered

—	—	—	—	—
27	14	6	22	31

The product of this puzzle's miracle was stored in the Most
____ Place (Exodus 26:34; Numbers 17:10)

—	—	—	—
19	8	34	26

7-1-19-36-34-31, 10-4-1 5-8-31 8-27 12-12-15-8-25

27-8-11 10-4-1 4-14-30-20-24 8-27 3-32-16-35

28-12-20 7-6-31-31-1-31, 12-22-31 7-9-8-6-13-4-33

27-8-11-23-4 7-17-31-20, 12-22-31 7-3-8-8-2-1-31

7-3-8-20-20-8-2-20, 12-22-31 26-35-18-34-31-18-31

12-34-21-14-25-31-20.

NUMBERS 17:8

WORD SEARCH
by Connie Troyer

DAGON'S DEFEAT
1 SAMUEL 5

ARK OF THE LORD

AROSE EARLY

ASHDOD

COASTS

CUT OFF

DAGON

DESTROYED

EBENEZER

EMERODS

FALLEN

GATH

GOD

GROUND

HAND OF THE LORD

HEAD

HOUSE

IN HIS PLACE

MORROW

PALMS OF HIS HANDS

PHILISTINES

PRIESTS

SET HIM

SMOTE THEM

SORE UPON US

STUMP

THRESHOLD

TO THE EARTH

TREAD

UPON HIS FACE

```
D T D A R K O F T H E L O R D A
A H T R A E E H T O T O L O M R
E R A L O W A D N U O R G W E E
R E P H I L I S T I N E S E H M
T S I E N Y E B E N E Z E R T E
Y H L A K I N H I S P L A C E R
L O I D E Y O R T S E D I N T O
R L U P O N H I S F A C E R O D
A D G P M U T S S E O L U C M S
E M O R R O W E K N L D O U S T
E A S D O P E T N A B A N R D S
S D N A H S I H F O S M L A P E
O F M G U S R I H T A G G O H I
R D Z O C R A M S F F O T U C R
A F H S O R E U P O N U S I E P
```

CRYPTOSCRIPTURE
by *Sharon Y. Brown*

━━━━━ A HIGHER POWER ━━━━━

If we keep our eyes on Jesus, our dreams can become reality. Crack these codes to uncover inspirational verses that will lift your heart and expand your mind!

MV EXDPMF ZUM VGES VLLSDSN FV QSUD FXS

MPGM VL TUGH; UGN KGFV FXST FXUF AVVW

LVD XPT MXUAA XS URRSUD FXS MSEVGN FPTS

ZPFXVKF MPG KGFV MUABUFPVG.

JKT LHOFO CWWPZKR FBWK SEHX OJZSE, MZSE

XHK ZS ZO ZXBWOOZVCH, VFS KWS MZSE RWT:

NWI MZSE RWT JCC SEZKRO JIH BWOOZVCH.

A STEW RENEWED

EASY

	A	B	C	D	E	F	G	H	I
1	M	E	R		L			B	
2		A		R	M				E
3	G	I		B	A		L		R
4		R				M	E	A	
5	N		E	L				I	
6			G		I	B			M
7		G			B	L			
8	R					I		L	B
9	I		L	M		R	G	E	A

Hint: Row 4

"But he said, Then _____ _____. And he cast it into the pot; and he said, Pour out for the people, that they may eat. And there was no harm in the pot" (2 Kings 4:41).

165

CROSSWORD
by David K. Shortess

▬▬▬ EASTER DISCOVERIES ▬▬▬

Ah, Easter. A time of renewal, hope, and joy, because He lives again! Work
this puzzle to uncover phrases relating to this uplifting day!

*In the end of the Sabbath. . .came Mary Magdalene
and the other Mary to see the sepulchre.*
MATTHEW 28:1

ACROSS

1 "The LORD hath _____ king over you"
   (1 Samuel 12:13) (2 words)
5 Play boisterously
9 "From the _____ of evil and cruel
   men" (Psalm 71:4 NIV)
14 Unit of matter
15 Charles Lamb's pen name
16 Sudsy brothers
17 "And joined the _____ of Egypt"
   (Joshua 15:4 NIV)
18 "And because I _____ you the truth"
   (John 8:45)
19 Ancient Greek marketplace
20 DISCOVERED ON THE FIRST EASTER
   MORN (Mark 16:4) (3 words)
23 "And _____ of them be gone astray"
   (Matthew 18:12)
24 Hair salon item
25 Radon or xenon
28 Female cat coat, sometimes
32 "Straightway ye shall find an _____
   tied" (Matthew 21:2)
35 DISCOVERED ON THE FIRST EASTER
   MORN (Luke 24:3) (2 words)
37 Tête topper
39 "And their round _____ like the moon"
   (Isaiah 3:18)
40 -Rain or -race preceder
41 "I am _____ for evermore, Amen"
   (Revelation 1:18)
42 "An _____ of wrath to bring" (Romans
   13:4 NIV)
43 DISCOVERED ON THE FIRST EASTER
   MORN (Matthew 28:6) (3 words)
45 "And upon the great _____" (Exodus
   29:20)
46 Corporate union
47 Naval officer (abbr.)

48 Resort
50 Ruby or Sandra
52 DISCOVERED ON THE FIRST EASTER
   MORN (John 20:12) (3 words)
61 Automaton
62 Stepped down
63 "But deliver us from _____" (Matthew
   6:13)
64 "_____ all that we ask or think"
   (Ephesians 3:20)
65 Philosopher Descartes
66 Highway hauler
67 "I will ransom them from the _____ of
   the grave" (Hosea 13:14)
68 "Mighty in _____ and word"
   (Luke 24:19)
69 "Let it become a _____" (Psalm
   69:22)

DOWN

1 "And put them under _____"
   (2 Samuel 12:31)
2 State (Fr.)
3 "Yea, and what have ye _____ with
   me" (Joel 3:4) (2 words)
4 Kind of acid
5 "They _____ before his thrashing" (Job
   41:25 NIV)
6 Margarine
7 "Two women shall be grinding at the
   _____" (Matthew 24:41)
8 Coffin cover
9 Forest opening
10 Royal
11 "Four men which have _____ on them"
   (Acts 21:23) (2 words)
12 Blood fluids
13 "Watch and _____" (Matthew 26:41)
21 Capsulate, biologically

22 Self, to Caesar
25 "Could not _____ the truth because of the uproar" (Acts 21:34 NIV) (2 words)
26 Pal (Sp.)
27 Overindulgence
29 "For, _____ winter is past" (Song of Solomon 2:11) (2 words)
30 Middle Eastern chief (var.)
31 "Good buddy's" radio (2 words)
32 "_____, my love, my fair one, and come away" (Song of Solomon 2:13)
33 How many sons had Sceva? (Acts 19:14)
34 British guns
36 How many sons had Haman? (Esther 9:10)
37 What Sarai was (Genesis 11:30)
38 "And brought the child to _____" (1 Samuel 1:25)
44 Tranquilized
46 Apple type, in short
48 Heater
49 "When _____ was come down out of the ship" (Matthew 14:29)
51 Opposite of ingest

52 "That he can _____ himself in it" (Isaiah 28:20)
53 King of the road
54 "For this cause _____ my knees" (Ephesians 3:14) (2 words)
55 Hog fat
56 Away from the wind
57 "These men shall _____ with me" (Genesis 43:16)
58 "Neither will he keep his anger for _____" (Psalm 103:9)
59 Ohio city or bean
60 "That my feet did not _____" (Psalm 18:36)

167

ACROSTIC
by Donna Maltese

BIRD FOOD

Crack the code to discover how the phrase "bird food" took on a whole new meaning for the prophet Elijah.

A small stream

—— —— —— —— ——
14 31 20 7   1

Elijah the prophet was a _____ (1 Kings 17:1)

—— —— —— —— —— —— —— ——
32 16 34 5   29 12 26 9

The region from which Elijah hailed (1 Kings 17:1)

—— —— —— —— —— ——
19 36 25 2   35 17

Elijah foretold of a _____ (1 Kings 17:1)

—— —— —— —— —— —— ——
13 24 8   27 33 22 3

An extreme scarcity of food

—— —— —— —— —— ——
6   18 28 15 23 11

Ahab looked for rain in _____

—— —— —— ——
10 30 4   21

35-21-17   3-5-2   31-18-10-9-23-34   14-24-7-27-19-22-32

22-16-28   29-24-9-18-13   35-21-17   6-25-11-34-22

12-23   26-5-2   28-20-31-23-15-23-33,   35-21-17

29-24-9-18-13   35-21-17   6-25-11-34-22   4-23   3-5-2

11-10-11-23-36-23-33;   35-21-17   5-2   13-31-30-23-1

20-6   26-5-2   14-24-8-8-1.

1 Kings 17:6

━━ A WOMAN FROM CANAAN ━━
Matthew 15:21–22, 28

Then Jesus went **thence**, and **departed** into the **coasts** of **Tyre** and **Sidon**. And, **behold**, a woman of **Canaan came** out of the **same** coasts, and **cried** unto him, **saying**, **Have mercy** on me, O **Lord**, thou son of **David**; my daughter is **grievously vexed** with a **devil**. . . . Then **Jesus answered** and **said** unto her, O **woman**, **great** is thy **faith**: be it unto **thee even** as **thou wilt**. And her **daughter** was **made whole from that very hour**.

```
Y R G T Y V E F S C V C U P I
P L U H H A V E P G Q M C V Q
Q L S O Y S W M E F O Z E Y M
K M T U H H U A A R A R F D K
E K E N O D I S F D Y I X L W
D R O L K V V D E S E T T O G
H N E C R I E D Y J A A M H F
L D S D N P E I C E H A G E I
D C E D A X Y Z R T N F C B R
A A K R E U N G E G N N O Q Z
V M T V E V G M M W E S A I D
I E E H T W I H I H V Q S H M
D G N I Y A S L T H E C T M L
K O I Z S Q T N E E W L S R Q
B O G A C A N A A N R Y G V E
```

SCRAMBLED CIRCLE
by Suzanne Stepp

━━ THE SPACE-TIME CONTINUUM ━━

It's a well-known fact that what goes up must come down.

1. ELVEBIE   5. REGRANTS

2. RATYR   6. LESUCEHRP

3. GNOLSRUF   7. DEMOMUCN

4. SIVONI   8. ENUOPDEDX

As their eyes were opened, Jesus did this.

1. _ _ _ _ _ Ⓞ _

2. _ Ⓞ _ _ _

3. _ _ _ _ _ Ⓞ _ _

4. _ _ _ Ⓞ _ _

5. Ⓞ _ _ _ _ _ _ _

6. _ _ _ _ _ _ Ⓞ _ _

7. _ _ _ _ _ _ Ⓞ _

8. _ _ _ _ _ _ Ⓞ _ _

Answer: _ _ _ _ _ _ _ _

172

ELIJAH'S CHALLENGE

It's one of the Bible's great miracle stories: Elijah's challenge to Jezebel's pagan priests. Can you unscramble the three phrases below from the story in 1 Kings 18?

A curl moment

_ _ _ _   _ _ _ _ _ _

A flappers booth

_ _ _ _ _ _ _ _

_ _   _ _ _ _

Scenic firing eave

_ _ _ _ _ _ _

_ _ _ _ _ _ _ _

CROSSWORD
by David K. Shortess

■ CELESTIAL SIGNS OF THE END TIMES ■

Although no one knows the exact date and time of the last days, we do have a description of what they will be like. Work this puzzle to learn more about this closing chapter in God's amazing plan.

[In] those days shall the sun be darkened, and the moon shall not give her light, and the stars shall fall from heaven.
MATTHEW 24:29

ACROSS
1 "And God _____ every thing that he had made" (Genesis 1:31)
4 Jonah follower
9 "The word is _____ thee, even in thy mouth" (Romans 10:8)
13 Asian nursemaid
15 Greek market
16 Referring to (2 words)
17 "As the _____ among thorns" (Song of Solomon 2:2)
18 Cold cream maker
19 Ivan or Peter
20 "God _____ his work which he had made" (Genesis 2:2)
22 "Go and walk through the land, and _____ it" (Joshua 18:8)
24 CELESTIAL SIGN (Joel 2:31) (3 words)
27 "Am I _____, or a whale" (Job 7:12) (2 words)
28 University of Oregon locale
31 Little (suffix)
34 Upbeat
36 "I _____ to those whose sin does not lead to death" (1 John 5:16 NIV)
37 CELESTIAL SIGN (Amos 8:9) (5 words)
41 Middle Eastern chieftain (var.)
42 Shop with ready-to-serve foods
43 They give TLC (abbr.)
44 Noted lean and fat noneaters
46 Iris locale
48 CELESTIAL SIGN (Revelation 8:10) (3 words)

54 Mascara applier
56 Set of steps over a fence
57 Cross or neuron (prefix)
58 Legume
61 Dutch cheese
62 "_____ are for kids"
63 Swelling from excess fluids
64 San _____, city in northern Italy
65 Unit of time (abbr.)
66 Four-door model, usually
67 "Water _____ round about the altar" (1 Kings 18:35)

DOWN
1 "And Melchizedek king of _____ brought forth" (Genesis 14:18)
2 Kind of organic acid
3 Ralph _____ Emerson
4 "As the men started on their way to _____ out the land" (Joshua 18:8 NIV)
5 "Because _____ to my Father" (John 16:10) (2 words)
6 Tenant-owned apartment, for short
7 Arabic unit of dry measure
8 Bother
9 Four-fifths of the atmosphere
10 "It's cold out here. . . . Why don't you go _____ a while?" (2 words)
11 Kind of bag
12 "And he said, Behold, I am _____, Lord" (Acts 9:10)
14 Serengeti laugher
21 Game player
23 Royal attendants

25 "And they _____ no candle, neither light of the sun" (Revelation 22:5)
26 Source of poi
29 It's a gas
30 European sea eagles
31 "To maintain good works for necessary _____" (Titus 3:14)
32 "A little leaven leaveneth the whole _____" (Galatians 5:9)
33 Peppy
35 Not away from (abbr.)
38 Transmission
39 Neither positive nor negative (abbr.)
40 Thomas _____ Edison
45 Apple and soy
47 "_____ the Fall," Miller play
49 Hebrew letter (var.)
50 "And came and _____ them into the pot of pottage" (2 Kings 4:39)
51 Duck known for its down
52 Alpaca's cousin
53 Detroit dud
54 Medics (abbr.)

55 Time long ago (poet.)
59 Grandma (Ger.)
60 Sure's rival

ACROSTIC
by Donna Maltese

▬▬ SAMSON'S BARE HANDS ▬▬

God's power can enable ordinary men to do the extraordinary. Crack the code to discover the bare facts of this truth!

To be mighty

___ ___ ___ ___ ___ ___ ___ ___
21 6 28 10 25 2 14 31

Bravery

___ ___ ___ ___ ___ ___ ___
20 36 3 30 15 24 33

This story takes place here (Judges 14:5)

___ ___ ___ ___ ___ ___ ___ ___
9 16 38 19 5 29 22 11

God gave Samson this

___ ___ ___ ___ ___ ___ ___ ___
12 37 23 1 35 17 39 8

Lion's head of hair

___ ___ ___ ___
13 32 4 26

To slay

___ ___ ___ ___
18 7 34 27

37-8-1   12-21-7-23-7-39   6-2   37-8-1   27-36-25-11

20-32-13-10   13-16-17-8-39-16-31-5   3-21-6-38   8-7-13,

15-4-11   8-1   30-19-4-37   8-7-13   15-12   8-1

28-6-14-34-11   8-15-9-33   30-19-4-37   15   18-7-11,

15-4-11   8-1   8-29-11   35-6-39-8-7-35-24   7-4   8-7-12

8-15-4-11.

JUDGES 14:6

— DISCIPLES AND THE MIRACULOUS —

Jesus performed miracles for many poor, nameless people of His time. But these spotty headlines describe three well-known disciples who experienced the miraculous. Can you solve each one?

DOUB●ING FI●H●●●AN ●ULLS IN ●NOUGH F●SH TO SI●K B●AT

_ _ _ _ _   _ _ _ _ _

●BSENT ●AN D●UB●S RE●URRECTION T●EORY

_ _ _ _ _ _

M●N WONDE●S HOW BOY'S LU●CH WILL F●E● A CRO●D

_ _ _ _ _ _

DIVINE REPORTS
OF CHRIST'S BIRTH

Christ's humble arrival upon the earth was heralded in many different ways by many different people. Solve the code to discover just a few.

ABC 2	MNO 6	MNO 6	ABC 2

DEF 3	JKL 5	GHI 4	QZ 0	ABC 2	ABC 2	DEF 3	TUV 8	GHI 4

JKL 5	MNO 6	PRS 7	DEF 3	PRS 7	GHI 4

MNO 6	ABC 2	PRS 7	WXY 9

PRS 7	GHI 4	DEF 3	PRS 7	GHI 4	DEF 3	PRS 7	DEF 3	PRS 7

PRS 7	GHI 4	MNO 6	DEF 3	MNO 6	MNO 6

QZ 0	ABC 2	ABC 2	GHI 4	ABC 2	PRS 7	GHI 4	ABC 2	PRS 7

PRISON SONG
ACTS 16:25–26

And at **midnight Paul** and **Silas prayed**, and **sang praises** unto God: and the **prisoners heard them**. And **suddenly there** was a **great earthquake**, so **that** the **foundations** of the prison were **shaken**: and **immediately** all the **doors** were **opened**, and **every one's bands were loosed**.

```
M T H P B F U O U Y V H S K N
M A C O R O A S L O O S E D T
I S Y T E U X N R S P A N W P
D M S E P N E K A H S L O J Q
N K M J K D E N E P O I Q R N
I T W E D A G W R S S S C J U
G J Z U D T U I O W E R E R V
H S S R A I S Q B R S K O U C
T S A H A O A L H O I A T O E
T E T E N N A T U T A Y H F D
H U B E V S B D E A R A E C G
E P R A Y E D B L L P A R R U
M S K H N P R I O G Y O E V G
M M L Y C D S Y F F W A O V F
E N B V I S S L G K T Z M H D
```

CROSSWORD
by David K. Shortess

▬▬▬ MIRACLES IN DANIEL ▬▬▬

The book of Daniel is full of miraculous acts of God (and we're not "lion").
Work this puzzle to find the answers to three theme clues relating to God's
awe-inspiring acts.

> *"[God] rescues and he saves; he performs signs
> and wonders in the heavens and on the earth."*
> DANIEL 6:27 NIV

ACROSS

1 "There is no _____ discerning and wise as you" (Genesis 41:39 NIV) (2 words)
6 Hearty's cohort
10 "For, lo, the winter is _____" (Song of Solomon 2:11)
14 Summer TV fare, often
15 Indigo plant
16 He was red all over (Genesis 25:25)
17 WHERE GOD INTERVENED TO SAVE DANIEL'S FRIENDS (Daniel 3:20–28) (3 words)
20 "But Jonathan was very _____ of David" (1 Samuel 19:1 NIV)
21 "And he will make her wilderness like _____" (Isaiah 51:3)
22 "Assyria has joined them _____ strength to the descendants of Lot" (Psalm 83:8 NIV) (2 words)
25 "Thou hast not _____ unto men, but unto God" (Acts 5:4)
26 Haw's opposite
29 In the distance
30 Accumulate
32 "Without _____ of brightness?" (Amos 5:20 NIV) (2 words)
33 "_____ a girl"
34 Oaf
35 "And in an hour that he is not _____ of" (Matthew 24:50)
36 WHERE GOD INTERVENED TO SAVE DANIEL (Daniel 6:16) (3 words)
40 Took a turn (2 words)
42 "Whither have ye made a _____ to day?" (1 Samuel 27:10)
43 "And _____ soul sin" (Leviticus 5:1) (2 words)
46 "_____ I trying to please men?" (Galatians 1:10 NIV) (2 words)

47 "Be self-controlled and _____" (1 Peter 5:8 NIV)
49 "And _____ hour he is not aware" (Luke 12:46) (2 words)
50 "Nor standeth in the _____ of sinners" (Psalm 1:1)
51 Made it home?
52 Go back
54 Bath powder
55 "The _____ came to Jesus by night" (John 3:2)
56 WHAT GOD WROTE ON THE WALL (Daniel 5:25 NIV) (3 words)
63 Where Isfahan is
64 "Go and _____ potter's earthen bottle" (Jeremiah 19:1) (2 words)
65 "Such knowledge _____ wonderful for me" (Psalm 139:6) (2 words)
66 Prohibitionists
67 Land of Seir (Genesis 32:3)
68 Depends on

DOWN

1 Table scrap (arch.)
2 Ezra follower (abbr.)
3 "And how long will it be _____ they believe me" (Numbers 14:11)
4 "That the Son of man must _____ many things" (Mark 8:31)
5 Leek relative
6 "It is _____ for thee to kick against the pricks" (Acts 26:14)
7 "And see if there be _____ wicked way in me" (Psalm 139:24)
8 "The _____ more than meat" (Luke 12:23) (2 words)
9 Slips away from
10 Quaker William
11 Jehoshaphat's father (1 Kings 15:24)

182

12 Biological pouch
13 Calendar abbreviation
18 "I will bring to an _____ the groaning she caused" (Isaiah 21:2 NIV) (2 words)
19 "By the way of the _____ sea" (Numbers 14:25)
22 _____ chi
23 "This do ye, as _____ as ye drink it" (1 Corinthians 11:25)
24 "And I will raise him up at the _____" (John 6:40) (2 words)
25 "I have _____ to no purpose" (Isaiah 49:4 NIV)
26 Monument rock
27 Give _____ to
28 Pink, at times
31 Pronoun (Fr.)
32 "But my heart standeth in _____ of thy word" (Psalm 119:161)
34 Game, _____, match
35 "Can _____ one cubit unto his stature" (Matthew 6:27)
37 Father of Canaan (Genesis 9:18)
38 "_____ standeth in the way of sinners" (Psalm 1:1)
39 Official under Darius (Daniel 6:1 NIV)
40 "Consider the lilies of the field, _____ they grow" (Matthew 6:28)

41 Jether's son (1 Chronicles 7:38)
44 "Be not _____ from me" (Psalm 38:21)
45 Sluggard's teacher? (Proverbs 6:6)
47 Maintain
48 "Dogs came and _____ his sores" (Luke 16:21)
49 Opposed to
51 "And he _____ down among the ashes" (Job 2:8)
53 Certain correspondence
54 Perfect scores, to some
55 Close forcefully
56 Naval officer (abbr.)
57 "They do alway _____ in their heart" (Hebrews 3:10)
58 "I tell you, _____: but, except ye repent" (Luke 13:3)
59 Ike's command (abbr.)
60 RR depot (abbr.)
61 It may be charged
62 Phone book listings (abbr.)

183

BIBLE QUOTATION
by Suzanne Stepp

━━ A MIRACLE ON A MOUNTAIN ━━
MARK 9:2

Work this Bible quotation puzzle to discover a mountaintop experience that left three disciples scared and speechless.

```
H   B   E   N   S   F   T   G   M   H   O   D
T   R   A   L   O   I   E   N   R   E   M
Y   N   M   D   I   P   E   K   T   S   N
J   D   T   N   U   E   A   J   V   E   U   B
T   A   N   F   D   R   H   O   M   A   U   S
S   E   I   H   E   M   P   J   I   W   E   M   S   E
N   W   R   U   H   G   H   A   T   N   P   A
T   A   S   H   S   A   D   I   U   A   E   T
A   E   I   N   A   H   S   L   H   T   E   H
    E   A   T   E       D   T   O
                        E   H   O
                            T
                            R
```

FROM THE ROOF

MARK 2:5

Others may fail us, but Jesus never will. Solve this puzzle to find out what
Jesus said to an invalid after his friends "let him down."

FELSITE	Best group	_____	1. ____ ____
OMINOUS	Not plus	_____	2. ____
REDSKIN	Traveled on snow	_____	3. ____ ____
GRATIFY	Godmother	_____	4. ____ ____
HAPPIER	Essay	_____	5. ____
VOCALLY	Not widespread	_____	6. ____
ELASTIN	Ancient language	_____	7. ____ ____
IGNOBLE	Sphere	_____	8. ____ ____
NOBLEST	Parts of ears	_____	9. ____
SELFISH	Document folders	_____	10. ____
BOUNDER	Circle	_____	11. ____
ENRAGED	Magnificent	_____	12. ____ ____

___ ___ ___ ___ ___ ___ ___ ___ ___ ___ ___ ___

___ ___ ___ ___ ___ ___ ___ ___ ___ ___ ___ ___
 1   2   3   4   5   6   7   8   9   10 11 12

── PRAYER FOR PETER IN PRISON ──
Acts 12:5–9

Peter therefore was kept in **prison**: but **prayer** was made **without ceasing** of the **church** unto God for him. And when **Herod** would have brought him forth, the same **night** Peter was **sleeping between** two **soldiers**, bound with two **chains**: and the **keepers** before the door kept the prison. And, **behold**, the **angel** of the Lord came upon him, and a **light shined** in the prison: and he **smote** Peter on the **side**, and raised him up, saying, **Arise** up **quickly**. And his chains **fell** off from his hands. And the angel said unto him, **Gird thyself**, and bind on thy **sandals**. And so he did. And he saith unto him, Cast thy **garment** about thee, and **follow** me. And he went out, and followed him; and wist not that it was **true** which was done by the angel; but **thought** he saw a **vision**.

```
P R I S O N B X A K P I T N R
J Q D L O H E B E H J P A I E
N P K A R I S E C L C V I G T
H W N D N Z P R Z H S I W H E
H I L N W E U U W O A S G T P
O T Y A R H L Y L K C I U Q T
W H H S C L B D G L L O N R T
Z O W Y L N I L D A F N U S H
X U R L S E R O F E R E H T G
Q T R G R E E E U O N M L N U
D S G S Y W L P R H L I E L O
A O I A K T Y F I L T L H N H
F C R D C E A S I N G D O S T
R P D E E B U R A N G E L W S
E T E P H S M O T E W U E E A
```

ACROSTIC
by Donna Maltese

━━━━ HAND IT TO MOSES ━━━━

Here's a puzzle that shows just how persuasive God can be when we doubt our own abilities.

He was raised by Pharaoh's daughter (Exodus 2:10)

___ ___ ___ ___ ___
6   27 13 24 17

This tribe was led out of Egypt

___ ___ ___ ___ ___ ___
15 21 28 8   12 10

It was burning when God called Moses

___ ___ ___ ___
20 3   5   23

To be unsure

___ ___ ___ ___ ___
11 29 4   25 19

Through miracles, God demonstrates His ____

___ ___ ___ ___ ___
2   18 14 9   26

What leprosy affects

___ ___ ___ ___
22 1   16 7

23-9   2-3-19   23-15-5   23-8-7-11   16-7-19-18

23-15-5   20-27-13-27-6:   8-7-11   14-23-9-7   23-9

19-29-29-1   16-19   18-4-19,   25-12-23-18-10-11,

23-15-5   23-8-7-11   14-8-22   10-24-2-26-18-3-17   8-22

21-7-18-14.

EXODUS 4:6

SUDOKU
by Sara Stoker

MIRACLE CHILD

EASY

	A	B	C	D	E	F	G	H	I
1	H	M	A			W		C	L
2			W			C			
3	C			A			W		D
4					R			L	
5	I		M	W	H		A	D	
6	L			M		D			C
7			I	H				A	
8	A					M		R	I
9	R		C			I	L		H

Hint: Column H

"And he went up, and lay upon the child. . .and he stretched himself upon the child; and the flesh of the _____ waxed _____" (2 Kings 4:34).

ORDER UP!

Daily fill yourself with Jesus, the Bread of Life.

1. EPESMTL

2. AETRSPU

3. MSAGNRTE

4. NNHTROER

5. LVYLAE

This was found on the ground, but it was good for eating.

1. _ _ O _ _ _ _

2. _ O _ _ _ _ _

3. _ _ _ _ _ O _ _

4. O _ _ _ _ _ _ _

5. _ O _ _ _ _

Answer: _ _ _ _ _

CROSSWORD
by David K. Shortess

MIRACLES OF JESUS

Jesus was one busy Man, performing miracle upon miracle among the people in the New Testament. Solve this puzzle to find phrases relating to four of them.

Jesus said to them, "I have shown you many great miracles from the Father."
JOHN 10:32 NIV

ACROSS

1 Separate
6 Miss or Mrs.
9 Last word in the Bible (Revelation 22:21)
13 Abraham's first wife (Genesis 17:15)
14 "But thou shalt give _____ now" (1 Samuel 2:16) (2 words)
16 Jacob's third son (Exodus 1:2)
17 "We are true men; we _____ spies" (Genesis 42:31) (2 words)
18 _____ Valley, CA
19 Chemical suffix (pl.)
20 MIRACLE (John 12:1) (2 words)
23 Organic compound
24 Shows or does (suffix)
25 He may save a lot
29 "For my yoke is _____" (Matthew 11:30)
31 Police charity (abbr.)
34 -Bus or -potent preceder
35 Psyche parts
36 Put one foot in front of the other
37 MIRACLE (Matthew 14:15–21) (3 words)
40 S-shaped moldings
41 Attention-getting word
42 "_____ of a Thousand Days"
43 Prof's lab helpers (abbr.)
44 Italian noble house
46 Took a turn in the lineup
48 Popular sandwich, briefly
49 Vessels (abbr.)
51 MIRACLE (Matthew 8:16) (3 words)
57 "They will _____ on wings like eagles" (Isaiah 40:31 NIV)
58 "Blessed are the _____ in spirit" (Matthew 5:3)
59 Get used to
61 Go bad, as fruit
62 Fairytale monster
63 "And, behold, Joseph was _____ the pit" (Genesis 37:29) (2 words)
64 Flying fish-eaters
65 "Calling on the _____ of the Lord" (Acts 22:16)
66 Long lock

DOWN

1 "Like _____ father pitieth his children" (Psalm 103:13) (2 words)
2 Catherine _____, last wife of Henry VIII
3 Kind of code
4 "Yet they _____ have not spoken to them" (Jeremiah 23:21) (2 words)
5 "But what things were gain. . . _____ counted loss" (Philippians 3:7) (2 words)
6 Mess up
7 MIRACLE (Mark 4:37–39) (3 words)
8 "A trap _____ him by the heel" (Job 18:9 NIV)
9 "Be on guard! Be _____! You do not know when" (Mark 13:33 NIV)
10 Beanery item
11 First lady and others
12 Serbian city
15 NYC museum (abbr.)
21 Direction from Tucson to Santa Fe (abbr.)
22 -How or -where preceder
25 "And who will _____ us?" (Isaiah 6:8) (2 words)
26 "I am Alpha and _____" (Revelation 1:8)

27 South American range
28 "The Lord is the strength of my _____" (Psalm 27:1)
30 Tennis great
31 Sow
32 C'est une _____ idee
33 "And all these things shall be _____ unto you" (Luke 12:31)
35 "Will _____ the flesh of bulls" (Psalm 50:13) (2 words)
36 Test taken by HS sophs (abbr.)
38 "Or to which of my creditors did _____ you?" (Isaiah 50:1 NIV) (2 words)
39 Old European game with three players and forty cards
45 "Who enter Dagon's temple at Ashdod _____ the threshold" (1 Samuel 5:5 NIV) (2 words)
47 Agree to
48 "Nor gather into _____" (Matthew 6:26)
50 Number of Noah's sons
51 "What, could ye not watch with me one _____?" (Matthew 26:40)
52 "And all who _____ their living from the sea" (Revelation 18:17 NIV)

53 "Whom are you pursuing? A dead _____ flea?" (1 Samuel 24:14 NIV) (2 words)
54 "So neither _____ my brethren, nor my servants" (Nehemiah 4:23) (2 words)
55 Like a kitten
56 Actor Kristofferson
57 Part of the names of many Quebec towns (abbr.)
60 Printers' measures

WORD SEARCH
by Connie Troyer

DAY VERSUS NIGHT
JOSHUA 10

AJALON

AMORITES

AVENGED

AZEKAH

BETH-HORON

CAMP

CAVE

DAY

DEBIR

DELIVERED

EGLON

ENEMIES

FIVE KINGS

FOUGHT

GILGAL

GIBEON

HAILSTONES

HEARKENED

HEAVEN

HEBRON

HID

ISRAEL

JASHER

JOSHUA

LORD

MAKKEDAH

MAN

MIDST

MIGHTY MEN

MOON

PIRAM

SLAUGHTER

SPAKE

STAND

STILL

SUN

VALLEY

VOICE

```
M I G H T Y M E N Y E L L A V
S D E N E K R A E H L O V M A
E Z B R E H S A J I P E N O S
I D E L I V E R E D N E N R E
M H E B R O N Y H G V O U I N
E S M A R I P A E A E H S T O
N D P C C C D D E B K R L E T
E M A A D E I H I T A A A S S
F I V E K I N G S E Z J U A L
O E T K S E I D L E L A G U I
U P A R I L I N K L T L H H A
G M A N G M R A I F O O T S H
H A O A K O H T E R A N E O T
T C L O K N S S D E B I R J M
E G L O N O N O R O H H T E B
```

TELEPHONE SCRAMBLE
by Connie Troyer

━━ HEALINGS ━━

Elisha, Elijah, and Jesus seemed to have the major share of the market when it came to healing others. Solve this puzzle to find words and names relating to these three major miracle workers.

PRS 7	GHI 4	JKL 5	MNO 6	ABC 2	MNO 6	
PRS 7	MNO 6	MNO 6	DEF 3	TUV 8	MNO 6	PRS 7
ABC 2	JKL 5	GHI 4	MNO 6	DEF 3		
JKL 5	DEF 3	PRS 7	DEF 3	PRS 7	PRS 7	
DEF 3	DEF 3	MNO 6	MNO 6	MNO 6	GHI 4	ABC 2
MNO 6	ABC 2	ABC 2	MNO 6	ABC 2	MNO 6	
PRS 7	DEF 3	PRS 7	TUV 8	ABC 2	MNO 6	TUV 8

━━━ MIRACLES OF FAITH ━━━

The combination of faith, expectation, and obedience produces amazing results. Crack these alphabet codes to discover two verses revealing a soldier and some servants who saw a miracle from Jesus.

MTY VYKMLNSZK GKWJYNYF GKF WGSF, BZNF,

S GH KZM JZNMTU MTGM MTZL WTZLBFYWM

VZHY LKFYN HU NZZC: ALM WRYGI MTY JZNF

ZKBU, GKF HU WYNDGKM WTGBB AY TYGBYF.

GOZ TMUZT QW GOZ WZXNG OXC GXNGZC

GOZ LXGZT GOXG LXN JXCZ LHVZ, XVC FVZL

VQG LOZVSZ HG LXN.

CROSSWORD
by David K. Shortess

═══ EGYPT'S PLAGUES ═══

Because he refused to let the Israelites go, Pharaoh wound up plagued with trouble. Can you find eight horrific events hidden within this puzzle?

"Let my people go. . .or this time I will send the full force of my plagues against you."
EXODUS 9:13–14 NIV

ACROSS

1 Kilauea product
5 Greek mountain
9 "Now the Valley of Siddim was full _____ pits" (Genesis 14:10 NIV) (2 words)
14 Elliptical
15 Dudley Do-Right's girlfriend
16 "I speak as a _____ am more" (2 Corinthians 11:23) (2 words)
17 THREE PLAGUES (Exodus 9:9; 8:21; 8:2) (3 words)
20 Have
21 Pre-Aztec Mexican tribe
22 Winglike structures
23 "Is any thing _____ hard for the LORD?" (Genesis 18:14)
24 "Who will _____ to every man according to" (Romans 2:6)
26 ANOTHER PLAGUE (Exodus 7:17) (3 words)
32 Dancer Castle of old
33 Bells ringing
34 "For this is the _____ and the prophets" (Matthew 7:12)
37 "Then Paul stood in the midst of _____ hill" (Acts 17:22)
38 One-hundredth of one liter (abbr.) (2 words)
39 Island east of Java
40 That has (suffix)
41 Nemesis
42 "And, lo, a great multitude, which no man _____ number" (Revelation 7:9)
43 ANOTHER PLAGUE (Exodus 12:29) (3 words)
45 Conversation (var.)
48 Born, in Bordeaux
49 1952 Winter Olympics site
50 "And did _____ showbread" (Mark 2:26) (2 words)
54 "Your lightning _____ up the world" (Psalm 77:18 NIV)
57 THREE MORE PLAGUES (Exodus 10:13; 9:22; 8:17) (3 words)
60 Related on mother's side
61 Close to, in a game
62 "I watch, and _____ a sparrow alone upon the house top" (Psalm 102:7) (2 words)
63 "And gave the _____, and caused them to understand the reading" (Nehemiah 8:8)
64 Sicilian volcano
65 "_____ harm yourself! We are all here!" (Acts 16:28 NIV)

DOWN

1 Gray wolf
2 "We have four men which have _____ on them" (Acts 21:23) (2 words)
3 "Shall _____ words have an end" (Job 16:3)
4 "They are _____ gone aside" (Psalm 14:3)
5 "They went through the flood _____" (Psalm 66:6) (2 words)
6 "Go and _____ that thou hast" (Matthew 19:21)
7 Narrow opening
8 Away from the wind
9 "And the publican, standing afar _____" (Luke 18:13)

10 "Looking _____ hasting unto the coming of the day of God" (2 Peter 3:12) (2 words)

11 "To prostitution, _____ wine and new" (Hosea 4:11 NIV) (2 words)

12 Pond organisms

13 Stair part

18 Candy or toy

19 "And the heavens shall be rolled together as a _____" (Isaiah 34:4)

23 Addition column

25 Greek dawn goddess

26 Hoarfrost

27 Persia, today

28 Like grass (Fr.)

29 "The watchman _____ the gate for him" (John 10:3 NIV)

30 "John Brown's Body" poet

31 On the _____

34 Praise

35 "If I give _____ possess to the poor" (1 Corinthians 13:3 NIV) (2 words)

36 "For _____ is the gate" (Matthew 7:13)

38 Walmart competitor

39 "A _____ of him shall not be broken" (John 19:36)

41 Personal profile, for short

42 Angler's basket

43 Disparages

44 "And they put _____ purple robe" (John 19:2) (3 words)

45 Distributes, with out

46 "This _____ of them" (Mark 14:69) (2 words)

47 Alaska Highway, once

51 "_____ forgive our debtors" (Matthew 6:12) (2 words)

52 "And God saw _____ it was good" (Genesis 1:10)

53 Small mountain lake

54 VIP transporter

55 "_____ do all things through Christ" (Philippians 4:13) (2 words)

56 "We should not _____ the Lord" (1 Corinthians 10:9 NIV)

58 "Ye shall not _____ me" (Luke 13:35)

59 Boy

199

HAIL TO THE
CONFEDERATED KINGS

"Hail to the king" takes on a whole new meaning in this encrypted miracle.

After Moses' death, Joshua was Israel's ____

___ ___ ___ ___ ___ ___
23 43 15 38   5 34

King of Jerusalem in Joshua 10:3

___ ___ ___ ___ ___ ___ ___ ___ ___ ___
 8 19 25   4 31 21 11 37   1 27

A body of soldiers

___ ___ ___ ___ ___ ___ ___
 3 39 26 18 41 13 35

Skirmish

___ ___ ___ ___ ___
10 36 29   6 20

Having won the battle

___ ___ ___ ___ ___ ___ ___ ___ ___ ___
28 14   2 42 33 17   9 24 30 12

More died from hailstones than Israel slew with this Old Testament weapon

___ ___ ___ ___ ___
40 22   7 32 16

20-6-1   23-7-32-16   2-15-12-42   19-39-22-13

29-34-43-8-42   40-42-24-4-11-40   10-17-33-26

6-5-41-28-5-4   30-18-25-4   20-6-1-26

30-4-42-7   8-21-5-27-8-6,   8-4-16   20-6-1-35

37-9-5-38.

JOSHUA 10:11

BIBLE QUOTATION
by Suzanne Stepp

▬ A SON RETURNED TO HIS MOTHER ▬
LUKE 7:14–15

Work this Bible quotation puzzle to discover a man who, after getting a rise out of Jesus, was returned to his mother.

M	T	B	N	D	R	S	E	Y	T	B	K
E	A	H	U	T	H	D	M	O	D	T	R
A	O	I	A	E	O	A	T	D	E	A	T
G	E	A	T	U	C	H	A	N	B	H	N
T	S	Y	I	M	H	A	E	A	G	U	E
S	T	W	L	H	C	Y	N	D	U	H	H
T	A	N	I	P		H	S	D	R	A	A
D		A	E	S		H	E	E	D	I	S
E		T	O	I		A	U	U		D	E
H		N	I	L		S	T	P		A	S
E		H	L	D		A	O	A			N
			D	T		E	A	D			
			T				N				

SPOTTY HEADLINE
by Sara Stoker

━━━ MEDICAL MIRACLES ━━━

Long before penicillin, CAT scans, and organ replacements, a few people enjoyed the benefits of true medical miracles. These spotty headlines describe three who came through serious physical trouble. Can you solve each one?

M●N S●RVIVES TERRIB●E SHIPWRECK AND VI●ER BITE

— — — —

KIND●EAR●ED SE●MSTRESS DIES, R●ISED TO L●FE ●Y PE●ER

— — — — — —

MAN DEAD FO●● D●YS COME● B●CK TO ●IFE WITH ●EST

— — — — — —

━━ BLIND MAN AT JERICHO ━━
MARK 10:46–47, 52

And **they came** to Jericho: and as he **went** out of **Jericho with** his **disciples** and a **great number** of **people, blind Bartimaeus**, the son of Timaeus, sat by the **highway side begging**. And **when** he **heard that** it was Jesus of **Nazareth**, he **began** to cry out, and say, Jesus, **thou** son of **David, have mercy** on me. . . . And Jesus **said** unto him, Go thy way; thy **faith hath made thee whole**. And **immediately** he **received** his **sight**, and **followed Jesus** in the way.

```
S  B  U  H  L  M  U  B  S  W  X  C  A  M  E
I  K  R  E  Y  A  W  H  G  I  H  C  U  L  B
G  R  E  A  T  L  N  U  C  G  F  T  P  Y  J
H  M  C  R  H  J  E  R  I  C  H  O  I  H  P
T  D  E  D  K  T  E  T  Z  B  E  T  H  A  T
C  E  I  A  Q  S  E  S  A  P  D  F  M  V  F
Q  W  V  S  A  X  T  R  U  I  Q  A  W  E  A
Y  O  E  I  C  N  T  M  A  S  D  H  V  U  N
R  L  D  H  E  I  A  F  L  Z  O  E  D  I  S
W  L  M  W  M  D  P  G  F  L  A  R  M  Z  D
X  O  Y  A  E  I  M  L  E  M  E  N  U  M  N
U  F  E  G  N  I  G  G  E  B  H  E  O  E  I
J  U  H  G  J  X  B  R  M  S  E  A  H  T  L
S  H  T  I  W  O  C  U  Q  H  H  W  T  T  B
K  O  A  M  I  Y  N  E  E  N  U  V  N  H  V
```

CROSSWORD
by David K. Shortess

━━━━━ JESUS AND THE SEA ━━━━━

Although Jesus was a peaceful Man, He often made great waves. Here are three theme clues relating to Jesus and the sea. Can you work this puzzle to uncover their answers? Note that of the long theme answers, only 17 Across is a direct quote from scripture. The other two, 41 and 65 Across, are not.

The same day went Jesus out of the house, and sat by the sea side.
MATTHEW 13:1

ACROSS

1 Georgetown jocks
6 One of two countries that claims Everest
11 "Which of you shall have. . .an ox fallen into a _____" (Luke 14:5)
14 Not hidden
15 "And if a man shall _____ pit. . .and not cover it" (Exodus 21:33) (2 words)
16 Jazz, for one
17 "AND IN THE FOURTH WATCH OF THE NIGHT JESUS WENT UNTO THEM, _____" (Matthew 14:25) (4 words)
20 "It shall be _____ with him" (Isaiah 3:11)
21 "Praise the _____" (Psalm 115:18)
22 "He _____ his meat and eats his fill" (Isaiah 44:16 NIV)
23 David, to many
24 Forks in the road
25 Leaf attachment point
28 "_____ art thou" (Genesis 27:32)
30 "Neither could any man _____ him" (Mark 5:4)
34 Hemoglobin deficiency
37 "And his word is not _____" (1 John 1:10) (2 words)
40 Shea spectator
41 WHAT HAPPENED WHEN A GREAT STORM AROSE ON THE SEA (Mark 4:39) (4 words)
44 NATO member (abbr.)
45 Edible plant of the genus Brassica
46 "But if thou _____ go down, go thou with. . .thy servant" (Judges 7:10) (2 words)
47 CIA operative
49 "Get up! Pick up your _____ and walk" (John 5:8 NIV)

51 "_____ John" (missive type)
52 "Barnabas they called _____" (Acts 14:12 NIV)
55 French 101 verb
58 "A young _____ and told Moses" (Numbers 11:27 NIV) (2 words)
61 _____ vera
62 "They that _____ in tears shall reap in joy" (Psalm 126:5)
65 WHAT PETER, JAMES, AND JOHN FOUND IN THEIR NETS (Luke 5:4–7) (5 words)
68 Vote cast
69 "In the first month, that is, the month _____" (Esther 3:7)
70 Clear the board
71 Poem of praise
72 Alamogordo's county
73 "Art thou a _____?" (Acts 22:27)

DOWN

1 "Consider _____ love thy precepts" (Psalm 119:159) (2 words)
2 Track shape
3 Give a holler
4 "Take up the _____ of the covenant" (Joshua 3:6)
5 Steps on a fence
6 "He causeth the grass _____ for the cattle" (Psalm 104:14) (2 words)
7 Trendy digital accessory
8 _____-oni, Rachel's son (Genesis 35:16–18)
9 "She crieth. . .at the _____ of the city" (Proverbs 8:3)
10 California/Nevada border lake
11 "And it came to _____" (Genesis 6:1)

12 "Through thy precepts _____ understanding" (Psalm 119:104) (2 words)
13 Herbal and green
18 Neither
19 "_____ of Eden," Steinbeck opus
23 Blood (prefix)
24 Habit
25 Follower of Micah
26 "As the Lord hath called every _____ let him walk" (1 Corinthians 7:17) (2 words)
27 Transferable picture
29 "And shall _____ multitude of sins" (James 5:20) (2 words)
31 "And the tongue is _____, a world of iniquity" (James 3:6) (2 words)
32 Devilfish
33 "There is a woman that hath a familiar spirit at _____" (1 Samuel 28:7)
35 Type
36 "Seeing I _____ stranger?" (Ruth 2:10) (2 words)
38 Most TV channels (abbr.)
39 Understand
42 "Under oaks and poplars and _____" (Hosea 4:13)
43 Trudge through

48 Old Testament scribe
50 "They should _____ man of him" (Mark 8:30) (2 words)
53 "Ye shall _____ manner of fat" (Leviticus 7:23) (2 words)
54 Not qualified
56 "It was _____ painful for me" (Psalm 73:16)
57 Direct toward
58 Minnesota clinic
59 "Ish-bosheth, who lay on _____ at noon" (2 Samuel 4:5) (2 words)
60 "These are a smoke in my _____" (Isaiah 65:5)
61 Like a wing
62 Burma neighbor, once
63 Greek mountain
64 "_____ I was a child" (1 Corinthians 13:11)
66 "_____ not vain repetitions" (Matthew 6:7)
67 "From going to and _____ in the earth" (Job 1:7)

207

ACROSTIC
by Donna Maltese

ABRAHAM'S
OFFERING GETS FIRED

Our God is a consuming fire, as He proves in performing this awesome feat.
Crack the code to learn more about this "hot" topic.

His name means "father of many" (Genesis 17:5)

___ ___ ___ ___ ___ ___ ___
26 12 37 20 7 31 15

Old Testament offering

___ ___ ___ ___ ___ ___ ___ ___ ___
17 32 6 36 28 10 40 4 21

This miracle sealed God's _____ to Abraham (Galatians 3:29)

___ ___ ___ ___ ___ ___ ___
19 38 24 1 30 43 13

A type of bird offered by Abraham (Genesis 15:9)

___ ___ ___ ___ ___ ___ ___ ___ ___ ___
3 16 27 33 8 39 22 5 18 11

Another type of bird offered by Abraham (Genesis 15:9)

___ ___ ___ ___ ___ ___
14 29 41 2 34 23

After this miracle, Abraham _____ God would keep His pledge

___ ___ ___ ___
9 25 42 35

35-7-2-23   3-7-2   17-16-25   35-13-23-3   22-5-35-23,

31-25-22   28-33   35-26-17   22-26-37-9,

12-11-7-24-8-22   31   43-1-34-9-40-25-41

10-16-36-23-31-6-13,   31-25-22   31

12-16-38-23-30-23-41   8-20-15-19   3-7-32-3

14-32-17-17-21-22   12-2-33-35-2-2-25   33-7-5-17-42

14-29-39-4-39-43.

GENESIS 15:17

CREATION

Miracle One was God's formation of the universe out of nothing. We've anagrammed three words or phrases from the creation account in Genesis 1–2. Can you unscramble them?

Ask nerds

_ _ _ _ _ _ _

On fanged deer

_ _ _ _ _ _   _ _   _ _ _ _

Half before it

_ _ _ _ _ _   _ _   _ _ _ _

MEALTIME MIRACLE

SEE MARK 6:44

Jesus was poor but managed to make enough bread to feed numerous people. Solve this puzzle to find out how many were nourished by Jesus while hanging out on a hillside.

LADLING	Organ	_____	1. ____ ____
OVERACT	Small amount	_____	2. ____ ____
AIMLESS	Loses weight	_____	3. ____ ____
VIBRANT	Intelligence	_____	4. ____ ____
ENGLISH	Shoe strap	_____	5. ____ ____
OLYMPUS	Swollen	_____	6. ____ ____
UNTWIST	Restrict	_____	7. ____
ELAPSED	Weakened	_____	8. ____ ____
APTERAL	Flower part	_____	9. ____ ____
ENDLESS	Snow runners	_____	10. ____ ____
FLANGED	Harvest	_____	11. ____ ____

__ __ __ __ __ __ __ __ __ __ __

__ __ __ __ __ __ __ __ __ __ __
1 2 3 4 5 6 7 8 9 10 11

━━ ONE GAVE GLORY TO GOD ━━
LUKE 17:15–19

And one of **them**, **when** he saw that he was **healed**, turned **back**, and with a **loud voice glorified** God, and **fell down** on his **face** at his **feet**, **giving** him **thanks**: and he was a **Samaritan**. And **Jesus answering** said, **Were** there not ten **cleansed**? but **where** are the **nine**? **There** are not **found** that **returned** to **give glory** to God, **save this stranger**. And he said unto him, **Arise**, go thy way: thy **faith hath made thee whole**.

```
H  Y  Y  Q  A  E  O  S  D  Q  N  H  D  X  A
C  A  D  I  R  N  E  J  E  S  U  S  E  R  L
X  W  T  E  E  F  S  F  L  W  T  A  I  P  E
T  T  H  H  S  Z  A  W  A  H  V  S  F  O  D
J  T  I  O  N  N  M  D  E  I  E  C  I  O  V
A  D  S  D  L  X  A  E  H  R  T  D  R  W  B
U  V  U  M  K  E  R  E  R  D  I  H  O  H  R
Q  O  A  O  G  C  I  E  L  H  D  N  L  E  D
Y  D  N  T  L  V  T  F  B  C  D  E  G  N  U
E  H  I  X  O  U  A  G  I  V  I  N  G  Q  L
M  V  W  E  R  E  N  D  K  E  A  I  U  K  L
X  V  A  N  Y  H  S  C  T  R  B  N  G  O  E
F  F  E  S  K  N  A  H  T  E  C  A  F  V  F
U  D  O  R  T  B  E  S  X  H  V  Z  I  Z  Y
O  G  B  B  N  M  C  D  O  W  N  G  R  H  G
```

CROSSWORD
by David K. Shortess

DONKEY BUSINESS

Donkeys appear in various roles in both the New and Old Testaments. Can you work this puzzle and solve the clues relating to these stubborn beasts of burden?

"You are now with child and you will have a son.
You shall name him Ishmael. . . . He will be a wild donkey of a man."
GENESIS 16:11–12 NIV

ACROSS

1 "Without an inhabitant, _____ this day" (Jeremiah 44:22) (2 words)
5 "As it _____ we had not delayed" (Genesis 43:10 NIV) (2 words)
9 "He shall gather the _____ with his arm" (Isaiah 40:11)
14 "The Jews of _____ sought to stone thee" (John 11:8)
15 "How _____ dispossess them?" (Deuteronomy 7:17) (2 words)
16 "There shall be _____ of Jesse" (Romans 15:12) (2 words)
17 WHAT SAMSON USED TO KILL A THOUSAND MEN (Judges 15:16 NIV) (3 words)
20 Presbyterian parsonage
21 "They _____ not, they spin not" (Luke 12:27)
22 "Sing unto him _____ song" (Psalm 33:3) (2 words)
23 Followes *printemp* (Fr.)
24 Caesar's "I"
26 "He planteth an _____" (Isaiah 44:14)
28 _____-cone
29 "I cannot find one _____ man among you" (Job 17:10)
31 "Why make ye this _____, and weep?" (Mark 5:39)
34 Formerly Siamese
37 "But as my beloved sons I _____ you" (1 Corinthians 4:14)
39 "The law is not _____ on faith" (Galatians 3:12 NIV)
41 WHAT HAPPENED WHEN BALAAM SAW THE ANGEL? (Numbers 22:27–28) (3 words)
44 "Watch ye and pray, lest ye _____ into temptation" (Mark 14:38)
45 "There was one Anna. . .of the tribe of _____" (Luke 2:36)
46 "Because I am a man of unclean _____" (Isaiah 6:5)
47 European theater of operations (abbr.)
48 "He _____ save himself!" (Mark 15:31 NIV)
50 "Give _____ king" (1 Samuel 8:6) (2 words)
52 "Under your arms to _____ the ropes" (Jeremiah 38:12 NIV)
53 Metro maker
54 "Thou sayest that I _____ king" (John 18:37) (2 words)
57 "Do not give _____ cry" (Joshua 6:10 NIV) (2 words)
60 "By this time there is a bad _____" (John 11:39 NIV)
63 Where Moses saw the burning bush (Exodus 3:1–2)
65 JESUS ENTERED JERUSALEM THIS WAY (Matthew 21:4–5 NIV) (4 words)
68 "Beast had _____ as a man" (Revelation 4:7) (2 words)
69 Hoodwink
70 Giant Mel's family
71 "When _____ with us" (Acts 20:14) (2 words)
72 "Their throat is an _____ sepulchre" (Romans 3:13)
73 Flag-maker Betsy

DOWN

1 "A blind man, or _____" (Leviticus 21:18) (2 words)
2 "He was _____ that saying" (Mark 10:22) (2 words)
3 "Slain by him _____ time" (1 Chronicles 11:11) (2 words)
4 "Captains over _____" (Deuteronomy 1:15)
5 "He casteth forth his _____ like morsels" (Psalm 147:17)
6 "Thus shall ye _____ David" (1 Samuel 18:25) (2 words)
7 "Give him drink: for _____ doing" (Romans 12:20) (2 words)

214

8 South Pacific country of 320 islands

9 "The _____ of the LORD is perfect" (Psalm 19:7)

10 Another name for *Hebron* (Genesis 35:27)

11 "Nor the _____ by night" (Psalm 121:6)

12 "A _____ of him shall not be broken" (John 19:36)

13 "Some bread and some lentil _____" (Genesis 25:34 NIV)

18 "This man Daniel. . .was found to have a _____ mind" (Daniel 5:12 NIV)

19 "_____ for the day!" (Joel 1:15)

25 "Her _____ is interwoven with gold" (Psalm 45:13 NIV)

27 First son of Cush (Genesis 10:7)

28 "A thousand shall fall at thy _____" (Psalm 91:7)

29 "Every day they _____ my words" (Psalm 56:5)

30 "Them that were entering _____ hindered" (Luke 11:52) (2 words)

31 "Whatever you _____ will give you" (Mark 6:23 NIV) (2 words)

32 "I sink in _____ mire" (Psalm 69:2)

33 Chances

34 "Make _____ an ark of gopher wood" (Genesis 6:14)

35 "Not be even a _____ of sexual immorality" (Ephesians 5:3 NIV)

36 "I speak _____ wise men" (1 Corinthians 10:15) (2 words)

38 A son of Ezer (Genesis 36:27)

40 "_____ man's ways seem right to him" (Proverbs 21:2 NIV) (2 words)

42 Free Willy, for example

43 "That was the _____ Light" (John 1:9)

49 "As _____ lappeth" (Judges 7:5) (2 words)

51 Fashionable London district

52 "Her _____ is far above rubies" (Proverbs 31:10)

53 "The vines with the tender _____" (Song of Solomon 2:13)

54 "Prepared an _____ the saving of his house" (Hebrews 11:7) (2 words)

55 "The church that _____ at their house" (1 Corinthians 16:19 NIV)

56 "Darkened by the smoke from the _____" (Revelation 9:2 NIV)

57 First son of Ulla (1 Chronicles 7:39)

58 "But his _____ looked back" (Genesis 19:26)

59 "As in _____ all die" (1 Corinthians 15:22)

61 "And whatsoever ye _____ it heartily" (Colossians 3:23) (2 words)

62 "He went _____ the mountain" (Exodus 24:18 NIV) (2 words)

64 _____ about (approximately) (2 words)

66 "He hath spread a _____ for my feet" (Lamentations 1:13)

67 "Ye have made it a _____ of thieves" (Luke 19:46)

SCRAMBLED CIRCLE
by Suzanne Stepp

━━━ SURPRISE VISIT ━━━

No matter where we go, God is always hot on our trail.

1. SUBTESEJI

2. MEDUNOSC

3. TREDES

4. ORGNUD

5. ESPTIR

6. NALD

7. NIHG

8. CAJBO

9. NURTDE

10. DESIA

11. LOEBDH

An angel of the Lord appeared here.

1. __ __ ◯ __ __ __ __ __ __

2. __ __ __ __ ◯ __ __ __

3. __ __ __ __ ◯ __

4. __ __ __ __ ◯ __

5. __ __ ◯ __ __ __

6. __ __ ◯ __

7. __ __ ◯ __

8. __ __ __ __ ◯

9. __ ◯ __ __ __ __

10. __ ◯ __ __ __

11. __ __ ◯ __ __ __

Answer: __ __ __ __ __ __ __   __ __ __ __

▬ MIRACLES CONCERNING ELIJAH ▬

Elijah definitely had a way with miracles. Decipher the telephone codes to uncover words and names that concern this prophet and his mysterious methods.

PRS 7	ABC 2	TUV 8	DEF 3	MNO 6	PRS 7

WXY 9	GHI 4	GHI 4	PRS 7	JKL 5	WXY 9	GHI 4	MNO 6	DEF 3

ABC 2	JKL 5	MNO 6	ABC 2	JKL 5

PRS 7	ABC 2	GHI 4	MNO 6

DEF 3	DEF 3	ABC 2	DEF 3

ABC 2	GHI 4	ABC 2	PRS 7	GHI 4	MNO 6	TUV 8

ABC 2	ABC 2	ABC 2	JKL 5

— MADE IN THE SHADE —

On Solomon's Porch, miracles abounded. Solve the puzzle to find out how those stricken with disease had it made in the shade.

Peter was a _____ of Jesus

—— —— —— —— —— —— —— ——
4   28   38   14   20   31   10   24

The disciples had this gift

—— —— —— —— —— —— ——
29   11   32   18   1   25   15

The author of Acts who was also a physician
(Colossians 4:14)

—— —— —— ——
19   36   5   30

Those healed _____ their diseases

—— —— —— —— —— —— —— ——
7   22   37   12   33   40   2   26

Term used to denote the twelve called by Jesus
(Acts 5:12)

—— —— —— —— —— —— —— ——
9   13   27   41   6   21   35   16

To unbelievers, miracles oftentimes seem _____ belief

—— —— —— —— —— ——
23   3   17   39   34   8

ACROSTIC
by Donna Maltese
(continued)

6-29-30-17   23-12-28-36-15-29-6   4-20-12-6-29   6-29-30

16-1-33-5   1-25-6-7   6-29-30   41-6-24-10-10-6-41,

9-34-8   38-32-1-8   6-29-30-2   7-25   23-11-8-16

9-34-8   33-7-36-33-29-37-16,   6-29-9-6   9-6   6-29-30

19-26-9-41-6   6-29-30   41-29-40-8-39-31   27-4

13-3-6-3-12   13-32-16-16-1-25-15   23-17   2-1-15-29-6

39-22-35-12-41-29-40-8-39-31   41-7-2-35.

ACTS 5:15

SUDOKU
by Sara Stoker

■ BATTLE OF THE GODS ■

MEDIUM

	A	B	C	D	E	F	G	H	I
1	L	H	A		M				
2				L	O	T	B	A	
3	B				P				S
4			O						M
5	M	P			H		A	O	
6	T								B
7		B		A			M		
8			H	M	T	O	S		
9	A				S			L	

Hint: Row 3

"And when they arose early on the morrow morning, behold, Dagon was fallen upon his face to the ground before the ark of the LORD; and the head of Dagon and _____ the _____ of his hands were cut off" (1 Samuel 5:4).

HIS GOD PROTECTED HIM

DANIEL 6:21–22

God can deliver us, even when we are faced with the fiercest of opposition.
Solve this puzzle to discover how God saved a man whose fate seemed
sealed.


```
N   E   U   T   O   K   D   R   A   L   M   I
M   Y   N   M   N   D   I   E   V   T   V   G
E   U   A   T   O   H   Y   H   G   A   T   L
N   E   O   F   D   T   H   E   N   T   T   I
V   H   N   A   O   E   T   H   T   E   R   E
S   T   N   G   R   R   I   A   S   I   L   O
A   N   T   T   H   U   N   N   H   A   E   H
S   L       I   D   T   H   H   A   K   E
    S       O       U   T   H   E   N
    G       T                   N
    S       T                   H
                                I
```

CROSSWORD
by Sarah Lagerquist Simmons

━━ SIGNS AND WONDERS ━━

Aren't you amazed at God's miraculous signs and wonders? They are a testimony to His heavenly work upon this earth. As you solve this puzzle, let your amazement be turned into praise for the workings of His mighty hand around and among us!

How great are his signs! and how mighty are his wonders!
DANIEL 4:3

ACROSS

1 GOD USED AN EARTHQUAKE TO GET PAUL AND SILAS OUT OF HERE (Acts 16:26)
5 Mimicked
9 "The magistrates. . .commanded to ____ them" (Acts 16:22)
13 "Fast. . .to ____ the heavy burdens" (Isaiah 58:6)
14 Platform where temple services are conducted
15 Inertia
16 Manner
17 GOD'S LIGHT BLINDED THIS PERSECUTOR ON THE ROAD TO DAMASCUS (Acts 9:3–9)
18 "The ____, because he cheweth the cud . . .is unclean" (Leviticus 11:5)
19 PHARAOH RECEIVED THESE WHEN HE TRIED TO TAKE ANOTHER MAN'S WIFE (Genesis 12:17)
21 "Their calls will ____ through the windows" (Zephaniah 2:14 NIV)
23 IT TOOK SOME GUTS TO GET THIS ANSWER TO GOD'S COMMAND (Jonah 3:3)
24 "____ them about thy neck" (Proverbs 6:21)
25 DEAD END THAT BECAME A SIGN OF GOD'S DELIVERANCE (Exodus 14) (2 words)
29 California (abbr.)
30 THE RAINBOW IS A SIGN ____ GOD THAT HE WILL NOT DESTROY THE EARTH WITH A FLOOD AGAIN (Genesis 9:14–15)
32 Extra phone line (abbr.)
33 Chart
36 "Like men condemned to die in the ____" (1 Corinthians 4:9 NIV)
37 Fuel
38 "Of the oaks of Bashan have they made thine ____" (Ezekiel 27:6)
39 To marry secretly
40 BEAUTIFUL WAS THE GATE WHERE THIS LEAPING MAN USED TO BE ____ (Acts 3:1–8)
41 Computer company (abbr.)
42 Fogs
43 Type of wood
44 Compass reading one point east of due north
45 "At ease from his youth. . .he hath settled on his ____" (Jeremiah 48:11)
46 Choke
47 WET ONE DAY, DRY THE NEXT, IT HELPED THIS MAN DO WHAT GOD SAID (Judges 6:37–40)
49 ____ Lanka
50 Compass point (abbr.)
53 Clothes, slang
55 "The ____ showed us unusual kindness; for they. . .made us all welcome" (Acts 28:2 NLV)
57 Caper
60 Idol
62 "The men. . .took two milch kine, and tied them to the ____" (1 Samuel 6:10)
63 DEFEATED BY RESURRECTION (Luke 24)
64 "I WILL CAUSE THE SUN TO GO DOWN AT ____, AND I WILL DARKEN THE EARTH IN THE CLEAR DAY" (Amos 8:9)
65 MOSES' HANDS HELD HIGH GAVE THE ISRAELITES THE ____ OVER THE AMALEKITES (Exodus 17:8–16)
66 Possesses
67 "Moses. . .sent me from Kadesh-barnea to ____ out the land" (Joshua 14:7)
68 Elk

DOWN

1 Skittish
2 Senile
3 "You are bringing some strange ____ to our ears" (Acts 17:20 NIV)

4 "WHEN THE CLOUD TARRIED ____ UPON THE TABERNACLE. . .THE CHILDREN OF THE LORD. . . JOURNEYED NOT" (Exodus 9:19)

5 Rappel

6 Legumes (arch.)

7 Large, flightless bird

8 "The valley of Shaveh. . .is the king's ____" (Genesis 14:17)

9 THIS HAD TO BE ON THE DOORPOST, OR THE FIRSTBORN WAS LOST (Exodus 12:7)

10 Billion years

11 THE ISRAELITES ____ MANNA FROM HEAVEN (Exodus 16:15–21)

12 "I am ____ shield" (Genesis 15:1)

15 Outline

20 US state

22 Hag

26 American sculptor

27 Tests

28 THE DISCIPLES WERE HERE WHEN THEY THOUGHT THEY SAW A GHOST (Matthew 14:22–26) (2 words)

29 Unit of frequency (abbr.)

30 PART OF THE SIGNS PLAGUING EGYPT (Exodus 8:3)

31 These fill the House (abbr.)

33 "The sun was ____ down" (Genesis 15:12)

34 "They said unto him, ____, (which is to say. . .Master)" (John 1:38)

35 "Ye will go ____ before the LORD to war" (Numbers 32:20)

36 Plant used in the mixture Nicodemus brought (John 19:39)

39 Improve

40 "Never ____ in zeal and in earnest endeavor" (Romans 12:11 AMP)

42 Slump

43 "Does a bird ever get caught in a trap that has no ___?" (Amos 3:5 NLT)

46 Mother's mother

48 Alterations

49 "He's sent these men to ____ around the city and size it up" (1 Chronicles 19:2 MSG)

50 "He didn't ____ the question. He told the plain truth" (John 1:19 MSG)

51 Fabric

52 Organic compound formed between acid and alcohol

54 Trigonometric function

56 Glazed

57 "Why make ye this ____, and weep?" (Mark 5:39)

58 "Bring forth the old because of the ____" (Leviticus 26:10)

59 Thrash

61 Another trigonometric function (abbr.)

223

WORD SEARCH
by David Austin

MIRACLES ABOUND

AARON
ABEDNEGO
AENEAS
BALAAM
BARNABAS
DAGON
DANIEL
DISCIPLES
ELIJAH
ELISABETH
ELISHA
EUTYCHUS
GIDEON
HANNAH

JAIRUS
JESUS
JONAH
LAZARUS
MALCHUS
MESHACH
MOSES
NAAMAN
PAUL
PETER
PRIESTS
SHADRACH
TABITHA
ZAREPHATH

```
H  X  A  P  I  S  T  J  Q  J  P  A  N  C  H
B  P  R  I  E  S  T  S  C  X  H  N  N  Z  Z
W  H  A  S  S  U  R  A  Z  A  L  L  W  U  J
W  O  O  U  Y  D  T  W  B  L  B  L  Z  N  O
W  M  G  L  L  X  J  Y  G  I  D  E  O  N  N
L  L  E  I  N  A  D  A  C  Z  T  G  R  S  A
G  E  N  L  U  N  S  E  A  H  A  H  U  H  H
R  S  D  H  I  U  A  R  L  D  U  H  A  A  C
K  U  E  Y  R  S  E  L  P  I  C  S  I  D  A
N  S  B  I  A  P  A  H  L  L  J  B  T  R  H
A  E  A  E  H  H  F  B  A  R  N  A  B  A  S
A  J  N  A  S  C  D  M  E  N  R  L  H  C  E
M  E  T  I  R  E  T  E  P  T  N  A  U  H  M
A  H  L  R  S  O  E  F  B  N  H  A  W  U  K
N  E  E  A  I  A  N  I  Q  A  U  M  H  A  H
```

━━━━ **UNDENIABLE MIRACLES** ━━━━

Those who witness irrefutable miracles are often awed by God's power. Solve these cryptoscripture puzzles to uncover two works of wonder that demonstrate the Lord's grace upon those He commissions.

XTP VZUT FXJW ZXP YXQZUEUP X LJTPWU RB

DQKGMD, XTP WXKP QZUO RT QZU BKEU, QZUEU

GXOU X CKFUE RJQ RB QZU ZUXQ, XTP BXDQUTUP

RT ZKD ZXTP.... XTP ZU DZRRM RBB QZU LUXDQ

KTQR QZU BKEU, XTP BUWQ TR ZXEO.

RWM AQHW RRCUW RWM RVV NQH

FQKVMCHW UT KXCRHV XRA IUXHX, YHQUVM,

NQH XDKW UT QKX TRFH XQUWH; RWM NQHP

AHCH RTCRKM NU FUIH WKBQ QKI.

SPOTTY HEADLINE
by Sara Stoker

━━━ MIRACULOUS LEPROSY ━━━

Sometimes, the miracle was in losing one's leprosy. Other times, it was in *getting* the dreaded disease. Can you solve these spotty headlines to figure out who did which?

LEPROUS SYRI●N ●RMY COM●●NDER CLEA●SED IN JORDA●

— — — — — —

MUR●UR●NG P●OPHETESS CO●ES DOWN W●TH TEMPOR●RY LEPROSY

— — — — — —

OVER●EALO●S KING F●NDS LEPROSY HA●ARD IN ●ANDLING PRIESTLY T●SK

— — — — — —

ACROSTIC
by Donna Maltese

■■■■■ JONAH'S ROTTEN GOURD ■■■■■

God sometimes uses the little things to teach us life lessons. Decode this puzzle to find out what was "bugging" Jonah and ended up souring his mood even more.

To have died

3	20	14	2	25	30	10

Jonah's calling

17	29	9	21	6	27	13

God sent Jonah on this

12	34	26	7	18	31	28

Nineveh escaped God's _____ (Jonah 3:9–10)

11	33	23	5	19

God's relenting to destroy Nineveh made
Jonah _____ (Jonah 4:1)

8	22	15	4	32

Jonah sat baking in the hot _____ (Jonah 4:8)

24	1	16

15-31-10   14-4-3-21-8-4-3-10   8   11-9-29-12

11-6-3-28   5-6-3   12-9-33-16-34-16-15   25-9-7-30

5-6-3   22-27-20-5   10-23-32,   8-22-10   2-5

24-12-9-13-3   5-6-3   15-9-1-4-10   5-6-8-5   2-5

11-18-13-6-30-4-30-10.

JONAH 4:7

CROSSWORD
by Sarah Lagerquist Simmons

━━ FEEDING THE HUNGRY ━━

When we long for His presence, God satisfies our soul, feeding us with His Word and His Spirit. Solve this puzzle and uncover God's hidden manna.

To him that overcometh will I give to eat of the hidden manna.
REVELATION 2:17

ACROSS
1   Shorten (abbr.)
4   Phloem
8   WHEN THE WIDOW WOMAN FED THIS PROPHET, HER MEAL AND OIL DID NOT RUN OUT (1 Kings 17)
14 Prior to (prefix)
15 "Thy husband. . .shall ____ over thee" (Genesis 3:16)
16 Scented ointment
17 "Thy oblation be a meat offering baken in a ____" (Leviticus 2:5)
18 "The LORD. . .brought you forth out of the ____ furnace" (Deuteronomy 4:20)
19 To fill with love
20 Rhododendrons
22 Graphical record of brain's electrical activity (abbr.)
23 Luxurious car, for short
24 "Her blossoms ____ forth" (Genesis 40:10)
27 "The ____ of Jehoshaphat was quiet" (2 Chronicles 20:30)
31 "I will ____ on softly" (Genesis 33:14)
33 Nigerian city
35 "He sailed to the ____ of Crete" (Acts 27:7 NIV)
36 By way of
38 "He shall take. . .one ____ of oil" (Leviticus 14:10)
39 Roman garment
40 "Ye shall ____ the feast of unleavened bread" (Exodus 12:17)
44 "EVEN THE ____ PERSON AMONG THEM GATHERED AT LEAST SIXTY BUSHELS [OF QUAIL]" (Numbers 11:32 MSG)
46 "A heart at peace gives life to the body, but envy ____ the bones" (Proverbs 14:30 NIV)
47 Period of time
49 "How long will it be ____ they believe me. . .?" (Numbers 14:11)

50 A ____ GAVE HIS LUNCH TO JESUS, AND IT FED 5,000 MEN (John 6:9–13)
51 "They humiliate Israel's king, slapping him around like a ____ doll" (Micah 5:1 MSG)
52 Flair
55 "Ye shall not ____, neither deal falsely" (Leviticus 19:11)
58 "[Hagar] said, 'I can't watch my son die.' As she sat, she broke into ____" (Genesis 21:14 MSG)
61 "Behold, the ____ of the temple was torn in two" (Matthew 27:51 NKJV)
63 "My accusers are a clothes ____ of threadbare socks and shirts" (Isaiah 50:9 MSG)
65 Arbiter
67 Motor
70 Small
71 Amount insurer will actually pay insured after a loss (abbr.)
72 Dwelling places
73 "Sinful self-interest in us. . .is at ____ with a free spirit" (Galatians 5:16 MSG)
74 Short peg used in golf
75 GOD USED THESE BIRDS TO FEED ELIJAH'S HUNGER (1 Kings 17:4)
76 "His feet thrust him into a net and he wanders into its ____" (Job 18:8 NIV)
77 Compass point (abbr.)

DOWN
1   To horrify or shock (var.)
2   South American country
3   "____ them 'Oaks of Righteousness' planted by GOD to display his glory" (Isaiah 61:1 MSG)
4   Soft cheese
5   Atmospheres
6   To flounder in water
7   "Joseph's ____ brethren went down to buy corn in Egypt" (Genesis 42:3)
8   Rapier with three-sided blade
9   Recluse

10 "In the _____ of God made he man" (Genesis 9:6)
11 Force in
12 Bustle
13 "IT TURNED OUT AS [ELIJAH] SAID— DAILY FOOD FOR. . ._____ FAMILY" (1 Kings 17:15 MSG)
21 JESUS BROKE THESE INTO ENOUGH PIECES TO FEED 5,000 MEN (Mark 6:44)
25 THIS WIDOW WOMAN SOUGHT HELP FROM ELISHA, AND GOD GAVE HER MORE _____ THAN SHE HAD VESSELS TO HOLD IT (2 Kings 4:3–6)
26 How the animals when into Noah's ark: by _____
28 A healing plant included in Nicodemus's spice mixture (John 19:39)
29 "His _____ are as pillars of marble" (Song of Solomon 5:15)
30 THE ISRAELITES CRIED OUT FOR _____, AND GOD RAINED DOWN QUAIL (Numbers 11:13–31)
32 Supervisor (abbr.)
34 Stare
37 Allege as fact
39 NUMBER OF BASKETS FILLED WITH LEFTOVER FOOD (John 6:13)
40 Spheres

41 "Every warrior's _____ used in battle and every garment rolled in blood will be destined for burning" (Isaiah 9:5 NIV)
42 Inflammation of eyelid
43 Divisions of geologic time
45 "Iron is taken from the earth, and copper is smelted from _____" (Job 28:2 NKJV)
48 "I knew a man in Christ above fourteen years _____" (2 Corinthians 12:2)
53 Expose to oxygen
54 Brother's daughters
56 "Return to thy place, and _____ with the king" (2 Samuel 15:19)
57 "Make. . .ten curtains of fine twined _____" (Exodus 26:1)
59 "He that hath the _____ is the bridegroom" (John 3:29)
60 "He. . ._____ rain on the righteous and the unrighteous" (Matthew 5:45 NIV)
62 Seawall
64 Cape
66 PART OF WHAT FED THE HUNGRY (Mark 6:41)
67 "Bow down thine _____, and hear" (2 Kings 19:16)
68 Sports association (abbr.)
69 Ruling body (abbr.)
70 Female parent

━━━━━━ **FULL OF FAITH** ━━━━━━
ACTS 6:8–10

And **Stephen**, **full** of **faith** and **power**, did **great wonders** and **miracles among** the **people**. **Then there arose certain** of the synagogue, which is **called** the **synagogue** of the **Libertines**, and **Cyrenians**, and **Alexandrians**, and of **them** of **Cilicia** and of **Asia**, **disputing** with Stephen. And **they were** not **able** to **resist** the **wisdom** and the **spirit** by **which** he **spake**.

```
Y L W V G N R N I A T R E C J
O M R T Y R N C I L I C I A E
B R H L E R E W I E L P O E P
G E E T I C H A T X X Z H M G
N S U W O B P Z T A G Z M E T
E I A G O M E F M N H C I H W
N S R U O P T R O D Y G R T X
T T O D T G S M T R N P A R I
B H S H H P A V E I W W C F O
Y I E C I T N N T A N D L O Y
W Y A R Y C I U Y N E E E A C
I A I Q E A P A B S N L S B G
M T S U N S Z S F U L L I L C
H W A S I A I C N S P A K E Y
W O N D E R S T N N Q C E E E
```

ACROSTIC
by Donna Maltese

═══ HEAVENLY SWEETENER ═══

Christ's cross is the tree that sweetens the bitter waters of our lives, a fact proven by this Old Testament miracle. Solve this puzzle to discover why.

The Jews wandered here

___ ___ ___ ___ ___ ___ ___ ___ ___ ___
12 31 4   21 14 26 7   19 10 2

This place had bitter waters (Exodus 15:23)

___ ___ ___ ___ ___
20 27 5   15 11

Leader of the Exodus

___ ___ ___ ___ ___
30 8   22 32 16

To be parched

___ ___ ___ ___ ___ ___
13 34 17 23 36 28

Moses led Israel through this desert (Exodus 15:22)

___ ___ ___ ___
29 33 6   24

A slender rod or twig

___ ___ ___ ___ ___ ___
1   35 3   18 25 9

ACROSTIC
by Donna Maltese
(continued)

9-14   25-26-3-19-21   6-7-28-8   18-9-14   4-8-5-21;

15-7-21   18-9-14   4-8-5-21   2-11-19-12-19-21

34-17-20   15   13-23-14-14,   12-33-31-25-33   35-9-14-7

9-14   34-27-21   25-27-10-18   3-7-28-8   18-9-14

35-27-13-32-24-1,   18-9-14   35-27-13-32-24-16

35-14-5-14   30-15-21-32   22-12-14-14-28.

EXODUS 15:25

235

ANAGRAM
by Paul Kent

━━ AFTER THE RESURRECTION ━━

Jesus' resurrection is the greatest miracle of all—with the largest implications to our lives today. The three anagrams below relate to the time immediately after Jesus returned to life. None of these exact terms is found in the King James Version, but you'll definitely recognize each one.

Boat might sound

_ _ _ _ _ _ _ _   _ _ _ _ _ _

To a sumo armed

_ _ _ _   _ _   _ _ _ _ _ _

Oh saint scene

_ _ _   _ _ _ _ _ _ _ _ _

SUDDENLY FREE!

ACTS 12:7

When we devote ourselves to prayer, God releases us from bondage. Solve this puzzle to discover the divine miracle wrought for a praying Peter.

S	D	Q	H	L	C	O	F	A	I	M	R
E	F	N	L	I	A	K	H	L	H	C	S
O	M	E	I	S	M	R	R	D	I	O	N
D	D	H	U	I	S	O	E	F	N	T	S
Y	I	E	G	A	N	D	N	A	E	N	A
P	E	R	H	I	M	L	I	S	A	P	F
M	H	P	N	E	L	O	T	Y	A	F	S
A	T	I	R	I	O	N	I	P		D	E
T	E	D	E	S	N	G	U	H		N	H
I	H	E	U	P	D	O	L	E		A	D
E	N	H		A	S		T	N		S	U
	H	E		O			I	H		I	A
				A			H	G		T	S
								R			

CROSSWORD

by Sarah Lagerquist Simmons

━━━━━━ MUD AND WATER ━━━━━━

Praise the Lord who heals us, in ways we could never think or imagine!
As you solve this puzzle, may your eyes be opened to God's miraculous
handiwork within the Bible, within the world, and within your own life.

*The Pharisees also asked him how he had received his sight. He said
unto them, He put clay upon mine eyes, and I washed, and do see.*
JOHN 9:15

ACROSS

1 Assemble
6 Fabulous
10 "If I make my ____ in hell, behold, thou art there" (Psalm 139:8)
13 Head (Latin)
15 MAN WAS FORMED FROM THIS (Genesis 2:7)
16 Adam's rib (Genesis 2:22)
17 "The cherubims ____ out their wings on high" (Exodus 37:9)
18 Type of pasta
19 NAAMAN DID ____ HIMSELF IN THE JORDAN SEVEN TIMES (2 Kings 5:14)
20 An unformed shape
22 AFTER NAAMAN'S HEALING, HE REFERRED TO HIMSELF AS ELISHA'S ____ (2 Kings 5:15)
24 "What is my ____ that it's all right to enter again the Sanctuary of GOD?" (Isaiah 38:21 MSG)
26 "He that findeth his life shall ____ it" (Matthew 10:39)
28 Exclamation
29 "____, my lord, I beseech thee" (Numbers 12:11)
30 BEVERAGE LACKING AT A BIBLICAL WEDDING (John 2:3)
31 Jeers
32 California city (abbr.)
33 "I'm not crazy. I'm. . .____" (Acts 26:25 MSG)
34 "At the ____ of forty days. . .Noah opened the window of the ark" (Genesis 8:6)
35 "Salt has lost its strength and has become saltless (____, flat)" (Luke 14:34 AMP)
37 Act of escape

41 Dot in Morse code
42 "Adam ____ Eve" (Genesis 4:1)
43 Computer system component (abbr.)
44 To set in place
47 Driving force
48 To solicit
49 God breathed life ____ Adam's nostrils (Genesis 2:7)
50 Reject
51 Protuberance of the human body
52 Eyelet
54 "One of the people might lightly have ____ with thy wife" (Genesis 26:10)
56 "Father of ____ Lord Jesus Christ" (Romans 15:6)
57 "Many. . .which used curious ____ brought their books together" (Acts 19:19)
59 "Jeroboam did not ____ power" (2 Chronicles 13:20 NIV)
63 "We ____ great plainness of speech" (2 Corinthians 3:12)
64 "You know nothing and have no ____" (John 4:32 AMP)
65 Exterior finish
66 "I heard ____ voice" (Genesis 3:10)
67 JESUS USED THIS TO GIVE SIGHT (John 9:6)
68 NO LESS, NO MORE DIPS WOULD HEAL LEPROSY (2 Kings 5:10)

DOWN

1 Society that organizes the Great American Smokeout (abbr.)
2 "The men started. . .to ____ out the land" (Joshua 18:8 NIV)
3 Spring month (abbr.)
4 Blockades
5 Stable (Dutch)

6 Axlike tool

7 Armor

8 _____ Lauder

9 "None is so fierce that dare _____ him up" (Job 41:10)

10 Besmear

11 Make evident

12 "The floods stood upright. . .and the _____ were congealed" (Exodus 15:8)

14 Shakespeare's Much _____ About Nothing

21 MUD RESTORED THE _____ MAN'S EYES (John 9:7)

23 Empty spaces

24 Gideon, from the poorest _____ in Manasseh, received his "dew" (Judges 6:15)

25 Major US airline (abbr.)

27 The waters under heaven were "gathered together unto _____ place" (Genesis 1:9)

29 Boxer Muhamad

30 "_____ on the LORD: be of good courage" (Psalm 27:14)

31 "Her judges are evening wolves; they _____ not the bones till the morrow" (Zephaniah 3:3)

33 FLUID JESUS USED TO HEAL THE BLIND MAN (John 9:6)

34 "The LORD shall reign for ever and _____" (Exodus 15:18)

36 Expression

37 To sign up (var.)

38 Figure

39 Musical composition

40 "God's kingdom is like a pine _____ that a farmer plants" (Matthew 13:31 MSG)

42 Partner of kaboodle

44 Overeat (2 words)

45 Forceful flow

46 One of the floors in a building (var.)

47 "It had been _____ for us to serve the Egyptians" (Exodus 14:12)

48 JESUS PUT SPIT ON THE _____ OF THE MAN WITH A SPEECH IMPEDIMENT (Mark 7:33)

50 Italian operatic composer

51 "Hand over any man before the accused _____ his accusers face to face" (Acts 25:16 NASB)

53 GIRL WHO TOLD NAAMAN ABOUT ELISHA WAS A _____ (2 Kings 5:2)

55 Federal tax agency (abbr.)

58 "The people _____ down to eat and to drink" (Exodus 32:6)

60 Amount an insurer will pay an insured after a loss (abbr.)

61 "Out of whose womb came the _____? and the hoary frost of heaven?" (Job 38:29)

62 No (Fr.)

WORD SEARCH
by Connie Troyer

ELIJAH AND BAAL
1 KINGS 18:17–46

AHAB
ALTAR
ANSWER
AWAKED
BLOOD
BULLOCKS
BURNT
CONSUMED
CRY ALOUD
FELL ON THEIR FACES
FIRE
FOUR BARRELS
ISRAEL
KISHON
KNIVES
MOCKED

MORNING
NAME OF THE LORD
NOON
PIECES
POUR
PROPHESIED
PROPHETS
REPAIRED
SACRIFICE
SLEEPETH
SLEW
TRENCH
TWELVE STONES
WATER
WOOD

```
D B U L L O C K S H O R P D M N
O S E V I N K E H C N E R T O N
O P E S O S I R C E R O K O C H
W R D R E W S N A I L N N E K T
F O U G Y N H M F E F T P I E E
O P O N P R O P H E S I E D D P
U H L I I L N T G D L A R O U E
R E A N E L F B S D E E H C C E
B T Y R C O R T E E P K I N A L
A S R O E C N M O A V S A G L S
R H C M S R U H I T R L G W T P
R O A O U S S R O A U R E J A O
E N V B N K E T E R E T A W R U
L B L O O D E L O O S L E W T R
S E C A F R I E H T N O L L E F
```

DROP TWO
by Dorothy Pryse

AN EVIL SPIRIT
MARK 5:2

Jesus saves the living from among the dead. Can you solve this drop two puzzle to see whom Christ encountered—and later rescued—in the middle of a graveyard?

MARCHED	Listened	_____	1. ___ ___
LOLLARD	Whimsical	_____	2. ___ ___
ENDEMIC	Physician	_____	3. ___ ___
WEATHER	Not here	_____	4. ___ ___
INVADER	Spoke wildly	_____	5. ___ ___
TRANSIT	Teach	_____	6. ___ ___
PERCHED	Religious belief	_____	7. ___ ___
ACINOSE	Pastry	_____	8. ___ ___
REDSKIN	Glided on snow	_____	9. ___ ___
INTRUDE	Style	_____	10. ___ ___
NATURAL	Related to ear	_____	11. ___ ___

___ ___ ___ ___ ___ ___ ___ ___ ___ ___ ___

1 2 3 4 5 6 7 8 9 10 11

━━━ MIRACLES IN JESUS' NAME ━━━

When Jesus' name is spoken, miracles are bound to follow. Work these
cryptoscripture puzzles to uncover men who worked wonders in His name.

YHNUUN E HDBEWTU QYKEVTU SEBS WUUH

NDHU WX BSUQ YI QEHYPUIB BD ETT BSUQ

BSEB NMUTT YH GUKOIETUQ; EHN MU VEHHDB

NUHX YB.

ZVJ AWDVD DLCM, XBKZCM UCY FBJ: XBK

JUWKW CD FB YLF OUCGU DULRR MB L

YCKLGRW CF YT FLYW, JULJ GLF RCQUJRT DSWLP

WICR BX YW.

ACROSTIC
by Donna Maltese

━━━━━ A STICKY SNAKE ━━━━━

Was Moses an ophidiophobe—a person who fears snakes? Solve this puzzle and find out!

In the beginning, Moses' _____ was weak

___ ___ ___ ___ ___
15 29   5 26 21

Title of the leader of Egypt (Exodus 6:11)

___ ___ ___ ___ ___ ___ ___
6   30 16 34 13 28   7

What Moses gained from this meeting with God

___ ___ ___ ___ ___ ___ ___
11 31 23   8   1 19 14

Fearlessness

___ ___ ___ ___ ___ ___ ___ ___
2   20 32 27 12 24 18   9

Another name for a shepherd's staff (Exodus 4:2)

___ ___ ___
22 35   4

His name means to "draw out" (Exodus 2:10)

___ ___ ___ ___ ___
10 25 17 33   3

30-14   3-29-5-27,   11-16-18-26   5-26   31-12   26-7-14

19-8-28-23-12-27.   13-12-4   21-14   11-16-18-26

5-26   31-12   26-7-14   19-8-28-23-12-27,   13-12-4

5-26   2-24-11-1-10-24   13   17-33-22-6-33-12-26;

13-12-4   10-20-9-33-9   15-32-24-4   15-22-35-10

2-24-15-25-34-24   5-26.

EXODUS 4:3

CROSSWORD
by Tonya Vilhauer

▰▰▰ THE GREAT ESCAPE ▰▰▰

Because he obeyed God, the tide was with Moses when he led the Israelites out of Egypt. Work this puzzle to find out more about how the children of God made their great escape and left Pharaoh seeing red.

By faith they passed through the Red sea as by dry land: which the Egyptians assaying to do were drowned.
HEBREWS 11:29

ACROSS
1 Christmas song
5 "Your _____ shall be without blemish" (Exodus 12:5)
9 Scorch
13 Christian association founded by Sir George Williams (abbr.)
14 "He filled the trench _____ with water" (1 Kings 18:35)
15 "Save the horses and mules _____ (1 Kings 18:5)
16 French Sudan
17 Artist Van _____
18 Lassoed
19 "SPEAK UNTO _____ KING OF EGYPT" (Exodus 6:11)
21 Prego's competition
23 Cap
24 Snake
25 Small pool of water
29 "Ye have made it a _____ of thieves" (Matthew 21:13)
30 "Then the _____ of the LORD fell" (1 Kings 18:38)
32 Suffer
33 "A great _____ knit at the four corners" (Acts 10:11)
36 Craze
37 Lyric: "I want my _____"
38 "GO IN UNTO PHARAOH, AND _____ HIM. . .LET MY PEOPLE GO" (Exodus 9:1)
39 Hewer of stones (1 Chronicles 22:2)
40 "Stop judging by _____ appearances" (John 7:24 NIV)
41 "There is _____ God" (James 2:19)
42 "A nurse of the Hebrew _____" (Exodus 2:7)
43 AARON'S BROTHER (Exodus 4:14)
44 United in one body (abbr.)

45 Fencing sword
46 THE _____ BECAME A SERPENT (Exodus 7:9)
47 "OUR _____ ALSO SHALL GO WITH US" (Exodus 10:26)
49 PHARAOH'S ARMY DROWNED IN THE RED _____ (Exodus 15:4)
50 Type of legume
53 "Fear of the LORD _____ length to life (Proverbs 10:27 NIV)
55 "Be perfect and entire, _____ nothing" (James 1:4)
57 Fabric resembling silk
60 "I will come and _____ him" (Matthew 8:7)
62 "STRETCH THINE HAND _____ THE LAND OF EGYPT" (Exodus 10:12)
63 Turn over
64 Nobleman
65 "And _____ of them believed" (Acts 17:4)
66 Fellow
67 PHARAOH'S _____ PURSUED THE ISRAELITES (Exodus 14:9)
68 Eye infection (var.)

DOWN
1 Lesser goddess
2 City in Nebraska
3 Acclaim
4 "He has left His _____ like the lion" (Jeremiah 25:38 NKJV)
5 Shallow sound
6 Hawaiian "hello"
7 Meat tenderizer (abbr.)
8 Danish physicist
9 "THE PILLAR OF THE _____ BY DAY" (Exodus 13:22)
10 "He smote them _____ and thigh" (Judges 15:8)
11 Farewell (Latin)

12 "MOSES BROUGHT ISRAEL FROM THE ____ SEA" (Exodus 15:22)
15 Disputer
20 To incite
22 "Put on an ____ , sit them at the table, and serve them" (Luke 12:35 MSG)
26 Ladies
27 Cubic decimeter (Brit.)
28 Pixies
29 Eastern state (abbr.)
30 Red signal flare
31 "From the midst of the furnace of ____" (1 Kings 8:51)
33 Unemotional
34 "My lover is to me a cluster of ____ blossoms" (Song of Solomon 1:14 NIV)
35 "Israel mine ____" (Isaiah 45:4)
36 "Immediately his ____ spread abroad" (Mark 1:28)
39 Sulked
40 Hip
42 Joined metal
43 "Howl like a jackal and ____ like an owl" (Micah 1:8 NIV)

46 Truly
48 Soil
49 "THERE CAME A GRIEVOUS ____ OF FLIES" (Exodus 8:24)
50 Revolve
51 "He delivered me from my strong ____" (Psalm 18:17)
52 "If two of you shall ____ on earth" (Matthew 18:19)
54 Former NY stadium
56 "Turn and ____ thee like a ball" (Isaiah 22:18)
57 Floor covering
58 Monkey
59 "GO NOW YE THAT ARE ____" (Exodus 10:11)
61 "The barley was in the ____" (Exodus 9:31)

TELEPHONE SCRAMBLE
by Connie Troyer

MISCELLANEOUS MIRACLES

Throughout the Bible, God has worked in mysterious ways, ofttimes using amazing methods. Solve this puzzle to uncover words and names that have to do with miscellaneous but nevertheless mystifying miracles.

| DEF 3 | TUV 8 | TUV 8 | WXY 9 | ABC 2 | GHI 4 | TUV 8 | PRS 7 |

| JKL 5 | ABC 2 | GHI 4 | PRS 7 | TUV 8 | PRS 7 |

| JKL 5 | MNO 6 | ABC 2 | TUV 8 | DEF 3 | PRS 7 |

| DEF 3 | JKL 5 | DEF 3 | DEF 3 | ABC 2 | DEF 3 |

| DEF 3 | MNO 6 | MNO 6 | ABC 2 | GHI 4 |

| DEF 3 | TUV 8 | PRS 7 | MNO 6 | ABC 2 | ABC 2 | DEF 3 |

| DEF 3 | MNO 6 | MNO 6 | JKL 5 | DEF 3 | WXY 9 |

WATER PURIFIER

MEDIUM

	A	B	C	D	E	F	G	H	I
1					S		A	R	
2			T	D					
3	A	S		L				T	O
4	I	H		S					
5			L					O	
6	R					A	T	S	H
7			R					H	
8	D		H		R			L	
9	T				D	L			I

Hint: Column E

"And he went forth unto the spring of the waters, and cast the salt in there, and said, Thus _____ the _____, I have healed these waters; there shall not be from thence any more death or barren land" (2 Kings 2:21).

WORD SEARCH
by Conover Swofford

━━━ THE BIRTH OF JESUS ━━━

ANGEL	HEROD
ANNA	JERUSALEM
BETHLEHEM	JOSEPH
CHILD	KING
CITY OF DAVID	MANGER
CLOTHES	MARY
DREAM	MULTITUDE
EAST	PROPHET
EGYPT	SHEPHERDS
EMMANUEL	SIMEON
ESPOUSED	STAR
FULFILLED	SWADDLING
GABRIEL	VIRGIN
GLORY	WISE MEN
HEAVENLY HOST	

```
T S H T S O H Y L N E V A E H
E G Y P T N I G R I V H A E H
D R M W I S E M E N H E A S T
H J D E L L I F L U F R M P R
G N I L D D A W S C E O J O S
E L S H T I B B H G H D H U I
D J H H M B V I N B H M P S M
U E E Y L H L A B M P G R E E
T R P S R D M B D L E L O D O
I U H T H A N N A F S O P B N
T S E A E N M M H J O R H E E
L A R R M G N I K J J Y E T H
U L D H H E M E H E L H T E B
M E S H C L O T H E S H H I M
E M M A N U E L E I R B A G C
```

A MAJOR SINKHOLE

Crack this code to discover how rebelling against authority was "the pits" for certain Israelites en route to the Promised Land.

What the Jews did in the wilderness

—— —— —— —— —— —— —— ——
16 30   4 23 12   9   3   7

This office was the Levites' inheritance (Joshua 18:7)

—— —— —— —— —— —— —— —— —— ——
 5 29 17 11 33 27   1 22 14 37

Moses' brother (Numbers 20:8)

—— —— —— —— ——
31 36 15   6 21

The rebels in this puzzle stood on shaky ____

—— —— —— —— —— ——
10 32 20 18   3 26

Dissatisfied with their leaders, these rebels ran

—— —— —— ——
13 25   8 34

This rebellion provoked Him (Numbers 16:30)

—— —— —— ——
24   2 28 19

27-1-11   35-13-9-27-1   20-5-12-3-12-37   1-11-29

25-8-18-27-1,   30-4-7   33-16-31-24-24-22-16-35-26

27-1-11-25   18-5,   30-4-7   27-1-11-17-28

1-14-18-33-12-33,   30-4-7   31-24-24   27-1-11   25-12-21

27-1-13-27   13-5-5-35-32-27-13-17-21-35-23   18-21-27-2

34-2-15-36-1,   30-4-7   31-24-24   27-1-11-17-28

10-6-6-19-33.

NUMBERS 16:32

SPOTTY HEADLINE
by Sara Stoker

━━━━━━━ **MIRACLE MISCELLANY** ━━━━━━━

These three miracles don't have any particular connection, other than that they were all pretty cool. Can you solve these spotty headlines by determining who was involved in each?

HAIRLE●S PROP●ET S●CS B●ARS ON L●UGHING ●ADS

— — — — —

PROP●ET TURNS B●CK ●UN'S SH●DOW FOR A●LING K●NG

— — — — —

FI●RY CHAR●OT ●ETS ●IVE PROP●ET TO HE●VEN

— — — — —

━━ WATERLOGGED ━━

With God in our lives, the sky is no limit!

1. SOECMNU

2. LEXTA

3. AEPELRUS

4. NSTERAV

5. EANRWS

6. RHIOPWS

7. RAUPETS

In the beginning, there was nothing to separate the water, until God created it. What was it? (NIV)

1. _ _ _ _ _ _ ◯

2. _ ◯ _ _ _

3. ◯ _ _ _ _ _ _ _

4. _ _ _ _ ◯ _ _

5. _ ◯ _ _ _ _

6. _ _ _ ◯ _ _ _

7. _ _ _ _ _ _ ◯

Answer: _ _ _ _ _ _ _ _

CROSSWORD
by Tonya Vilhauer

■ FIRE FROM HEAVEN ■

When it comes to dealing with the faithful (and sometimes the unfaithful), God can't help but get all fired up. Work this puzzle to find the life-*altaring* changes God wrought in the lives of His people, through a blaze of glory and power!

For the LORD thy God is a consuming fire.
DEUTERONOMY 4:24

ACROSS

1 Pocket
4 Sends
9 "THE ____ RAN ROUND ABOUT THE ALTAR" (1 Kings 18:35)
14 Mutt
15 "Many knew him, and ran ____" (Mark 6:33)
16 "Vineyards and ____ trees. . .thou plantedst not" (Deuteronomy 6:11)
17 "Copper is smelted from ____" (Job 28:2 NIV)
18 Long poem division
19 Caught with a lasso
20 "Deliver thyself. . .as a bird from the hand of the ____" (Proverbs 6:5)
22 World treaty alliance (abbr.)
24 "The truth shall make you ____" (John 8:32)
25 "There is but a ____ between me and death" (1 Samuel 20:3)
27 Bambi
31 LOT'S WIFE BECAME A PILLAR OF ____ (Genesis 19:26)
32 LOT ____ THE PLAIN OF JORDAN (Genesis 13:11)
33 Luau dish
34 "THE LORD DESTROYED ____ AND GOMORRAH" (Genesis 13:10)
36 Fable writer
38 Move
40 Protruded
42 Unfitting
43 "ELIJAH REPAIRED THE ____ OF THE LORD" (1 Kings 18:30)
44 A mental system for permanently storing information (abbr.)

45 Student of farming
47 "And now my life ____ away" (Job 30:16 NIV)
51 "Punish the men that are settled on their ____" (Zephaniah 1:12)
53 "A ____ sleep fell upon Abram" (Genesis 15:12)
54 "Thy word is ____" (Psalm 119:160)
55 Dock
57 Wacky
59 HE FORMED THE MOLTEN CALF OUT OF GOLD (Exodus 32)
62 "Israel did eat ____ forty years" (Exodus 16:35)
65 Drink
66 Rickety
67 Playing field
68 "They did ____ and drink" (Genesis 24:54)
69 Rubber
70 Stairway post
71 "If any man will ____ thee at the law" (Matthew 5:40)

DOWN

1 "The fool rages and ____" (Proverb 29:9 NIV)
2 Dawn
3 Embroidery yarn
4 Spice
5 "They saw him ____ off" (Genesis 37:18)
6 Charged particle
7 "____. . .PITCHED HIS TENT TOWARD SODOM" (Genesis 3:12)
8 "WITH THE ____ HE BUILT AN ALTAR" (1 Kings 18:32)

9 St. John's _____

10 "My friends stand _____ from my sore" (Psalm 38:11)

11 "Dip the _____ of his finger in water" (Luke 16:24)

12 "For Adam was first formed, then _____" (1 Timothy 2:13)

13 "On the shore of the _____ sea" (1 Kings 9:26)

21 Abates (2 words)

23 Gorilla

25 "Put off thy _____ from thy foot" (Isaiah 20:2)

26 Male turkey

28 Recess

29 THE FIRE CONSUMED THE _____ (1 Kings 18:38)

30 Chill

32 Scenic trail along the Continental Divide (abbr.)

35 Grain

36 Wing

37 Herons

38 Stake

39 "ALL THE PEOPLE _____ NEAR UNTO HIM" (1 Kings 18:30)

40 Radar spot

41 Southwestern Indian

42 "Love worketh no _____ to his neighbour" (Romans 13:10)

43 Joshua was old and "stricken in _____ " (Joshua 23:1)

45 Hoopla

46 European language

48 Savages

49 Agency

50 Tranquilize

52 "THE COUNTRY WENT UP AS THE _____ OF A FURNACE" (Genesis 19:28)

56 "They wrought _____ stones" (Exodus 39:6)

57 Green Gables orphan

58 "ELIJAH SAID UNTO THE PROPHETS OF _____ " (1 Kings 18:25)

59 American sign language (abbr.)

60 Expression of surprise

61 Lab animal

63 "Even the goodliest, _____ mine" (1 Kings 20:3)

64 "Neither do men put _____ wine into old bottles" (Matthew 9:17)

▬ A WOMAN OF GOOD WORKS ▬
Acts 9:36–37, 40

Now there was at **Joppa** a **certain disciple named Tabitha**, which by **interpretation** is **called Dorcas**: this **woman** was **full** of **good works** and **almsdeeds which** she did. And it **came** to **pass** in **those days**, that she was **sick**, and **died**. . . . But Peter put **them** all **forth**, and **kneeled down**, and **prayed**; and **turning** him to the **body said**, Tabitha, **arise**. And she **opened** her **eyes**: and **when** she saw **Peter**, she sat up.

```
D T Y S I A I N S H W N W Z K
R N H H D D L A F W C O U A H
W I M O I K K M H J R I H F M
S K C I S N P E S K M T H E R
E E E D A E N D S D I A H W R
W L Y M T E W L H B E T C P F
V W O E F L O C A M E E N R R
W W R D I E D T R S R R D R N
S A C R O D L D O T F P E S O
A N D E Y A R P A S M R L O J
I G E S F P P I I H P E L J X
D G N S D O N B L C L T A F A
O O E A I L R V N L S N C A O
J O P P A R R T U R N I N G X
Y D O B X U A F H S Y A D Z C
```

ACROSTIC
by Donna Maltese

━━━ JEHOVAH VS. THE ASSYRIANS ━━━

God is ready to fight our battles. Crack the code to discover how one man's prayer delivered God's people in a mighty way!

A weapon of the Israelites

___ ___ ___ ___ ___
13 41 33 25   4

In this battle, 185,000 Assyrians were ____

___ ___ ___ ___ ___ ___ ___ ___ ___ ___ ___
 5 18 34 23   9 27 14 30   7 20 11

Hezekiah ____ to God for deliverance (2 Kings 15–19)

___ ___ ___ ___ ___ ___
12 28   1 35 22 17

These littered the battlefield

___ ___ ___ ___ ___ ___ ___
10 26 38 15 42 29   2

Time of day when victory was discovered (2 Kings 19:35)

___ ___ ___ ___ ___ ___ ___
24 39   6 43 36 31 19

The Lord was Israel's best ____

___ ___ ___ ___ ___ ___ ___
32   3 40 21 16 37   8

ACROSTIC

by Donna Maltese
(continued)

34-43-4   36-14   10-1-24-30   14-33   12-1-5-5

14-27-1-14   31-36-9-27-14,   14-27-1-14   14-27-20

34-43-19-22-18   26-40   14-27-29   18-39-7-11

41-3-31-14   33-23-14,   34-43-17   13-24-33-14-21

36-16   14-27-8   10-1-24-15   26-40   14-27-8

1-2-42-35-6-36-1-16-37.

2 Kings 19:35

MIRACLE TOOLS

On occasion, the Bible's miracle workers used "props" to do their amazing things. Can you solve these three anagrammed miracle tools? Hint: The first is from Acts, the other two from the Gospels.

Chief Ed shrank

— — — — — — — — — — —

Fools have fit views

— — — —   — — — — —'

— — —   — — — —

Worst pies tax

— — —   — — — — —   — — — —

▬▬ **GIVEN A SIGN** ▬▬

God works in mysterious ways, sometimes giving us miraculous signs. Solve the puzzles below to uncover a servant's dream and a king's request, given as harbingers of things to come.

BGA QW ZBHY WT MBXX, BX SY

QGWYEMEYWYA WT PX, XT QW CBX; HY SY

EYXWTEYA PGWT HQGY TOOQZY, BGA SQH SY

SBGKYA.

VKR OSWSEGVO VKMPSTSR, GL GM V FGBOL

LOGKB NHT LOS MOVRHP LH BH RHPK LSK

RSBTSSM: KVC, XQL FSL LOS MOVRHP TSLQTK

XVAEPVTR LSK RSBTSSM.

CROSSWORD
by *Tonya Vilhauer*

━━━ THE MASTER'S TOUCH ━━━

When we seek the Lord and commune with Him, He touches us in our place of greatest need, making us whole once more. Ah, the Master's touch. There is nothing more miraculous than that.

[They] besought him. . .and as many as touched him were made whole.
MARK 6:56

ACROSS
1 Electric spark
4 "THY ____ HATH MADE THEE WHOLE" (Matthew 9:22)
9 Retire from military service (abbr.)
14 "They shall not hurt ____ destroy" (Isaiah 65:25)
15 "It is not good that the man should be ____" (Genesis 2:18)
16 "Thou art a stranger, and also an ____ " (2 Samuel 15:19)
17 Flightless bird
18 Ray
19 Tired
20 "Ye call me ____ and Lord" (John 13:13)
22 Dirt
24 "Ye shall not enter ____ the kingdom of heaven" (Matthew 18:3)
25 Tinter
27 "HE SENT THEM. . .TO HEAL THE ____" (Luke 9:2)
31 Society (abbr.)
32 Assess
33 Female deer
34 "THEY SAW THE DUMB TO ____" (Matthew 15:31)
36 "JESUS. . .A MAN APPROVED OF GOD ____ YOU BY MIRACLES" (Acts 2:22)
38 JESUS WAS ABOUT ____ YEARS OF AGE (Luke 3:23)
40 Unstable
42 "HER DAUGHTER WAS MADE ____ FROM THAT VERY HOUR" (Matthew 15:28)
43 God confounded their language at this tower (Genesis 11:9)
44 "I ____ MEN AS TREES, WALKING" (Mark 8:24)
45 Belonging to Eve's husband

47 "____ ye of all his wondrous works" (Psalm 105:2)
51 "As far as the east is from the ____" (Psalm 103:12)
53 "That ____ with their teeth" (Micah 3:5)
54 Hautbois
55 "Kill him, that the inheritance may be ____" (Luke 20:14)
57 Renter
59 ____ HEALED THEIR SICK (Matthew 14:14)
62 Right angle to a ship's length
65 "When the sun did ____" (Mark 1:32)
66 "And he came ____, and drew near" (2 Samuel 18:25)
67 Domain
68 Annex
69 "An hundred ____ of oil" (Ezra 7:22)
70 "SON OF DAVID, HAVE ____ ON US" (Matthew 9:27)
71 Henna

DOWN
1 Deficiency in blood
2 Bible book following Acts
3 Pastry shells
4 "HIS ____ WENT THROUGHOUT ALL SYRIA" (Matthew 4:24)
5 Wing-shaped
6 Cation
7 Dynamite (abbr.)
8 JESUS ____ THE CHILD (Luke 9:42)
9 ____ vu
10 Tests
11 Central
12 Bravo (Sp.)
13 "SICK OF THE PALSY, LYING ON A ____" (Matthew 9:2)
21 Tissue near the pharynx
23 Lode yield

25 Cart for hauling heavy things
26 Talk
28 False god
29 Ice cream receptacle
30 Small barrel
32 "____ thee behind me, Satan" (Luke 4:8)
35 Before (prefix)
36 Lincoln
37 ____ Bradley, the game company
38 "MASTER, I WILL FOLLOW ____" (Matthew 8:19)
39 Garden tools
40 "BLIND RECEIVE THEIR SIGHT, AND THE ____ WALK" (Matthew 11:5)
41 Stomach muscles (abbr.)
42 Compass point (abbr.)
43 Flying rodent
45 Reduce (abbr.)
46 Take away weapons
48 "Whosoever shall exalt himself shall be ____" (Matthew 23:12)
49 Solitary
50 "He struck it into the pan, or ____" (1 Samuel 2:14)

52 "IF I MAY BUT ____ HIS GARMENT" (Matthew 9:21)
56 "Maintain good works for necessary ____" (Titus 3:14)
57 Baby powder
58 TV award
59 Strike
60 Gives protection of our surroundings (abbr.)
61 BLIND BARTIMAEUS ____ BY THE SIDE OF THE HIGHWAY (Mark 10:46)
63 Stinger
64 "He that hath an ____, let him hear" (Revelation 2:7)

265

WORD SEARCH
by Connie Troyer

━━━ NO LAUGHING MATTER ━━━
Genesis 15–21

ABRAHAM	LAUGHED
AFRAID	LORD
BEAR	MAMRE
BLESS	MANY NATIONS
CANAAN	MOTHER
CHILD	MULTIPLY
COVENANT	NINETY
DARKNESS	SARAH
EVERLASTING	SEED
FATHER	SON
FURNACE	STARS
GENERATIONS	TENT
HEAVEN	TIME APPOINTED
HEIR	VISITED
HUNDRED	WAXED OLD
ISAAC	YEARS
LAMP	

```
A G N S E S S E N K R A D I A
D E A F R A I D C A A S I U S
E N A E L A U G H E D O U B N
T E N T O N T E N E V A E H O
N R A R E Y A S E S Z A E Y I
I A C G N I T S A L R E V E T
O T A C W A X E D O L D I A A
P I B H R T D R N T I Y S R N
P O R I E H E F N I L E I S Y
A N A L E H U A T P N R T R N
E S H D T R N N I L S M E E A
M O A O N E X T D S A A D H M
I N M A V A L A E R I M R T H
T A C O W U E L V A E H P A R
M E C R M U B A L O R D R F H
```

BIBLE QUOTATION
by Suzanne Stepp

━━━ TAKING A LAST LOOK ━━━
Acts 1:11

Work this Bible quotation puzzle to discover wise words spoken by heavenly angels to earthly gazers.

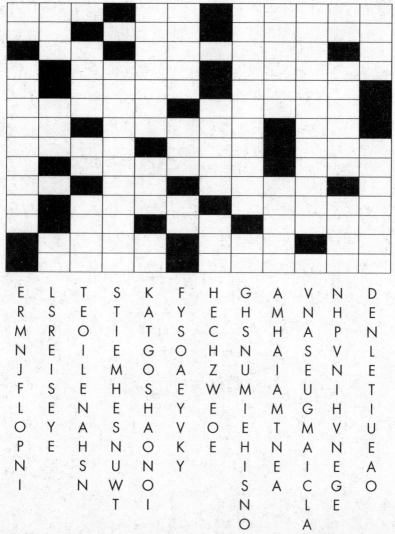

E	L	T	S	K	F	H	G	A	V	N	D
R	S	E	T	A	Y	E	H	M	N	H	E
M	R	O	I	T	S	C	S	H	A	P	N
N	E	I	E	G	O	H	N	A	S	V	L
J	I	L	M	O	A	Z	U	I	E	N	E
F	S	E	H	O	E	W	M	A	U	I	T
L	E	N	E	H	Y	E	I	M	G	H	I
O	Y	A	S	A	V	O	E	T	M	V	U
P	E	H	N	O	K	E	H	N	A	N	E
N		S	U	N	Y		H	E	I	E	A
I		N	W	O			I	A	C	G	O
			T	I			S	L	L	E	
							N	A			
							O				

TELEPHONE SCRAMBLE
by Connie Troyer

▬ MIRACLES CONCERNING WATER ▬

In some places around the world, clear, cool water is itself a miracle, but thousands of years ago, it was involved in even more notable phenomena. Go with the flow in solving this puzzle of miracles concerning water.

| PRS 7 | MNO 6 | ABC 2 | JKL 5 | | | |

| WXY 9 | GHI 4 | MNO 6 | DEF 3 | | | |

| PRS 7 | ABC 2 | PRS 7 | TUV 8 | DEF 3 | DEF 3 | |

| WXY 9 | ABC 2 | JKL 5 | JKL 5 | GHI 4 | MNO 6 | GHI 4 |

| PRS 7 | TUV 8 | MNO 6 | PRS 7 | MNO 6 | | |

| JKL 5 | MNO 6 | PRS 7 | DEF 3 | ABC 2 | MNO 6 | |

| MNO 6 | DEF 3 | TUV 8 | PRS 7 | | | |

ACROSTIC
by Donna Maltese

AN OPEN WOMB

This miracle proves that with God, we can "expect" anything!

These two sisters were Jacob's _____ (Genesis 29:25–28)

___ ___ ___ ___ ___
18 24 5   34 12

The name of Jacob's father-in-law (Genesis 29:21–23)

___ ___ ___ ___ ___
29 11 33 20 4

The wife Jacob loved (Genesis 29:28–30)

___ ___ ___ ___ ___ ___
3   28 15 22 10 31

Leah traded her son's _____ for time alone with Jacob
(Genesis 30:16)

___ ___ ___ ___ ___ ___ ___ ___ ___
2   17 36 9   25 32 6   21 13

To be with child

___ ___ ___ ___ ___ ___ ___ ___
14 30 8   27 19 35 1   26

The often painful part of childbirth

___ ___ ___ ___ ___
7   38 16 23 37

28-1-9 27-23-9 3-8-2-8-2-33-8-3-8-9 3-35-15-22-10-7,

28-1-9 27-23-9 22-8-20-30-6-8-19-8-9 26-23

22-34-30, 11-1-9 23-14-8-4-8-9 22-34-30 18-23-2-16.

11-1-9 13-22-8 15-23-36-15-21-24-5-21-9, 38-1-9

33-17-25-21 32 12-23-36.

GENESIS 30:22–23

CROSSWORD
by Tonya Vilhauer

━━━ DADDY, I'M HUNGRY ━━━

God always takes care of us, whether it's by providing physical food (like meat and potatoes) or spiritual food (like Jesus). Solve this puzzle to discover the many ways God and His Son, Jesus, fed those who hungered.

> *"Your forefathers ate manna and died,*
> *but he who feeds on this bread will live forever."*
> JOHN 6:58 NIV

ACROSS

1 "I will put my _____ into their hearts" (Hebrews 10:16)
5 "The diligent _____ only to plenteousness" (Proverbs 21:5)
9 A heavy noise
13 Double-reed instrument
14 Pennsylvania Canal
15 Engage
16 Torah table
17 "Woe unto them that draw. . .sin as it were with a cart _____" (Isaiah 5:18)
18 "Rejoice at the sound of the _____" (Job 21:12)
19 "JESUS TOOK BREAD, AND_____ IT" (Matthew 26:26)
21 Bartlett
23 Japanese money
24 Native of (suffix)
25 Ideal person
29 Wing
30 "The women _____ hangings" (2 Kings 23:7)
32 Anger
33 Fracas
36 Removes
37 "_____ the kine to the cart" (1 Samuel 6:7)
38 Small brook
39 Hiker's nemeses
40 Barrel
41 Compass point (abbr.)
42 "RAINED DOWN _____ UPON THEM TO EAT" (Psalm 78:24)
43 Ezekiel and the valley of dry _____ (Ezekiel 37:1)
44 Poisonous snake
45 Time periods
46 "HERE IS A _____ WITH. . .BARLEY LOAVES" (John 6:9 NIV)

47 Remove bony projections from the head of cattle
49 "THOSE _____ . . .HAD SEEN THE MIRACLE THAT JESUS DID" (John 6:14)
50 Greek goddess of the dawn
53 "THEY CAUGHT SUCH A LARGE NUMBER OF _____" (Luke 5:6 NIV)
55 Free of germs
57 Above
60 Off-Broadway award
62 "Obey them that have the _____ over you" (Hebrews 13:17)
63 Employs
64 Kick
65 Very first garden in the Bible (Genesis 2:8)
66 Short for shorten
67 "Thine _____ did see my substance" (Psalm 139:16)
68 Saucy

DOWN

1 Foyer
2 White poplar
3 "FOUR THOUSAND MEN, BESIDE _____ AND CHILDREN" (Matthew 15:38)
4 Gathering together of the waters (Genesis 1:10)
5 Mother _____
6 Wear away
7 Tweak
8 "LAUNCH OUT INTO THE _____, AND LET DOWN YOUR NETS" (Luke 5:4)
9 _____ cotta (clay)
10 Harpy
11 Uncle Sam's nation (abbr.)
12 Daniel and the lions' _____
15 "HE TOOK THE FIVE _____ AND THE TWO FISHES" (Luke 9:16)

20 "_____ me this day thy birthright" (Genesis 25:31)
22 Roof overhang
26 Giant
27 "_____, and take up thy bed" (Mark 2:11)
28 Stinks
29 Hole-making tool
30 Alerts
31 Vegetable
33 "RAVENS BROUGHT HIM _____ AND FLESH" (1 Kings 17:6)
34 Wash off
35 First letter in Hebrew alphabet
36 Bonito
39 "So shall thy _____ be filled with plenty" (Proverbs 3:10)
40 Bashful
42 Deserves
43 "This is now _____ of my bones" (Genesis 2:23)
46 Hems in
48 "To _____ a sacrifice" (Luke 2:24)
49 Northeastern state
50 Music used as practice
51 Cargo ship

52 "The _____ thereof shall be as the wine" (Hosea 14:7)
54 "Thou art my _____ in the day of evil" (Jeremiah 17:17)
56 Secondary school (abbr.)
57 Expression of triumph
58 Movement that seeks a group's equal rights (informal)
59 Bolus
61 "_____ the truth, and sell it not" (Proverbs 23:23)

THE RAISING OF LAZARUS

JOHN 11:1–44

ABODE	LAZARUS
ASK	LIGHT
AWAKE	LIVETH
BETHANY	LORD
BROTHER	LOVEST
CHRIST	MAN
DEATH	MARTHA
DISCIPLES	MARY
GLORIFIED	OINTMENT
GLORY	RESURRECTION
GOD	SICK
GRAVE	STONE
HOURS	THOMAS
JERUSALEM	TWELVE
JESUS	WALK
JUDEA	WEEPING

```
H  B  N  V  G  J  L  B  I  B  E  S  E  S  B
T  T  N  O  U  L  R  I  M  E  N  E  V  I  J
E  B  H  D  I  O  O  E  G  T  A  L  A  D  Z
V  K  E  O  T  T  L  R  H  H  M  P  R  B  W
I  A  A  H  M  A  C  L  Y  A  T  I  G  O  D
L  Y  E  W  S  A  O  E  E  N  F  C  M  C  E
A  R  C  U  A  R  S  I  R  Y  C  S  O  H  D
V  D  R  T  D  G  Y  Z  N  R  W  I  K  R  O
D  E  A  T  H  O  N  N  H  T  U  D  E  I  B
J  G  L  O  R  I  F  I  E  D  M  S  J  S  A
S  U  R  A  Z  A  L  B  P  V  K  E  E  T  H
W  Z  J  M  A  R  T  H  A  E  L  C  N  R  O
A  T  S  E  V  O  L  D  W  K  E  E  I  T  U
L  E  N  O  T  S  J  E  S  U  S  W  W  S  R
K  M  M  H  H  X  E  A  Y  R  A  M  N  T  S
```

SUDOKU
by Sara Stoker

━ BREAKING THE LAW—OF PHYSICS ━

DIFFICULT

	A	B	C	D	E	F	G	H	I
1	D				S			C	
2			S				T		
3	C	T	N	O				W	
4		W		T	N			S	
5						W		T	
6	T	S						N	
7		N		I				K	O
8		D				N		I	T
9		K					N		

Hint: Row 1

"And he cut _____ a _____, and cast it in thither; and the iron did swim" (2 Kings 6:6).

A CRIPPLED WOMAN
SEE LUKE 13:11

While teaching in a synagogue one Sabbath, Jesus noticed a woman who was attending services even though she was ill. Can you discover her malady?

WHITING   A thought   _____   1. ____ ____

TROOPER   Lassoer   _____   2. ____ ____

MOODILY   Lace scarf   _____   3. ____ ____

FEMORAL   Mushroom   _____   4. ____ ____

NOISOME   Hoofed mammal   _____   5. ____ ____

NARTHEX   Additional   _____   6. ____ ____

FANTASY   Restless   _____   7. ____ ____

DISPOSE   Sheriff's group   _____   8. ____ ____

AROUSED   Drench   _____   9. ____ ____

STAMPED   Recorded   _____   10. ____ ____

PAPRIKA   Hooded jacket   _____   11. ____ ____

INGRATE   Stove   _____   12. ____ ____

REGALLY   Lawful   _____   13. ____ ____

— — — — — — — — — — — — —

— — — — — — — — — — — — —
1   2   3   4   5   6   7   8   9   10   11   12   13

ACROSTIC
by Donna Maltese

━━ A DISCIPLE GETS CARRIED AWAY ━━

When we're under the Spirit's leading, anything can happen. Crack this code and see how one disciple rose up in God's power.

The country of a unique eunuch (Acts 8:27)

—— —— —— —— —— —— —— ——
22 45 3 27 36 9 31 16

Philip was a _____ of Jesus

—— —— —— —— —— —— —— ——
4 25 37 42 7 32 20 13

Following an angel's directions, Philip _____ the eunuch

—— —— —— —— ——
35 47 39 15 44

Baptism is a Christian _____

—— —— —— —— —— —— —— —— ——
17 8 30 43 11 48 40 23 2

Third person of the Trinity

—— —— —— —— —— —— —— —— ——
24 6 33 18 12 29 5 46 21

Given official authority

—— —— —— —— —— —— —— —— ——
14 41 26 38 1 19 34 28 10

1-24-22-15   2-3-22-18   1-40-34-40   30-47-41-13

39-26   36-39-45   6-35   2-3-22   1-16-21-14-34,

2-3-22   17-32-7-43-7-45   6-35   2-3-22   20-5-43-4

42-11-39-12-29-45   8-1-8-18   9-29-31-33-27-9,   2-3-8-2

2-3-22   19-39-23-39-42-29   37-11-1   24-25-48   23-5

41-38-43-28.

ACTS 8:39

CROSSWORD
by Dorothy Pryse

THE SYNAGOGUE LEADER'S DAUGHTER

When Jairus, the synagogue leader, was faced with a seemingly impossible situation, Jesus gave him hope. As you solve this puzzle, remember that no matter how things appear, you need not despair, but only believe—because Jesus is by your side!

As soon as Jesus heard the word that was spoken, he saith unto the ruler of the synagogue, Be not afraid, only believe.
MARK 5:36

ACROSS

1 Compass direction (abbr.)
4 "Only ____ the harlot shall live" (Joshua 6:17)
9 Popular TV show about forensic scientists
12 Literary form found in Psalms
14 "Not that I have now attained [this ____], or. . .been made perfect" (Philippians 3:12 AMP)
15 "The ____ is now shut" (Luke 11:7)
16 Mountain range
17 Type of code
18 European monetary unit
19 "The people. . .saw that Jesus was ____" (John 6:24) (2 words)
21 "I was ____ in iniquity; and in sin did my mother conceive me" (Psalm 51:5)
23 Keats' poem: "____ on a Grecian Urn"
24 Do needlework
25 AFTER JESUS RAISED JAIRUS'S DAUGHTER, "THE ____ ABOUT THIS SPREAD" (Matthew 9:26 AMP)
28 Ruling official of Ottoman Empire
31 Thick carpet
34 JESUS SAID TO THE MOURNERS, "WHY. . .WEEP? THE ____ IS NOT DEAD" (Mark 5:39)
36 "As a ____ returneth to his vomit, so a fool returneth to his folly" (Proverbs 26:11)
38 WHEN JESUS ARRIVED AT JAIRUS'S HOUSE, HIS DAUGHTER APPEARED TO BE THIS (Matthew 9:24) (abbr.)
40 Assert
41 "I desire to speak to the Almighty and to ____ my case with God" (Job 13:3 NIV)
43 JAIRUS "FELL ____ AT JESUS' FEET" (Luke 8:41)
44 "WHILE HE ____ SPAKE, THERE COMETH ONE FROM [JAIRUS'S] HOUSE" (Luke 8:49)

45 "For in ____ season we shall reap" (Galatians 6:9)
46 "Jesus came out wearing the ____ crown" (John 19:5 AMP)
48 "Two of the sons of Jacob, Simeon and ____" (Genesis 34:25)
51 Guess (abbr.)
53 Sea eagles
54 "But the ____ is not by and by" (Luke 21:9)
56 Largest New Deal agency (abbr.)
58 Constellation
61 Cheers
66 JAIRUS URGED JESUS TO "COME AND LAY THY HAND ____ HER" (Matthew 9:18)
67 "They wondered every one ____ things which Jesus did" (Luke 9:43) (2 words)
69 Olive tree
70 "Rejoice. . .that I may be ____ sorrowful" (Philippians 2:28)
71 "Our enemies totally lost their ____" (Nehemiah 6:15 MSG)
72 "AND HE ____ THE DAMSEL BY THE HAND" (Mark 5:41)
73 "And ____ us make three tabernacles" (Mark 9:5)
74 South American mountains
75 Compass point (abbr.)

DOWN

1 "Goliath. . .whose height was six cubits and a ____" (1 Samuel 17:4)
2 Alone
3 WHEN JESUS CAME TO JAIRUS'S HOUSE, HE SAW "THE TUMULT, AND THEM THAT ____" (Mark 5:38)
4 Coated with ice
5 "They ____ and exalted and praised and thanked God" (Acts 21:20 AMP)
6 "Behold, I stand ____ by the well of water" (Genesis 24:13)

7 Science degree (abbr.)
8 Revered
9 Sudden takeover
10 "They were _____ afraid" (Mark 9:6)
11 "His bedstead was a bedstead of _____" (Deuteronomy 3:11)
13 Mountain time
15 JAIRUS TOLD JESUS, "MY LITTLE DAUGHTER LIETH AT THE POINT OF _____" (Mark 5:23)
20 Nylons
22 BEFORE HEALING JAIRUS'S DAUGHTER, JESUS HEALED ANOTHER WOMAN, TELLING HER, "DAUGHTER, YOUR FAITH _____ MADE YOU WELL" (Mark 5:34 NJKV)
25 "Thy _____ is like a round goblet" (Song of Solomon 7:2)
26 Express
27 Compass point (abbr.)
29 "Shoulderpieces. . .joined at the two _____" (Exodus 28:7)
30 JESUS SAID TO JAIRUS'S DAUGHTER, "I SAY TO ___, GET UP!" (Mark 5:41 NIV)
32 "Women _____ themselves in modest apparel" (1 Timothy 2:9)
33 Ball dresses
34 "Rejoice ye in that _____" (Luke 6:23)
35 "There is a _____ here" (John 6:9)
37 "_____ thee behind me, Satan" (Mark 8:33)

39 "THERE CAME FROM [JAIRUS'S HOUSE ONE] WHICH SAID, . . .WHY TROUBLEST THOU THE MASTER _____ FURTHER?" (Mark 5:35)
42 "Ye tithe mint and _____ and all" (Luke 11:42)
43 "Neither did Manasseh drive out. . .the inhabitants of _____ (Judges 1:27)
47 "When they _____, [they] receive the word with joy" (Luke 8:13)
49 Blood carriers
50 [He] "brought him to an _____" (Luke 10:34)
52 WHEN JESUS HEALED JAIRUS'S DAUGHTER, SHE WAS _____ YEARS OLD (Mark 5:42)
55 "They cried out, saying, Great _____ of the Ephesians" (Acts 19:28)
57 Fence stakes
58 Sea bird
59 Dueling sword
60 "Jesus, thou Son of the _____ high" (Mark 5:7)
61 "Children, how _____ is it?" (Mark 10:24)
62 Small child
63 "_____, a Zebulonite, judged Israel" (Judges 12:11)
64 Florescent
65 "He entreated Abram well for her _____" (Genesis 12:16)
68 "There met him _____ men" (Luke 17:12)

SCRAMBLED CIRCLE
by Suzanne Stepp

OBEYING JESUS

Once we decide to follow Jesus, our souls are in no danger of being eternally "repossessed."

1. ROTHAITUY
2. STUDQEOINE
3. ENTRCIDO
4. ULDO
5. YOEB
6. ECAPE

7. DENSHASTIO
8. NAGYSUEGO
9. DAEPSR
10. SEBIRCS
11. OIRNGE
12. NROT

Jesus rebuked this to come out.

1. _ ◯ _ _ _ _ _ _ _
2. _ _ _ _ _ _ _ ◯ _ _
3. _ _ ◯ _ _ _ _ _
4. ◯ _ _ _
5. _ _ ◯ _
6. _ _ ◯ _ _
7. _ _ _ _ ◯ _ _ _ _ _
8. ◯ _ _ _ _ _ _ _ _
9. _ ◯ _ _ _ _
10. _ _ _ ◯ _ _ _
11. ◯ _ _ ◯ _ _
12. ◯ _ _ _

Answer: _ _ _ _ _ _ _ _ _ _ _ _ _ _ _

SPOTTY HEADLINE
by Sara Stoker

— OLD TESTAMENT MIRACLE MEN —

God can do some pretty amazing things to get people's attention. Can you solve these spotty headlines to discover three Old Testament men who experienced the miraculous?

DIS●BEDIENT PROPHET E●DURES T●REE DAYS
IN ●UMBO FISH'S STOM●CH

— — — — —

W●AK MAN SUB●UES MI●HTY ARMY
W●TH ●NLY THREE HU●DRED MEN

— — — — — —

M●N'S DONKEY SC●●DS HI●
IN HE●REW L●NGU●GE

— — — — — —

283

THE FISH'S SHEKEL
Matthew 17:24–27

And when they were come to **Capernaum**, they that received **tribute money came** to **Peter**, and said, Doth not your **master pay** tribute? He saith, Yes. And when he was come into the **house, Jesus prevented him**, saying, What thinkest **thou, Simon**? of whom do the **kings** of the **earth** take **custom** or tribute? of their own **children**, or of **strangers**? Peter saith unto him, Of strangers. Jesus **saith** unto him, Then are the children **free**. Notwithstanding, **lest** we should **offend them**, go thou to the **sea**, and **cast** an **hook**, and **take** up the **fish** that **first cometh** up; and when thou **hast opened** his **mouth**, thou **shalt find** a **piece** of money: that take, and **give unto** them **for me and thee**.

```
S A A T E N E R D L I H C E G
A S H E A T H E M H P I S I R
B R E T S A M A T L A I V I U
F E D S J E S U S E Y E E D F
O G E H I K O H K I N G S C R
R N N A R M H O A C E M A L E
M A E L H F O D I S U S E U Y
E R P T I H N N W A T S O N E
A T O R M I D A N O T O T T N
N S S U F E N R E T E P R O O
D T D E T N E V E R P U I H M
T A K E I P F A A R O T B H O
H E R G A V F E R H H O U S E
E M A C M K O H T I A S T O U
E T E C O M E T H F R E E F S
```

ACROSTIC
by Donna Maltese

━━━━ A LOT OF SALT FOR A WIFE ━━━━

Decipher this puzzle to discover who else, besides a cat, was killed by curiosity.

Lot to Abraham (Genesis 12:4)

　　　　　　 __11__ __25__ __30__ __3__ __21__ __17__

Fire and _____ (Genesis 19:24)

__6__ __13__ __18__ __29__ __1__ __33__ __26__ __8__ __22__

Angels _____ Lot

　　　　 __19__ __2__ __14__ __24__ __9__ __28__ __12__

Lot was saved for Abraham's _____ (Genesis 19:29)

　　　　　　　　 __4__ __10__ __27__ __31__

Lot was told not to stay in this place (Genesis 19:17)

　　　　 __15__ __20__ __32__ __5__ __34__

One last look sealed Lot's wife's _____

　　　　　　 __23__ __7__ __35__ __16__

6-9-35   3-5-14   17-5-23-16   20-26-26-27-31-12

6-10-24-27   23-13-26-29   6-28-3-5-8-12   3-5-29,

7-11-12   1-3-2   6-22-24-32-29-21   7   30-18-20-20-32-19

26-23   4-7-20-33.

GENESIS 19:26

HEALED BY JESUS

When it came to miracles, Jesus was "the man." Besides calming storms and turning water into wine, He also specialized in healings. Can you unscramble these three? Note: None are proper names.

Rent sleep

_ _ _   _ _ _ _ _ _

Fourth jaguar dies

_ _ _ _ _ _ _ _   _ _

_ _ _ _ _ _

Nor active stunners

_ _ _ _ _ _ _ _ _

_ _ _ _ _ _ _

TELEPHONE SCRAMBLE
by Connie Troyer

═══ MIRACULOUS EVENTS ═══

God's miracles pave the way for amazing events. Solve this puzzle to uncover words regarding places, happenings, visions, and people inextricably linked with the miraculous.

ABC 2	ABC 2	ABC 2	DEF 3	JKL 5

PRS 7	DEF 3	MNO 6	TUV 8	DEF 3	ABC 2	MNO 6	PRS 7	TUV 8

JKL 5	DEF 3	PRS 7	GHI 4	ABC 2	GHI 4	MNO 6

PRS 7	PRS 7	MNO 6	PRS 7	GHI 4	DEF 3	TUV 8	GHI 4	ABC 2

PRS 7	JKL 5	ABC 2	GHI 4	TUV 8	DEF 3	PRS 7

PRS 7	ABC 2	PRS 7	TUV 8	TUV 8	PRS 7	DEF 3

MNO 6	ABC 2	PRS 7	WXY 9

CROSSWORD
by Dorothy Pryse

■ THE SICK WOMAN IS HEALED ■

Talk about issues! This sick woman certainly had them, but she also had faith, and *that's* what made her whole. Solve this puzzle to find out more about this woman who approached Jesus in faith and got immediate results in healing.

> *But Jesus turned him about, and when he saw her, he said,*
> *Daughter, be of good comfort; thy faith hath made thee whole.*
> *And the woman was made whole from that hour.*
> MATTHEW 9:22

ACROSS

1 "The Pharisees began to ____ him vehemently" (Luke 11:53)
5 WHEN JESUS FELT "THAT VIRTUE HAD GONE OUT OF HIM," HE TURNED "TO SEE HER THAT HAD DONE THIS ____" (Mark 5:30, 32)
10 Taxi
13 "The ____ ways shall be made smooth" (Luke 3:5)
15 "____, the son of Beeri" (Hosea 1:1)
16 "The screech ____ also shall rest there" (Isaiah 34:14)
17 "The Jordan is at flood ____ all during harvest" (Joshua 3:15 NIV)
18 More capable
19 Buddhist
20 Aviation (prefix)
21 River in Italy
23 Subway system
25 Russian name (abbr.)
26 MINUTES BEFORE JESUS MET THE WOMAN, "A LARGE CROWD FOLLOWED AND ____ AROUND HIM" (Mark 5:25 NIV)
28 Shoveled
31 "Lift up now ____ eyes" (Genesis 13:14)
32 "What ____ thee, O thou sea, that thou fleddest?" (Psalm 114:5)
33 Break in friendship
34 Lotus 1-2-3 file name extension (abbr.)
37 "Wilt thou ____ it up?" (John 2:20)
38 Ultima ____, a remote goal or ideal
40 Eight, Roman numeral
41 Promos
42 "He ____ hath ears to hear, let him hear" (Mark 4:9)
43 "He took. . .a cake of ____ bread" (Leviticus 8:26)
44 Hunt illegally
45 THE WOMAN HAD SUFFERED FOR ____ YEARS (Luke 8:43)
46 Explore caves
49 "Even the ____ and the sea obey him?" (Mark 4:41)
50 "He made ____ of the church" (Acts 8:3 NKJV)
51 "The valley of Shaveh. . .is the king's ____" (Genesis 14:17)
52 Doctors' organization (abbr.)
55 Mimic
56 "Are there not twelve ____ in the day?" (John 11:9)
59 "Scribes. . .desire to walk in long ____" (Luke 20:46)
61 Average
62 "Take it, and ____ it ____" (Revelation 10:9) (2 words)
63 ONLY AFTER JESUS HAD ASKED, "WHO TOUCHED MY CLOTHES?" DID THE WOMAN ____ (Mark 5:30–33)
64 City in England, noted for its cathedral
65 "I have taken. . .even the ____ of the cup" (Isaiah 51:22)
66 Building extensions

DOWN

1 ____ Major (Big Dipper)
2 Learning method
3 Cluster bean
4 "Is there any taste in the white of an ____?" (Job 6:6)
5 "I ____ thee, O Father" (Matthew 11:25)
6 Tramp
7 Universal mode of communication for the deaf (abbr.)
8 Maiden name
9 HIS WAS TOUCHED BY THE SICK WOMAN (Luke 8:44)

10 "Thirty milch camels with their _____" (Genesis 32:15)
11 AT FIRST, JESUS DID NOT SEEM TO BE _____ OF WHO TOUCHED HIM (Luke 8:45)
12 THIS ISSUED FORTH FROM THE WOMAN (Matthew 9:20)
14 AS SOON AS THE SICK WOMAN CAME INTO CONTACT WITH JESUS, "SHE FELT IN HER BODY THAT SHE WAS _____" (Mark 5:29)
22 "By faith they passed through the _____ sea" (Hebrews 11:29)
24 Compass point (abbr.)
25 "And Arad and _____" (1 Chronicles 8:15)
26 TV's Mr. Donahue
27 "Extortion is _____, robbery is epidemic" (Ezekiel 22:29 MSG)
28 "_____ obeyed Abraham" (1 Peter 3:6)
29 Motley
30 "_____, who shall live when God doeth this!" (Numbers 24:23)
31 THE WOMAN FELL DOWN BEFORE JESUS, "AND TOLD HIM ALL THE _____" (Mark 5:33)
34 THE WOMAN THOUGHT, "IF I JUST TOUCH HIS CLOTHES, I _____ BE HEALED" (Mark 5:28)
35 Capital of the Ukraine
36 THIS SCENE WITH THE WOMAN BEGINS "WHEN JESUS WAS PASSED OVER AGAIN BY SHIP UNTO THE OTHER _____" OF THE SEA (Mark 5:21)

38 "To love him. . .is more _____ all whole burnt offerings" (Mark 12:33)
39 Chop
40 Contended
42 JESUS' QUESTION AMID THE CROWD: "WHO _____ ME?" (Luke 8:45)
43 "The _____ thereof said. . .Why loose ye the colt?" (Luke 19:33)
44 Political movement once chaired by Arafat (abbr.)
45 Up to the time of (poet.)
46 "The Holy Ghost descended in a bodily _____ like a dove" (Luke 3:22)
47 Relating to the Roman Catholic Church
48 AFTER THE HEALING OF THE SICK WOMAN AND A LITTLE GIRL, THE DISCIPLES WENT OUT "PREACHING. . . AND HEALING _____ WHERE" (Luke 9:6)
49 Stinging insects
51 "_____ yourselves so you feel nothing" (Isaiah 29:9 MSG)
52 "_____ was a keeper of sheep" (Genesis 4:2)
53 "Make ready quickly three measures of fine _____" (Genesis 18:6)
54 "Everyone who _____ receives" (Matthew 7:8 NJKV)
57 "All that handle the _____, the mariners" (Ezekiel 27:29)
58 Shoshonean
60 Unlock (poet.)

291

WORD SEARCH
by John Hudson Tiner

━━━ FOUR MEN WALKING ━━━
DANIEL 3:25–26

He **answered** and said, Lo, I see four men **loose**, **walking** in the midst of the fire, and **they have** no **hurt**; and the **form** of the **fourth** is **like** the Son of God. Then **Nebuchadnezzar** came **near** to the **mouth** of the **burning fiery furnace**, and **spake**, and **said**, Shadrach, Meshach, and Abednego, ye **servants** of the **most high** God, come forth, and **come hither**. **Then Shadrach**, **Meshach**, and **Abednego**, **came forth** of the **midst** of the **fire**.

```
R D I A S B E X N T P M M J D
E A K P P L V M T G L G Y Z F
H K Z F A U Z G A B H R S G O
T S I Z K T H E N C E A T H B
I W E L E R W J A I H R Z G M
H L K R C N I R F T K H E I V
G T I D V M D G C S F L J H F
J F U V M A Z A Y O Q L A U V
S V G O H J N S H M M V B W H
H F N S M S A T R C E I E X H
F I I R W L O O S E U S D D U
K O N E A R F Q T C R B N S R
F U R N A C E H C A H S E M T
B E U T U E E M O C E F G N P
D Q B Z H Y R K H T R U O F I
```

by David Austin and Sharon Y. Brown

ALL THINGS
BRIGHT AND BEAUTIFUL

God's glory can be clearly seen in the beauty that surrounds us. Work these puzzles to read more about His shining creativity, which filled the dark and formless void!

QPW KIW NQXW, JZG GSZAZ YZ JXKSG: QPW

GSZAZ RQN JXKSG.

GC GRBG IRNC BGC CRYBG EH GKM DQVCY,

GC GRBG CMBREUKMGCN BGC VQYUN EH

GKM VKMNQI, RTN GRBG MBYCBZGCN QOB

BGC GCRFCTM EH GKM NKMZYCBKQT.

THE FIFTH PLAGUE

DIFFICULT

	A	B	C	D	E	F	G	H	I
1					I		K		V
2	I			V	K	L			
3	V	K		C	S		E		L
4		L	V						C
5				T				K	
6		C	K				I	V	
7		T	L	I	V	E			
8		I	S		L			E	T
9				S	T	C			

Hint: Column A

The fifth plague was upon this: _____ (Exodus 9:4 NIV).

ACROSTIC
by Donna Maltese

━━ SAMSON THIRSTS NO MORE ━━

Solve this acrostic to find out how God used the natural to perform the supernatural.

He was a miracle baby, raised a Nazarite
(Judges 13:3–5)

___ ___ ___ ___ ___ ___
2   23   34   12   27   18

Samson later fell in love with this woman in the
Valley or Sorek (Judges 16:4)

___ ___ ___ ___ ___ ___ ___
13   24   7   33   16   28   3

To refresh or renew

___ ___ ___ ___ ___ ___
9   22   35   17   31   4

A cavity containing gold, water, or gas

___ ___ ___ ___ ___ ___
15   29   5   20   8   26

A natural thirst-quencher

___ ___ ___ ___ ___
6   21   36   11   32

Before kings, Israel was ruled by ____

___ ___ ___ ___ ___ ___
10   19   30   1   25   14

1-27-30   5-16-23-31-22   21-18   3-29-7-7-29-6

15-16-21-5-24   36-3-28-36   6-28-2   17-18   36-3-4

10-28-6,   21-18-13   36-3-4-9-4   5-23-34-25

6-28-26-8-32   36-3-4-32-4-27-19-36;   21-18-13

6-3-11-18   3-4   3-28-13   13-9-19-18-20,

3-33-12   14-15-33-9-33-26   5-23-34-25

23-1-23-17-18.

JUDGES 15:19

CROSSWORD
by Dorothy Pryse

═══ JESUS WALKS ON WATER ═══

If we keep our eyes on Jesus and not our circumstances, we can do the impossible. Unfortunately, we sometimes lose our focus and begin to slide into the deep end, which is what happened to the disciple in this story. Have fun solving!

When he saw the wind boisterous, he was afraid; and beginning to sink, he cried, saying, Lord, save me. And immediately Jesus stretched forth his hand, and caught him.
MATTHEW 14:30–31

ACROSS

1 "They should take nothing for their journey, save a _____ only" (Mark 6:8)
6 "THE SEA AROSE BY REASON OF A GREAT WIND _____ BLEW" (John 6:18)
10 ONE DARING DISCIPLE CRIED OUT TO THE LORD FOR _____ (Matthew 14:30)
14 Eastern religion
15 "[He] _____ seen in a vision a man named Ananias" (Acts 9:12)
16 "The _____ seemed good to me" (Deuteronomy 1:23 NIV)
17 "Whether is greater, the gift, or the _____" (Matthew 23:19)
18 Away from the wind
19 "They _____ their clothes" (Acts 14:14)
20 Teensy
21 Country road
23 Stretches
25 "They lost all control of the ship. It was a _____ in the storm" (Acts 27:13 MSG)
26 "As a _____ gathereth her chickens" (Matthew 23:37)
27 "They have killed Your prophets. . .and _____ am left" (Romans 11:3 NKJV) (2 words)
30 Resist separation (2 words)
34 "One _____ is needful" (Luke 10:42)
35 "He's trotting behind her, like a calf led to the butcher _____" (Proverbs 7:22 MSG)
36 Switchboard worker (abbr.)
38 Prongs
39 Germanic god of war and the sky
40 "As one opened his sack to give his _____ provender. . ._____ espied his money" (Genesis 42:27) (2 words)
42 "Copper is smelted from _____" (Job 28:2 NKJV)
43 "THE _____ WAS CONTRARY" (Matthew 14:24)

44 "I will _____ mine arrows upon them" (Deuteronomy 32:23)
45 "They cast four _____ out of the stern" (Acts 27:29)
48 JESUS TOLD THE DISCIPLES, "BE NOT _____" (Mark 6:50)
49 "Give _____ to his commandments" (Exodus 15:26)
50 Maneuver
51 Rich fabric
54 "Don't _____ off to the right or the left" (Deuteronomy 5:32 MSG)
55 "How long will it be _____ thou be quiet?" (Jeremiah 47:6)
58 Chills
59 Monogram (abbr.)
61 "When thou prayest, _____ into thy closet" (Matthew 6:6)
63 Composer of "Rule, Britannica"
64 River in England
65 Echolocation
66 "Jesus Christ our Lord, which was made of the _____ of David" (Romans 1:3)
67 Movie_____
68 "They shall be snares and _____" (Joshua 23:13)

DOWN

1 George Bernard _____
2 "Son of man, take thee a _____" (Ezekiel 4:1)
3 Stake
4 Food regulating agency (abbr.)
5 "Emmaus. . .was from Jerusalem about threescore _____" (Luke 24:13)
6 "I _____ my God" (Philemon 1:4)
7 "Give diligence. . .lest he _____ thee" (Luke 12:58)
8 "I _____ no pleasant bread" (Daniel 10:3)

9 "HE CONSTRAINED HIS DISCIPLES TO GET INTO ____" (Mark 6:45) (2 words)

10 "You have been unfaithful to your God, ____ yourselves out like prostitutes" (Hosea 9:1 NLT)

11 "This land. . .is become like the garden of ____" (Ezekiel 36:35)

12 "The Egyptians. . .____ unto them such things as they required" (Exodus 12:36)

13 Gestures of affection

22 "THOSE WHO WERE IN THE BOAT. . . WORSHIPED HIM, SAYING, 'TRULY YOU ____ THE SON OF GOD' " (Matthew 14:33 NKJV)

24 "He. . .owed him ____ thousand talents" (Matthew 18:24)

25 Pine tree fruit

27 "He commanded ____ be given her" (Matthew 14:9) (2 words)

28 "The captain. . .of Naphtali shall be ____" (Numbers 2:29)

29 "The armies. . .followed him. . .clothed in fine ____" (Revelation 19:14)

30 Protruding part of lower jaws

31 "He. . .turned back, and with a ____ voice glorified God" (Luke 17:15)

32 ONE DISCIPLE BEGAN ____ WALK ON THE ____ (Matthew 14:29) (2 words)

33 "And ____ and Gaha" (Joshua 18:24)

35 ONCE THE DISCIPLES WERE ON THE WATER, THE WIND DID ____ UP THE SEA (Matthew 14:24)

37 Make tidy

40 "Mine heritage is unto me ____ a lion in the ____" (Jeremiah 12:8) (2 words)

41 Energetic

43 "Let him labour, ____ with his hands" (Ephesians 4:28)

46 "WHEN THEY WERE COME INTO THE SHIP, THE WIND ____" (Matthew 14:32)

47 "Because he ____ set his love upon Me, therefore I will deliver him" (Psalm 91:14 NKJV)

48 Brew

50 THIS "ROCK" COULDN'T STAY AFLOAT

51 First European to round the Cape of Good Hope

52 "An half ____ of land, which a yoke of oxen might plow" (1 Samuel 14:14)

53 "The writing that was written. . .____, TEKEL, UPHARSIN" (Daniel 5:25)

54 "I am the true ____" (John 15:1)

55 Volcano

56 "I ____ where I sowed not" (Matthew 25:26)

57 "He who hurries his footsteps ____" (Proverbs 19:2 NASB)

60 Recent (prefix)

62 "Your adversaries shall not be able to gainsay ____ resist" (Luke 21:15)

299

HEALING A LEPER

LUKE 5:13

Jesus' healing touch often produced instantaneous results. Solve this drop two puzzle to discover what happened immediately after Jesus ministered to an outcast.

RADDLED	Combined	_____	1. ___ ___
TRAIPSE	Twins	_____	2. ___ ___
PEASANT	Claus	_____	3. ___ ___
DRABBLE	Tower city	_____	4. ___ ___
FERMION	Coal extractor	_____	5. ___ ___
SHORTLY	Fiery	_____	6. ___ ___
OVERLAY	Large basin	_____	7. ___ ___
MADDEST	In place	_____	8. ___ ___
EUCHRED	Restored	_____	9. ___ ___
PITYING	Knotting	_____	10. ___ ___
MACABRE	Hold steady	_____	11. ___ ___

___ ___ ___ ___ ___ ___ ___ ___ ___ ___ ___

___ ___ ___ ___ ___ ___ ___ ___ ___ ___ ___
1   2   3   4   5   6   7   8   9   10   11

THE LORD LEADS HIS PEOPLE

EXODUS 13:21

Twenty-four hours a day, God goes before us, leading the way. Work this puzzle to uncover the miracle of His guidance as the Israelites walked through the wilderness of life.

F	N	T	L	B	I	T	G	R	A	Y	O
N	P	D	I	E	L	F	H	A	N	E	T
H	R	M	W	P	B	L	O	N	Y	T	F
E	L	N	H	G	I	R	H	D	E		B
I	N	E	A	D	Y	O	D	A	R		T
T	E	A	O	L	E	T	L	I	D		W
O	H	T	M	A	O	Y	U	T	M		O
A	E	G		N	A	I	G	E	D		A
H		E		B	Y	G	A	H	T		I
Y		I		T	H	L	R	R	V		T
		E		C	L		O	D	F		
		A						O			
								I			

FEAR NOT

DEUTERONOMY 31:3, 6

The **LORD thy God**, he will go **over before thee**, and he will **destroy these nations** from before thee, and **thou shalt possess them**: and **Joshua**, he shall go over before thee, as the LORD **hath** said. . . . Be **strong** and of a **good courage**, <u>fear not</u>, **nor** be **afraid** of them: for the LORD thy God, he it is **that doth** go with thee; he **will** not **fail** thee, nor **forsake** thee.

```
C R S Y O R T S E D I A R F A
T H Y Z B D H A T O T R S S P
A N O I U S O V E L O B N E O
T E L G G S B T A E R O F E B
H W V O H E E H H R I T S H O
E E D V R E S K T T E U E T G
M K G O O D S E A I D V C A R
E L I A F L E N H S I N O Q D
I G H T R O S U T T R A J B Y
L R P H I U S R O Y U O V I C
P O E K T H O U J E S U F O T
S N Y B O N P C R H Y S I C W
R U E T G P M E U O L P R I T
O I L T O N R A E F H S L R F
B C E W T T Y W R A D L A I R
```

━━━━━━━ **MOSES HOLDS UP** ━━━━━━━

God assured victory to Israel as Moses stood on the hill and Joshua led the troops below. Solve the puzzle with Exodus 17 to find out how Israel won the battle—hands *up*!

Where the Israelites fought Amalek

___ ___ ___ ___ ___ ___ ___ ___
13   27   19   7   30   23   15   3

One man who held up Moses' hands

___ ___ ___ ___ ___
2   28   17   24   33

The other man who held up Moses' hands

___ ___ ___
21   5   12

During this battle, Moses sat on a ____

___ ___ ___ ___ ___
10   25   16   1   20

Israel was the ____ over Amalek

___ ___ ___ ___ ___ ___
22   32   8   29   11   4

Moses ____ in God's ways

___ ___ ___ ___ ___ ___
18   31   6   14   26   9

ACROSTIC
by Donna Maltese
(continued)

2-33-9   30-25   8-28-3-27   29-11   19-28-10-10,

18-7-20-1   3-24-10-27-10   7-20-6-23   2-33-9

18-7-20-1   7-20   6-20-29   23-16-18-1   21-32-10

7-2-33-9,   2-3-2-6-20-14   19-17-26-22-31-15-6-26-23.

Exodus 17:11

CROSSWORD
by Dorothy Pryse

THE HEALING OF THE BOY WITH SEIZURES

Jesus did some pretty amazing things while He was here on earth, and even though we no longer see Him, He continues to work wonders in our lives. As you solve this puzzle, let praise be upon your lips as you marvel at the mighty power of Jesus then, now, and forevermore.

They were all amazed at the mighty power of God. LUKE 9:43

ACROSS

1 "STRAIGHTWAY THE SPIRIT ____ HIM" (Mark 9:20)
5 "It hath no ____: the bud shall yield no meal" (Hosea 8:7)
10 "They ____ lifted up their eyes" (Matthew 17:8)
13 "O death, where is thy ____?" (1 Corinthians 15:55)
15 Muscular male (hyph.)
16 Wrath
17 Sailing (2 words)
18 Edible seaweed
19 Dream cycle (abbr.)
20 Wild barley
21 Naval rank (abbr.)
23 Poetry muse
25 Ballet movement
26 "She came. . .to hear the wisdom of ____" (Matthew 12:42)
28 IT WAS REBUKED BY JESUS (Mark 9:25)
31 "He ____ to have seen some miracle done by him" (Luke 23:8)
32 Flowering shrub
33 "He observed times, and ____ enchantments" (2 Chronicles 33:6)
34 Woman's undergarment (abbr.)
37 "If he's not an enemy, he's an ____" (Mark 9:39 MSG)
38 "What thinkest thou, ____?" (Matthew 17:25)
40 Nail
41 "She answered and said unto him, ____, Lord" (Mark 7:28)
42 Movie: Finding ____
43 "IF YOU HAVE ____. . .NOTHING WILL BE IMPOSSIBLE FOR YOU" (Matthew 17:20 NIV)
44 Echo sounder

45 WHEN THE BOY HAD SEIZURES, HIS MOUTH DID THIS (Luke 9:39)
46 "Gideon had threescore and ten sons of ____ begotten" (Judges 8:30) (2 words)
49 Pretty child
50 Native of the East
51 "IF YE HAVE FAITH AS A GRAIN OF MUSTARD ____" (Matthew 17:20)
52 Alphabet run following *L*
55 "If a man is lazy, the rafters ____" (Ecclesiastes 10:18 NIV)
56 Couch
59 "His hand took hold on ____ heel" (Genesis 25:26)
61 Beige
62 "Greet ye one another with ____ of charity" (1 Peter 5:14) (2 words)
63 BECAUSE OF THIS, THE DISCIPLES COULD NOT CURE THE BOY (Matthew 17:20)
64 South Sea (abbr.)
65 "____ reproved kings for their sakes" (1 Chronicles 16:21) (2 words)
66 "But the ____ took oil in their vessels" (Matthew 25:4)

DOWN

1 Russian monarch (var.)
2 Lawyer (abbr.)
3 "Sleep, and ____ night and day" (Mark 4:27)
4 Carbon compound (suffix)
5 "The Lord is thy ____ upon thy right hand" (Psalm 121:5)
6 "He aborts the schemes of. . .crooks, so that none of their plots come to ____" (Job 5:8 MSG)
7 Physicians organization (abbr.)
8 Criminal's rapid escape

9 THE BOY'S FATHER PRAYED AND _____ TO JESUS (Matthew 17:14)

10 "And _____ king of Tyre sent his servants unto Solomon" (1 Kings 5:1)

11 "ALL THINGS _____ POSSIBLE _____ HIM THAT BELIEVETH" (Mark 9:23)

12 ANOTHER NAME FOR THE ENTITY JESUS CAST OUT OF THE BOY

14 "We ate in Egypt. . . onions and _____" (Numbers 11:5 NIV)

22 Small island (Brit.)

24 "Thy _____ and thy staff" (Psalm 23:4)

25 SOME DEMONS CANNOT BE CAST OUT UNLESS YOU _____ AND FAST (Mark 9:29)

26 Passable (hyph.)

27 "I will _____ my mouth in parables" (Matthew 13:35)

28 "Some of them they shall _____ and persecute" (Luke 11:49)

29 "I will even make the _____ for fire great" (Ezekiel 24:9)

30 "They are free from the burdens. . .not plagued by human _____" (Psalm 73:5 NIV)

31 "You can afford to _____ an occasional fool who happens along" (2 Corinthians 11:19 MSG)

34 "Fill the waterpots with water. . .up to the _____" (John 2:7)

35 "And gather at a certain _____ every day" (Exodus 16:4)

36 Neurological disorder (abbr.)

38 "He. . .began to _____ them forth by two and two" (Mark 6:7)

39 "Utterance may be given. . .that _____ open my mouth" (Ephesians 6:19) (2 words)

40 "Jeroboam. . .served _____, and worshipped him" (1 Kings 16:31)

42 "They. . .grope in the _____ as in the night" (Job 5:14)

43 "Elijah took his mantle and _____ it together and struck the waters" (2 Kings 2:8 NASB)

44 Agency that supports mom-and-pop stores (abbr.)

45 "He saved them from the hand of the _____" (Psalm 106:10 NIV)

46 "Make _____, and get thee quickly out of Jerusalem" (Acts 22:18)

47 "My covenant will I establish with _____" (Genesis 17:21)

48 "Except ye see _____ and wonders, ye will not believe" (John 4:48)

49 "He saw _____ smoke rising from the land" (Genesis 19:28 NIV)

51 Waistband

52 Hawaiian island

53 Small protuberances

54 German river

57 Eisenhower's nickname

58 By way of

60 "Thou shalt not _____ thy vineyard with divers seeds" (Deuteronomy 22:9)

SPOTTY HEADLINE
by Sara Stoker

━━━ MISSIONARY MIRACLES ━━━

God gave His special servants special powers in Bible times. These spotty headlines describe three people who experienced the miraculous—for good or ill—in the early missionary era. Can you solve each one?

MAS●●VE EARTHQU●KE FREES ●ESSER-KNOWN MAN FROM PRI●ON

— — — — — —

A●OSTLE PA●L HEAL● ●EDR●DDEN FATHER OF IS●AND R●LER

— — — — — — —

FA●SE PROPH●T CUR●ED BY P●UL, ●EANDERS BLINDL●

— — — — — —

308

■ KNOWING YOUR BIBLE ■

Our end will be but a beginning.

1. ANRE	7. NDOEIRSI
2. EGNER	8. NCOIANT
3. EIGES	9. RSECATT
4. SRRUEL	10. TPIY
5. SGERLID	11. UHSOE
6. ESRITS	12. NAEHEHT

What is it that all believers will experience?

1. _ _ _ O

2. _ _ O _ _

3. O _ _ _ _

4. _ O _ _ _ _

5. _ _ O _ _ _ _

6. _ _ _ _ _ O

7. _ O _ _ _ _ _ _

8. O _ _ _ _ _ _

9. _ _ _ _ O _ _

10. _ O _ _

11. _ O _ _ _

12. _ _ _ _ _ _ O

Answer: _ _ _ _ _ _ _ _ _ _ _ _ _

WORD SEARCH
by David Austin

PASSOVER

AARON
BLOOD
BREAD
DELIVERED
DESTROY
DESTROYER
EGYPT
EXECUTE
FEAST
FIRSTBORN
GENERATIONS
HOUSES

JUDGMENT
MEMORIAL
MOSES
OBSERVE
ORDINANCE
OVER
PASS
PHARAOH
PLAGUE
SEVEN DAYS
SMITE
UNLEAVENED

```
S  F  P  H  A  R  A  O  H  T  U  H  E  N  K
E  G  Y  P  T  M  B  A  M  R  T  L  E  Y  E
V  L  W  G  K  S  E  E  R  U  E  G  M  H  O
E  J  U  Q  E  J  F  M  N  O  B  Z  O  F  O
N  Q  A  R  V  N  D  L  O  Z  N  J  S  V  F
D  R  V  K  D  D  E  S  T  R  O  Y  E  R  T
A  E  O  B  T  A  L  R  E  U  I  R  S  O  O
Y  F  D  B  V  P  I  I  A  S  Q  A  R  B  Q
S  V  E  E  T  A  V  F  Y  T  U  D  L  R  X
A  W  N  A  M  S  E  O  O  H  I  O  M  E  J
L  E  M  L  S  S  R  V  V  N  O  O  H  A  J
D  P  S  M  I  T  E  I  A  D  L  U  N  D  I
T  X  M  Q  S  K  D  N  F  Q  P  P  R  S  S
Q  W  M  E  X  E  C  U  T  E  U  G  A  L  P
J  U  D  G  M  E  N  T  P  N  V  B  T  B  G
```

ACROSTIC
by Donna Maltese

— THE ROCK THAT FLOATS —

Solve this acrostic to discover how keeping our eyes on Jesus can buoy ourselves and our faith.

Another name for Peter (Matthew 10:12)

$\overline{}$ $\overline{}$ $\overline{}$ $\overline{}$ $\overline{}$
5 21 1 18 11

A small body of water

$\overline{}$ $\overline{}$ $\overline{}$ $\overline{}$
24 7 30 9

Those who power a boat

$\overline{}$ $\overline{}$ $\overline{}$ $\overline{}$ $\overline{}$ $\overline{}$
10 28 31 14 25 2

"O thou of little ____" (Matthew 14:31)

$\overline{}$ $\overline{}$ $\overline{}$ $\overline{}$ $\overline{}$
16 3 20 27 12

Jesus practiced what He ____

$\overline{}$ $\overline{}$ $\overline{}$ $\overline{}$ $\overline{}$ $\overline{}$ $\overline{}$ $\overline{}$
13 33 26 32 29 22 17 6

When Peter began to sink, Jesus ____ his faith

$\overline{}$ $\overline{}$ $\overline{}$ $\overline{}$ $\overline{}$ $\overline{}$
8 23 19 15 4 34

7-11-6   12-9   5-3-21-19,   29-18-1-14.   32-11-6

31-12-4-11   13-26-27-26-10   31-7-2   29-18-1-17

19-28-31-11   28-23-27   28-16   27-12-9   5-12-20-13,

12-14   31-3-24-30-14-6   28-11   27-22-9   31-32-27-4-34,

27-18   15-18   27-18   8-26-2-23-2.

MATTHEW 14:29

Answers

DROP TWOS

BORN AGAIN
BLEAT, SATIN, HATED, PLANT, ANGLE, GAILY, ARCED, PLATE, BOLES, BELLY, SHAVE, ADMIT
"Nicodemus, a ruler of the Jews." John 3:1

SOWING SEEDS
WIDER, ACTED, BLAND, GRAIN, ARDOR, REMIT, CANAL, DRAWN, DRONE, VALET, EIGHT, CRATE
"When he sowed, some seeds fell." Matthew 13:4

WATER PROVIDED
CLEAN, MIDST, STAIN, CREAK, HOLEY, ROBES, NAMED, WANDS, BLAME, RAZED, TAINT, TRITE, TRICE
"Smite the rock, people may drink." See Exodus 17:6

PETER JAILED
GRANT, SCOUT, FIERY, ROVES, ODDER, DOWRY, SPADE, SHARP, STEIN, PRATE, FLOOR
"So Peter was kept in prison." See Acts 12:5

THE BIRTH OF JESUS
TRAIL, PENAL, PARTS, RIDER, BASIC, WAGED, ETHER, GREED, ALONE, CORAL, CAIRN, TARNS, EIGHT
"Found the babe lying in a manger." See Luke 2:16

PAUL'S JOURNEYS
DRAIN, USING, TIMED, NAKED, SALES, ZONED, LATER, ROUGH, DINED, HIKED, PANES, AMBLE, SHEER
"The ship was caught up into wind." See Acts 27:15

FROM THE ROOF
ELITE, MINUS, SKIED, FAIRY, PAPER, LOCAL, LATIN, GLOBE, LOBES, FILES, ROUND, GRAND
"Son, thy sins be forgiven thee." Mark 2:5

MEALTIME MIRACLE
GLAND, TRACE, SLIMS, BRAIN, SLING, LUMPY, STINT, PALED, PETAL, SLEDS, GLEAN
"Loaves were five thousand." See Mark 6:44

AN EVIL SPIRIT
HEARD, DROLL, MEDIC, THERE, RAVED, TRAIN, CREED, SCONE, SKIED, TREND, AURAL
"Man with an unclean spirit." Mark 5:2

A CRIPPLED WOMAN
THING, ROPER, DOILY, MOREL, MOOSE, EXTRA, ANTSY, POSSE, DOUSE, TAPED, PARKA, RANGE, LEGAL
"Woman had a spirit of infirmity." See Luke 13:11

HEALING A LEPER
ADDED, PAIRS, SANTA, BABEL, MINER, HOTLY, LAVER, STEAD, CURED, TYING, BRACE
"Leprosy departed from him." Luke 5:13

ACROSTICS

ASP FOR HEALING
FIERY, COMPLAINED, VENOMOUS, TYPE, PERISH, BETWEEN
"And Moses made a serpent of brass, and put it upon a pole, and it came to pass, that if a serpent had bitten any man, when he beheld the serpent of brass, he lived." Numbers 21:9

SPINNING WHEELS
VISION, BABYLON, PROPHET, FACES, WINGS, DUMB
"When the living creatures went, the wheels went by them: and when the living creatures were lifted up from the earth, the wheels were lifted up." Ezekiel 1:19

MISCOMMUNICATION
TOGETHER, HUMANS, BUILD, TONGUE, SCATTER, FOIL
"Therefore is the name of it called Babel; because the LORD did there confound the language of all the earth." Genesis 11:9

NAAMAN'S LUCKY 7
CAPTAIN, LEPROSY, ELISHA, JEW, MAID, FORGIVENESS
"Then went he down, and dipped himself seven times in Jordan, according to the saying of the man of God." 2 Kings 5:14

A GATED COMMUNITY
APOSTLES, VISION, GARNISHED, CHALCEDONY, FAITHFUL, TWELVE
"The twelve gates were twelve pearls: every several gate was of one pearl: and the street of the city was pure gold, as it were transparent glass." Revelation 21:21

A STORY, A STORY
VASHTI, CITIES OF REFUGE, NAZARITE, MEPHIBOSHETH, FIRSTBORN, WILDERNESS
"For whatsoever things were written aforetime were written for our learning, that we through patience and comfort of the scriptures might have hope." Romans 15:4

A SIGN OF THINGS TO COME
KING, AMOZ, ASSYRIA, RECOVERED, HELP, WATERCOURSE
"In those days Hezekiah was sick to the death, and prayed unto the LORD: and he spake unto him, and he gave him a sign." 2 Chronicles 32:24

A HOT TOPIC
PARABLES, NETHERWORLD, CRUMB, TESTIFY, ZERO, GRIEVE
"Father Abraham, have mercy on me, and send Lazarus, that he may dip the tip of his finger in water, and cool my tongue." Luke 16:24

REDEEMING LOVE
MAIZE, HANDFUL, GATHER, BARLEY, CLAN, LABORS
"Said Boaz unto Ruth, Hearest thou not, my daughter? Go not to glean in another field, neither go from hence, but abide here fast by my maidens." Ruth 2:8

A BEWITCHING TALE
PHILIP, WITCH, CRAFT, DEMONS, BEMUSE, SLY
"There was a certain man, called Simon, which beforetime in the same city used sorcery, and bewitched the people of Samaria." Acts 8:9

ONE GREAT CATCH
TIBERIAS, FISHERMEN, DIRECTION, PETER, CAUGHT, WHOLLY
"Cast the net on the right side of the ship, and ye shall find. They cast therefore, and now they were not able to draw it for the multitude of fishes." John 21:6

TALK ABOUT JOB LOSS!
SERVANT, HEDGE, MISFORTUNE, BLEAK, WAY, CURSED
"Naked came I out of my mother's womb, and naked shall I return thither: the LORD gave, and the LORD hath taken away; blessed be the name of the LORD." Job 1:21

A HAIR-RAZING TALE
PHILISTINES, WEB, MANOAH, FIGURE, DAILY, CUT
"Delilah said to Samson, Tell me, I pray thee, wherein thy great strength lieth, and wherewith thou mightest be bound to afflict thee." Judges 16:6

ONE, TWO, THREE, TESTING

VALOUR, MIDIANITES, WOOLY, NAPHTALI, CONFIRMING, BAAL

"Let me prove, I pray thee, but this once with the fleece; let it now be dry only upon the fleece, and upon all the ground let there be dew." Judges 6:39

MAKING WAVES

SHIP, WATER, DOUBT, CALAMITY, KNOWLEDGE, FAITH

"And when the disciples saw him walking on the sea, they were troubled, saying, It is a spirit; and they cried out for fear." Matthew 14:26

IT'S A FAMILY AFFAIR

KING DAVID, COUSIN, WAX, FATHER, LYING, MOROSE

"Amnon was so vexed, that he fell sick for his sister Tamar; for she was a virgin; and Amnon thought it hard for him to do anything to her." 2 Samuel 13:2

TROUBLED WATERS

SABBATH, WHOLE, PASSOVER, LAME, DURATION, LIE

"The impotent man answered him, Sir, I have no man, when the water is troubled, to put me into the pool." John 5:7

WAKING THE DEAD

BETHANY, AMAZE, DIDYMUS, GLORIFIED, WEPT, STINK

"These things said he: and after that he saith unto them, Our friend Lazarus sleepeth; but I go, that I may awake him out of sleep." John 11:11

A BUDDING ENTERPRISE

TWELVE, BROTHER, MURMURING, STAVE, FOUND, HOLY

"Behold, the rod of Aaron for the house of Levi was budded, and brought forth buds, and bloomed blossoms, and yielded almonds." Numbers 17:8

BIRD FOOD

BROOK, TISHBITE, GILEAD, DROUGHT, FAMINE, VAIN

"And the ravens brought him bread and flesh in the morning, and bread and flesh in the evening; and he drank of the brook."
1 Kings 17:6

SAMSON'S BARE HANDS
POWERFUL, COURAGE, VINEYARD, STRENGTH, MANE, KILL
"The Spirit of the LORD came mightily upon him, and he rent him as he would have rent a kid, and he had nothing in his hand."
Judges 14:6

HAND IT TO MOSES
MOSES, ISRAEL, BUSH, DOUBT, POWER, SKIN
"He put his hand into his bosom: and when he took it out, behold, his hand was leprous as snow." Exodus 4:6

HAIL TO THE CONFEDERATED KINGS
LEADER, ADONIZEDEK, COMPANY, FIGHT, VICTORIOUS, SWORD
"The LORD cast down great stones from heaven upon them unto Azekah, and they died." Joshua 10:11

ABRAHAM'S OFFERING GETS FIRED
ABRAHAM, SACRIFICE, PROMISE, TURTLEDOVE, PIGEON, KNEW
"When the sun went down, and it was dark, behold a smoking furnace, and a burning lamp that passed between those pieces." Genesis 15:17

MADE IN THE SHADE
FOLLOWER, HEALING, LUKE, OVERCAME, APOSTLES, BEYOND
"They brought forth the sick into the streets, and laid them on beds and couches, that at the least the shadow of Peter passing by might overshadow some." Acts 5:15

JONAH'S ROTTEN GOURD
EXPIRED, PROPHET, MISSION, WRATH, ANGRY, SUN
"God prepared a worm when the morning rose the next day, and it smote the gourd that it withered." Jonah 4:7

HEAVENLY SWEETENER
WILDERNESS, MARAH, MOSES, THIRST, SHUR, SWITCH
"He cried unto the LORD; and the LORD shewed him a tree, which when he had cast into the waters, the waters were made sweet." Exodus 15:25

A STICKY SNAKE
FAITH, PHARAOH, COURAGE, BOLDNESS, ROD, MOSES
"He said, Cast it on the ground. And he cast it on the ground, and it became a serpent; and Moses fled from before it." Exodus 4:3

A MAJOR SINKHOLE
WANDERED, PRIESTHOOD, AARON, GROUND, AMOK, LORD
"The earth opened her mouth, and swallowed them up, and their houses, and all the men that appertained unto Korah, and all their goods." Numbers 16:32

JEHOVAH VS. THE ASSYRIANS
SWORD, SLAUGHTERED, PRAYED, CORPSES, MORNING, DEFENSE
"And it came to pass that night, that the angel of the LORD went out, and smote in the camp of the Assyrians." 2 Kings 19:35

AN OPEN WOMB
WIVES, LABAN, RACHEL, MANDRAKES, PREGNANT, LABOR
"And God remembered Rachel, and God hearkened to her, and opened her womb. And she conceived, and bare a son." Genesis 30:22–23

A DISCIPLE GETS CARRIED AWAY
ETHIOPIA, DISCIPLE, FOUND, SACRAMENT, HOLY GHOST, EMPOWERED
"When they were come up out of the water, the Spirit of the Lord caught away Philip, that the eunuch saw him no more." Acts 8:39

A LOT OF SALT FOR A WIFE
NEPHEW, BRIMSTONE, RESCUED, SAKE, PLAIN, FATE
"But his wife looked back from behind him, and she became a pillar of salt." Genesis 19:26

SAMSON THIRSTS NO MORE
SAMSON, DELILAH, REVIVE, POCKET, WATER, JUDGES
"God clave an hollow place that was in the jaw, and there came water thereout; and when he had drunk, his spirit came again." Judges 15:19

MOSES HOLDS UP
REPHIDIM, AARON, HUR, STONE, VICTOR, WALKED

"And it came to pass, when Moses held up his hand, that Israel prevailed: and when he let down his hand, Amalek prevailed." Exodus 17:11

THE ROCK THAT FLOATS
SIMON, LAKE, ROWERS, FAITH, PREACHED, JUDGED

"And he said, Come. And when Peter was come down out of the ship, he walked on the water, to go to Jesus." Matthew 14:29

WORD SEARCHES

Samson Defeats the Philistines

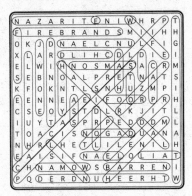

Ladder to Heaven

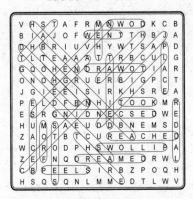

The Ark of the Covenant

Stephen's Witness

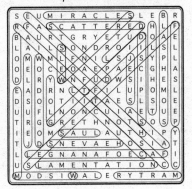

God Is Faithful in
the Old Testament

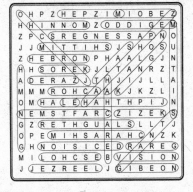

God Is Faithful in
the New Testament

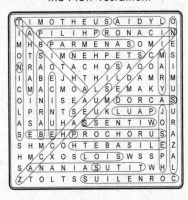

Joseph and Mary

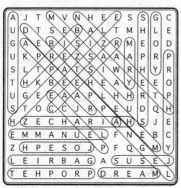

Nathan's Parable

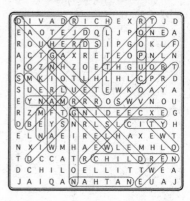

The Voyage Begins

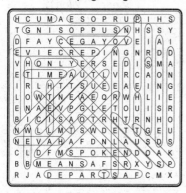

No Longer Doubting

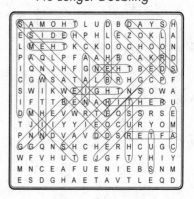

Sodom and Gomorrah

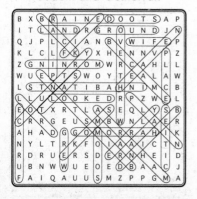

The Promised Land

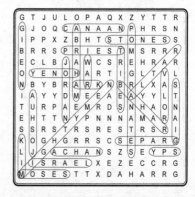

The Betrayer

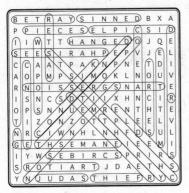

Aaron's Golden Calf

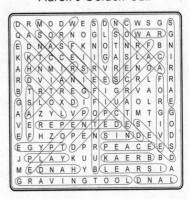

Army of One

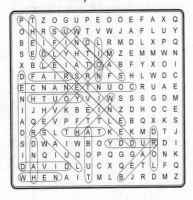

Shipwrecked

Bringing Up the Axe

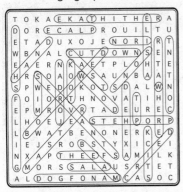

Ark of Bulrushes

Dagon's Defeat

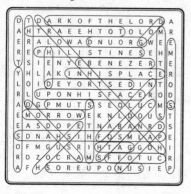

A Woman from Canaan

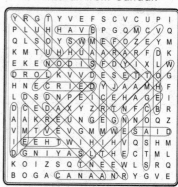

Prison Song

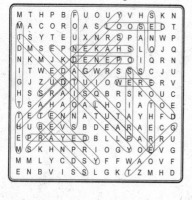

Prayer for Peter in Prison

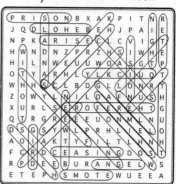

Day versus Night

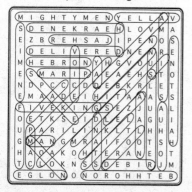

Blind Man at Jericho

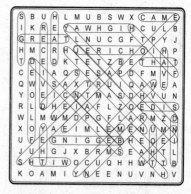

One Gave Glory to God

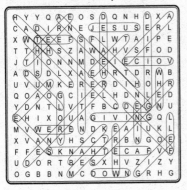

Miracles Abound

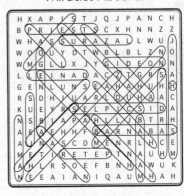

Full of Faith

Elijah and Baal

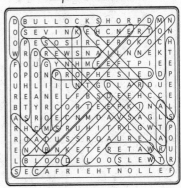

The Birth of Jesus

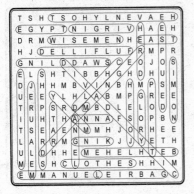

A Woman of Good Works

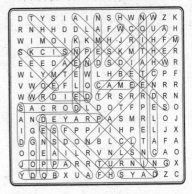

No Laughing Matter

The Raising of Lazarus

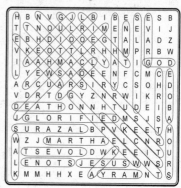

The Fish's Shekel

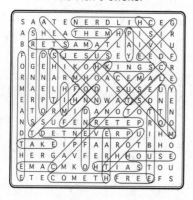

Four Men Walking

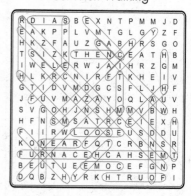

Fear Not

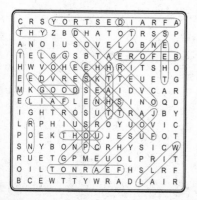

Passover

CRYPTOSCRIPTURES

IN THE DAYS OF NOAH

"And God said unto Noah, The end of all flesh is come before me; for the earth is filled with violence through them; and, behold, I will destroy them with the earth." Genesis 6:13

"And of every living thing of all flesh, two of every sort shalt thou bring into the ark, to keep them alive with thee; they shall be male and female." Genesis 6:19

BEFORE THE THRONE

"In the year that king Uzziah died I saw also the LORD sitting upon a throne, high and lifted up, and his train filled the temple." Isaiah 6:1

"Then said I, Woe is me! for I am undone; because I am a man of unclean lips, and I dwell in the midst of a people of unclean lips: for mine eyes have seen the King, the LORD of hosts." Isaiah 6:5

THE PROPHET AND THE HARLOT

"And the LORD said to Hosea, Go, take unto thee a wife of whoredoms and children of whoredoms: for the land hath committed great whoredom, departing from the LORD." Hosea 1:2

"So he went and took Gomer the daughter of Diblaim; which conceived, and bare him a son. And the LORD said unto him, Call his name Jezreel." Hosea 1:3–4

TO SHOW THE WAY

"And the LORD went before them by day in a pillar of a cloud, to lead them the way; and by night in a pillar of fire, to give them light; to go by day and night." Exodus 13:21

"And she shall bring forth a son, and thou shalt call his name JESUS: for he shall save his people from their sins." Matthew 1:21

ZECHARIAH'S SEVENTH VISION
"And I turned, and lifted up mine eyes, and looked, and, behold, there came four chariots out from between two mountains; and the mountains were mountains of brass." Zechariah 6:1

"And the angel answered and said unto me, These are the four spirits of the heavens, which go forth from standing before the LORD of all the earth." Zechariah 6:5

THE FINAL MOMENTS
"And Pilate wrote a title, and put it on the cross. And the writing was, JESUS OF NAZARETH THE KING OF THE JEWS." John 19:19

"And when Jesus had cried with a loud voice, he said, Father, into thy hands I commend my spirit: and having said thus, he gave up the ghost." Luke 23:46

A HIGHER POWER
"So Christ was once offered to bear the sins of many; and unto them that look for him shall he appear the second time without sin unto salvation." Hebrews 9:28

"And Jesus looking upon them saith, With men it is impossible, but not with God: for with God all things are possible." Mark 10:27

MIRACLES OF FAITH
"The centurion answered and said, Lord, I am not worthy that thou shouldest come under my roof: but speak the word only, and my servant shall be healed." Matthew 8:8

"The ruler of the feast had tasted the water that was made wine, and knew not whence it was." John 2:9

UNDENIABLE MIRACLES
"And when Paul had gathered a bundle of sticks, and laid them on the fire, there came a viper out of the heat, and fastened on his hand. . . . And he shook off the beast into the fire, and felt no harm." Acts 28:3, 5

"And when Aaron and all the children of Israel saw Moses, behold, the skin of his face shone; and they were afraid to come nigh him." Exodus 34:30

MIRACLES IN JESUS' NAME
"Indeed a notable miracle hath been done by them is manifest to all them that dwell in Jerusalem; and we cannot deny it." Acts 4:16

"But Jesus said, Forbid him not: for there is no man which shall do a miracle in my name, that can lightly speak evil of me." Mark 9:39

GIVEN A SIGN
"And it came to pass, as he interpreted to us, so it was; me he restored unto mine office, and him he hanged." Genesis 41:13

"And Hezekiah answered, It is a light thing for the shadow to go down ten degrees: nay, but let the shadow return backward ten degrees." 2 Kings 20:10

ALL THINGS BRIGHT AND BEAUTIFUL
"And God said, Let there be light: and there was light." Genesis 1:3

"He hath made the earth by his power, he hath established the world by his wisdom, and hath stretched out the heavens by his discretion." Jeremiah 10:12

SUDOKU

Ehud's Death

	A	B	C	D	E	F	G	H	I
1	S	E	D	A	T	C	L	O	F
2	C	T	O	L	S	F	D	E	A
3	L	A	F	O	E	D	S	C	T
4	A	S	T	F	L	O	E	D	C
5	O	F	E	C	D	T	A	S	L
6	D	C	L	S	A	E	T	F	O
7	E	D	C	T	F	L	O	A	S
8	F	L	A	D	O	S	C	T	E
9	T	O	S	E	C	A	F	L	D

FAT CLOSED

Jesus' Triumphal Entry

	A	B	C	D	E	F	G	H	I
1	O	E	T	D	S	N	A	K	Y
2	K	S	D	Y	A	O	N	T	E
3	Y	N	A	K	T	E	O	S	D
4	E	A	Y	T	D	S	K	O	N
5	S	T	N	E	O	K	Y	D	A
6	D	O	K	A	N	Y	S	E	T
7	A	D	S	N	K	T	E	Y	O
8	N	Y	O	S	E	D	T	A	K
9	T	K	E	O	Y	A	D	N	S

SAT/DONKEY

The Philistines and the Ark

	A	B	C	D	E	F	G	H	I
1	T	H	E	L	O	W		I	N	G
2	I	L	O	E	N	G	W	H	T
3	N	W	G	I	H	T	L	O	E
4	H	I	N	W	E	O	T	G	L
5	W	E	T	H	G	L	O	I	N
6	G	O	L	N	T	I	H	E	W
7	L	G	I	O	W	N	E	T	H
8	E	N	W	T	I	H	G	L	O
9	O	T	H	G	L	E	N	W	I

THE LOWING

334

Jezebel's Death

	A	B	C	D	E	F	G	H	I
1	D	I	W	T	R	S	O	A	H
2	H	S	T	A	I	O	W	D	R
3	A	R	O	W	H	D	T	S	I
4	R	W	D	O	A	I	H	T	S
5	O	T	H	R	S	W	D	I	A
6	S	A	I	D	T	H	R	O	W
7	I	H	R	S	D	T	A	W	O
8	W	D	S	H	O	A	I	R	T
9	T	O	A	I	W	R	S	H	D

SAID THROW

Preparing Moses

	A	B	C	D	E	F	G	H	I
1	O	C	R	D	G	A	T	U	H
2	G	A	H	T	C	U	D	O	R
3	D	U	T	O	H	R	G	A	C
4	U	G	D	C	R	O	H	T	A
5	R	H	C	A	D	T	U	G	O
6	A	T	O	H	U	G	R	C	D
7	T	R	A	U	H	O	C	D	G
8	C	O	G	R	T	D	A	H	U
9	H	D	U	G	A	C	O	R	T

CAUGHT/ROD

The Philistines and God's Judgment

	A	B	C	D	E	F	G	H	I
1	H	O	N	T	R	G	K	A	E
2	R	K	E	A	O	N	T	G	H
3	G	A	T	H	E	K	R	O	N
4	O	R	G	N	T	H	A	E	K
5	E	H	A	G	K	O	N	R	T
6	T	N	K	R	A	E	G	H	O
7	K	T	H	E	G	A	O	N	R
8	N	G	O	K	H	R	E	T	A
9	A	E	R	O	N	T	H	K	G

GATH/EKRON

A Stew Renewed

	A	B	C	D	E	F	G	H	I
1	M	E	R	I	L	G	A	B	N
2	L	A	B	R	M	N	I	G	E
3	G	I	N	B	A	E	L	M	R
4	B	R	I	N	G	M	E	A	L
5	N	M	E	L	R	A	B	I	G
6	A	L	G	E	I	B	R	N	M
7	E	G	M	A	B	L	N	R	I
8	R	N	A	G	E	I	M	L	B
9	I	B	L	M	N	R	G	E	A

BRING MEAL

Miracle Child

	A	B	C	D	E	F	G	H	I
1	H	M	A	I	D	W	R	C	L
2	D	I	W	R	L	C	M	H	A
3	C	R	L	A	M	H	W	I	D
4	W	H	D	C	R	A	I	L	M
5	I	C	M	W	H	L	A	D	R
6	L	A	R	M	I	D	H	W	C
7	M	L	I	H	C	R	D	A	W
8	A	D	H	L	W	M	C	R	I
9	R	W	C	D	A	I	L	M	H

CHILD/WARM

Battle of the Gods

	A	B	C	D	E	F	G	H	I
1	L	H	A	S	M	B	O	P	T
2	S	M	P	L	O	T	B	A	H
3	B	O	T	H	P	A	L	M	S
4	H	A	O	P	B	L	T	S	M
5	M	P	B	T	H	S	A	O	L
6	T	S	L	O	A	M	P	H	B
7	O	B	S	A	L	H	M	T	P
8	P	L	H	M	T	O	S	B	A
9	A	T	M	B	S	P	H	L	O

BOTH/PALMS

Water Purifier

	A	B	C	D	E	F	G	H	I
1	H	L	I	O	S	T	A	R	D
2	O	R	T	D	A	H	S	I	L
3	A	S	D	L	I	R	H	T	O
4	I	H	A	S	T	O	L	D	R
5	S	T	L	R	H	D	I	O	A
6	R	D	O	I	L	A	T	S	H
7	L	A	R	T	O	I	D	H	S
8	D	I	H	A	R	S	O	L	T
9	T	O	S	H	D	L	R	A	I

SAITH/LORD

Breaking the Law—of Physics

	A	B	C	D	E	F	G	H	I
1	D	O	W	N	S	T	I	C	K
2	K	I	S	D	W	C	T	O	N
3	C	T	N	O	I	K	S	W	D
4	O	W	K	T	N	I	D	S	C
5	N	C	D	S	O	W	K	T	I
6	T	S	I	K	C	D	O	N	W
7	W	N	T	I	D	S	C	K	O
8	S	D	O	C	K	N	W	I	T
9	I	K	C	W	T	O	N	D	S

DOWN/STICK

The Fifth Plague

	A	B	C	D	E	F	G	H	I
1	L	S	C	E	I	O	K	T	V
2	I	E	T	V	K	L	C	O	S
3	V	K	O	C	S	T	E	I	L
4	E	L	V	K	O	I	T	S	C
5	S	O	I	T	C	V	L	K	E
6	T	C	K	L	E	S	I	V	O
7	O	T	L	I	V	E	S	C	K
8	C	I	S	O	L	K	V	E	T
9	K	V	E	S	T	C	O	L	I

LIVESTOCK

CROSSWORDS

Climbing the Walls

F	L	O	G		A	R	A	S	H		L	E	B	O
L	I	N	E		S	O	M	M	E		A	N	E	W
U	P	O	N	T	H	E	T	O	W	N	W	A	L	L
		T	O	E		O	N	E		M	I	E		
S	A	W	I	N		I	S	T		T	R	E	A	T
A	H	O	L	E	I	N	T	H	E	W	A	L	L	
L	A	K	E		D	O	A		G	A	Y			
A	B	E		C	A	R	N	I	E	S		O	W	L
	A	A	H		D	D	S		A	S	E	A		
W	A	L	L	O	F	B	E	T	H	S	H	A	N	
C	H	I	L	I		L	Y	S		A	H	A	R	D
O	O	S		C	I	A		E	T	A				
W	A	L	L	O	F	T	H	E	T	E	M	P	L	E
A	R	E	A		A	L	E	R	T		E	L	E	V
T	E	S	S		S	Y	E	N	E		D	O	T	E

Beauty Contest

J	E	W	S		F	O	A	L	S		P	A	M
I	R	A	N		R	A	T	I	O		E	L	S	E
F	A	R	O		A	R	O	M	A		M	A	I	D
			B	P	M		M	O	R	D	E	C	A	I
A	G	O		H	E	M				A	R	E	N	A
B	E	N	A	D	R	Y	L		D	R	Y	S		
B	A	C	H			R	U	P	E	E				
A	R	E	A		A	R	R	O	W		C	R	O	P
			N	I	H	I	L			P	U	R	E	
	E	V	I	L		D	I	S	E	A	S	E	S	
A	R	S	O	N				O	I	L		E	S	T
B	E	T	T	E	R	E	D		N	F				
A	C	H	E		A	D	O	R	E		O	R	A	L
S	U	E	D		R	E	N	E	W		V	O	L	T
E	R	R			E	N	E	M	Y		E	D	A	M

Nations in the Promised Land

J	U	S	T		N	A	H	U	M		S	A	T	A
A	R	A	B		I	R	A	T	E		O	M	E	R
C	A	N	A	A	N	I	T	E	S		L	O	S	T
O	N	E		D	E	S		H	E	A	R	T	S	
B	I	L	L	S		E	G	G		M	C	I		
S	A	Y	S		G	N	A	R		B	E	T	T	A
			T	O	R		L	I	M	O		E	O	N
H	U	H		H	I	V	I	T	E	S		S	O	D
I	S	I		I	D	O	L		A	S	H			
M	E	T	T	O		L	E	N	T		A	R	F	S
		T	W	A		T	E	A		A	M	E	R	E
A	L	I	E	N	S			T	E	D		S	I	N
D	A	T	E		P	E	R	I	Z	Z	I	T	E	S
A	C	E	D		A	D	O	O	R		G	E	N	E
M	E	S	S		T	O	W	N	A		O	D	D	S

Characters of Parables and Stories

C	L	A	S	P		W	A	R	E		C	R	A	G
R	I	G	O	R		A	T	O	M		H	E	R	R
A	M	I	N	O		G	O	B	I		R	A	C	E
M	A	N		D	E	E	P		T	R	O	P	H	Y
			P	I	G	S			T	O	M			
V	I	R	A	G	O		S	T	E	W	A	R	D	
A	C	U	R	A		P	O	O	R		H	A	G	
L	I	B	E	L		T	U	G		A	M	I	G	O
E	N	E			R	A	T	S		T	E	N	O	N
G	N	O	M	I	S	H		S	T	R	O	N	G	
			W	A	C		T	R	U	E				
S	T	A	N	C	H		C	H	I	N		M	C	G
H	O	W	E		M	A	L	I		I	D	A	H	O
A	G	A	R		A	K	I	N		N	A	M	E	D
W	A	Y	S		N	A	P	E		G	N	A	W	S

Windows of Opportunity

R	C	A		R	E	V		O	K	A		M	A	D
A	A	R		A	V	I	O	N	I	C		O	F	A
T	I	E		J	E	Z	R	E	E	L		N	O	V
O	R	N	O		O	S	A	V	E		T	R	I	
N	O	A	H	S	A	R	K		A	A	H	E	D	
			M	E	L			M	T	N	S			
A	S	A		E	L	A	T	E	R		T	I	L	E
T	O	W	A	R	D	J	E	R	U	S	A	L	E	M
E	X	E	C		I	A	T	E	I	T		L	I	T
		N	E	E	R		S	O	N					
T	O	W	E	L		D	A	M	A	S	C	U	S	
R	U	E		I	Z	A	R	S		F	A	T	E	
O	T	S		J	E	R	I	C	H	O		L	I	E
A	T	A		A	R	E	P	O	O	R		E	L	A
S	O	W		H	I	D		T	E	A		B	E	N

Animal Stories

M	A	R	C		A	L	U	L	A		S	U	B
A	G	U	A		P	I	P	E	R		B	O	L	O
N	O	E	L		O	Z	O	N	E		I	N	T	O
			F	M	G		N	O	A	H	S	A	R	K
B	O	N		P	E	A				I	O	T	A	S
A	P	O	T	H	E	G	M		E	T	N	A		
B	E	A	U			G	O	A	T	S				
A	C	H	E		G	R	A	T	A		S	W	A	Y
			L	I	O	N	S			O	H	I	O	
	R	A	I	N		S	E	C	E	D	I	N	G	
A	L	A	M	O				A	U	G		P	T	A
D	E	M	A	N	D	E	D		T	O	N			
O	A	R	S		O	D	O	R	S		E	R	M	A
B	R	O	S		G	I	V	E		B	O	A	R	
E	N	D		S	T	E	P	S		E	C	K		

338

Three Monetary Lessons

```
AROMA  GPA  ABBA
LUZON  RAW  CLOD
ALOSTCOINFOUND
KENT  RAN  ARENA
ERE  BEN  OWN
   TEE  BAN  TAJ
BATHE  GET  ARLO
ACOININTHEFISH
DENS  HAS  DAGON
ESE  HOT  FOR
   TOP  RAM  SPA
STRIP  SON  MAIN
THEWIDOWSMITES
AREA  OWE  AMOCO
BUDS  END  LINEN
```

Good Guys and Villains

```
CARL  CROP  HARP
ALOE  SWAMI  AGUE
LAMA  NASAL  TD
FRESCO  PHARAOH
   HOWL  ATOM
FAO  HEAD  EDICT
LTD  EDGAR  ROBE
ALIGN  EVE  HEROD
PAUL  RIFLE  NNE
SMIRK  DEAN  YEN
   MIND  RIND
SAPPORO  CAESAR
GALS  COPRA  MACE
EASE  KNEEL  OGLE
TROD  SEND  SAUL
```

Alpha-Numeric Mix-up

```
ASA  SPIN  SNACKS
NAN  AURA  CABANA
DIN  SPUR  EDISON
3DAYSAND3NIGHTS
   EYE  OER
DAMP  SIR  ITIS
ISA  THOR  SORROW
ANDTHESE3AREONE
NEARER  NOTE  VIE
ARMY  TEN  HEAT
   USA  HOE
3MEASURESOFMEAL
MILLER  LAST  ABA
ERMINE  ALEE  SLY
NESTOR  MEAN  YES
```

On Trial

```
SNOBS  JOSE  BALD
CARAT  EBON  EPEE
APERY  SIDE  RAVE
MESA  CUE  MARRED
   BIAS  PILATE
WOBBLY  SEEP
AURAL  HARSH  EHF
CROSS  AGO  A  LIE
SSW  GNAT  BASTE
   DUDS  DETEST
ABS  IS  CITE
UPLIFT  DAM  LOSS
SHAM  ACAD  AISLE
DIDO  RULE  BELOW
ADEN  SPIT  CROWN
```

Biblical Big Boys

```
GUAM  SALEM  BARE
AGRA  OCALA  ENOS
THEREWEREGIANTS
   ABET  MORT
NET  BRIM  GALORE
ALOG  CEO  EREI
MEREST  SHEA  ASO
GOLIATHOFGATH
WAN  PROA  TENORS
ANTS  PCF  DREI
STOWED  HULA  YDS
   AREA  LESS
THELANDOFGIANTS
HAVE  TENIA  NOWA
EYES  SNELL  DROP
```

A Double Portion

```
CREAM  FMG  ESAU
HALSA  AIL  ISLES
ICIER  UNO  STARE
DEJA  ELISHA  MOD
FRA  CST  SEAM
   SHARP  ALCAIDE
BAN  ARM  NOEL
JACOB  STY  STUCK
AGAR  OLE  ALL
POTTAGE  POETS
SIRE  SSW  APT
CAW  DEPUTE  BRIE
OCHRE  ESE  TETRA
BREAD  REV  STAIR
BEND  SSE  PARTY
```

Sowing the Word

Overcomers

A Snake in the Grass

Stories with a Purpose

Bethlehem's Visitors

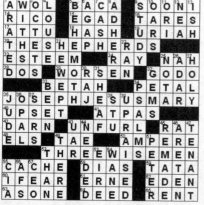

Some Parables of Jesus

Easter Discoveries

```
S E T A . R O M P . G R A S P
A T O M . E L I A . L E V E R
W A D I . T E L L . A G O R A
S T O N E R O L L E D A W A Y
. . . O N E . . . G E L . . .
G A S . C A L I C O . . A S S
E M P T Y T O M B . B E R E T
T I R E S . T E R . A L I V E
A G E N T . H E I S R I S E N
T O E . M E R G E R . E N S .
. . . S P A . . . D E E . . .
W H I T E C L A D A N G E L S
R O B O T . A L I T . E V I L
A B O V E . R E N E . S E M I
P O W E R . D E E D . T R A P
```

Celestial Signs of the End Times

```
S A W . M I C A H . N I G H
A M A H . A G O R A . I N R E
L I L Y . P O N D S . T S A R
E N D E D . . D E S C R I B E
M O O N I N T O B L O O D . .
. . . A S E A . . E U G E N E
U L E . P E R T . R E F E R .
S U N G O D O W N A T N O O N
E M E E R . D E L I . R N S .
S P R A T S . . U V E A . . .
. . G R E A T S T A R F E L L
E Y E B R U S H . . S T I L E
M O T O . C A R O B . E D A M
T R I X . E D E M A . R E M O
S E C . . S E D A N . . R A N
```

Miracles in Daniel

```
O N E S O . H A L E . P A S T
R E R U N . A N I L . E S A U
T H E F I E R Y F U R N A C E
. . . F O N D . E D E N . . .
T O L E N D . L I E D . G E E
A F A R . A M A S S . A R A Y
I T S . S L O B . A W A R E .
. . T H E L I O N S D E N . .
H A D A T . R O A D . I F A .
O R A M . A L E R T . A T A N
W A Y . S L I D . R E V E R T
. . T A L C . S A M E . . . .
M E N E T E K E L P A R S I N
I R A N . G E T A . I S T O O
D R Y S . E D O M . L E A N S
```

Miracles of Jesus

```
A P A R T . M S . S . A M E N
S A R A H . I T M E . L E V I
A R E N O . S I M I . E N E S
R A I S E D L A Z A R U S . .
. . . E N O L . E N T . . . .
G O A L I E . E A S Y . P B A
O M N I . . I D S . . P L O D
F E D F I V E T H O U S A N D
O G E E S . A H E M . A N N E
R A S . E S T E . B A T T E D
. . . B L T . S T R S . . . .
H E A L E D T H E S I C K . .
S O A R . P O O R . E N U R E
T U R N . O G R E . N O T I N
E R N S . N A M E . T R E S S
```

Egypt's Plagues

```
L A V A . O S S A . O F T A R
O V A L . N E L L . F O O L I
B O I L S F L I E S F R O G S
O W N . T O L T E C . A L A E
. . . T O O . . R E N D E R .
R I V E R T O B L O O D . . .
I R E N E . P E A L S . L A W
M A R S . T E N M L . B A L I
E N T . B A N E . C O U L D .
. . F I R S T B O R N D I E .
D I A L O G . . N E E . . . .
O S L O . E A T T H E . L I T
L O C U S T S H A I L L I C E
E N A T E . W A R M . A M A S
S E N S E . E T N A . D O N T
```

Jesus and the Sea

```
H O Y A S . T I B E T . P I T
O V E R T . O P E N A . A G E
W A L K I N G O N T H E S E A
I L L . L O R D . R O A S T S
. . . H E R O . W Y E S . . .
N O D E . W H O . . T A M E .
A N E M I A . I N U S . F A N
H E C A L M E D T H E W I N D
U S A . K A L E . F E A R T O
M O L E . M A T . D E A R . .
. . Z E U S . E T R E . . . .
M A N R A N . A L O E . S O W
A B O A T F U L L O F F I S H
Y E S . N I S A N . E R A S E
O D E . O T E R O . R O M A N
```

Donkey Business

```
A S A T # I S I F # L A M B S
L A T E # C A N I # A R O O T
A D O N K E Y S J A W B O N E
M A N S E # T O I L # A N E W
E T E # E G O # # A S H # # #
# # # S N O # W I S E # A D O
T H A I # W A R N # B A S E D
H I S D O N K E Y T A L K E D
E N T E R # A S E R # L I P S
E T O # C A N T # U S A # # #
# # # P A D # G E O # A M A #
A W A R # O D O R # H O R E B
R I D I N G O N A D O N K E Y
A F A C E # D U P E # O T T S
H E M E T # O P E N # R O S S
```

Signs and Wonders

```
J A I L # A P E D # B E A T
U N D O # B E M A # S L O T H
M I E N # S A U L # C O N E Y
P L A G U E S # E C H O # # #
Y E S # T I E # R E D S E A #
# # C A L # F R O M # E X T #
G R A P H # A R E N A # G A S
O A R S # E L O P E # L A M E
I B M # S M O G S # B A L S A
N B E # L E E S # G A G # # #
G I D E O N # S R I # E S E #
# # # D U D S # N A T I V E S
A N T I C # I C O N # C A R T
D E A T H # N O O N # E D G E
O W N S # E S P Y # D E E R #
```

Feeding the Hungry

```
A B R # B A S T # E L I J A H
P R E # R U L E # P O M A D E
P A N # I R O N # E N A M O R
A Z A L E A S # E E G # # # #
L I M O # S H O T # R E A L M
# L E A D # I W O # L E E # #
# # V I A # L O G # T O G A #
O B S E R V E # S L O W E S T
R O T S # E R A # E R E # # #
B O Y # R A G # E L A N # # #
S T E A L # S O B S # V E I L
# # B I N # R E F E R E E # #
E N G I N E # M I N I # A C V
A B O D E S # O D D S # T E E
R A V E N S # M E S H # E S E
```

Mud and Water

```
A M A S S # A C E S # B E D #
C A P I T A # D U S T # E V E
S P R E A D # Z I T I # D I P
# # # G L O B # S E R V A N T
C U E # L O S E # O U C H # #
A L A S # W I N E # G I B E S
L A # S A N E # E N D # # # #
I N S I P I D # E V A S I O N
# # # D I T # K N E W # C P U
P O S I T # B I R R # T O U T
I N T O # V E T O # M O N S #
G R O M M E T # L I E N # # #
O U R # A R T S # R E G A I N
U S E # I D E A # S T U C C O
T H Y # D I R T # S E V E N #
```

The Great Escape

```
N O E L # L A M B # C H A R
Y M C A # A L S O # A L I V E
M A L I # G O G H # R O P E D
P H A R A O H # R A G U # # #
H A T # B O A # P U D D L E #
# # D E N # F I R E # A I L #
S H E E T # F U R O R # M T V
T E L L # M A S O N # M E R E
O N E # W O M E N # M O S E S
I N C # E P E E # R O D # # #
C A T T L E # S E A # P E A #
# # # A D D S # W A N T I N G
R A M I E # H E A L # O V E R
U P E N D # E A R L # S O M E
G E N T # A R M Y # S T Y E #
```

Fire from Heaven

```
S A C # M A I L S # W A T E R
C U R # A F O O T # O L I V E
O R E # C A N T O # R O P E D
F O W L E R # N A T O # # # #
F R E E # S T E P # F A W N #
S A L T # C H O S E # P O I #
# # # S O D O M # A E S O P #
A C U A T E # B U L G E D # #
I N A P T # A L T A R # # # #
L T M # A G G I E # E B B S #
L E E S # D E E P # T R U E #
# # # M O O R # A B S U R D #
A A R O N # M A N N A # T E A
S H A K Y # A R E N A # E A T
L A T E X # N E W E L # S U E
```

The Master's Touch

ARC FAITH DEMOB
NOR ALONE EXILE
EMU MANTA JADED
MASTER LOAM
INTO DYER SICK
ASSN GRADE DOE
SPEAK AMONG
THIRTY LABILE
WHOLE BABEL
SEE ADAMS TALK
WEST BITE OBOE
OURS TENANT
JESUS ABEAM SET
APACE REALM ELL
BATHS MERCY DYE

Daddy, I'm Hungry

LAWS TEND THUD
OBOE ERIE LEASE
BEMA ROPE ORGAN
BLESSED PEAR
YEN ESE AVATAR
ALA WOVE IRE
BRAWL TAKES TIE
RILL BURRS CASK
ENE MANNA BONES
ASP ERAS BOY
DEHORN MEN EOS
FISH ASEPTIC
ALOFT OBIE RULE
HIRES PUNT EDEN
ABBR EYES PERT

The Synagogue Leader's Daughter

SSW RAHAB CSI
POEM IDEAL DOOR
ALPS MORSE EURO
NOTTHERE SHAPEN
ODE TAT
NEWS DEY SHAG
DAMSEL DOG DOA
AVOW ARGUE DOWN
YET DUE THORNY
LEVI EST ERNS
END WPA
GEMINI HEARTENS
UPON ATALL OLEA
LESS NERVE TOOK
LET ANDES NNE

The Sick Woman Is Healed

URGE THING CAB
ROUGH HOSEA OWL
STAGE ABLER LAO
AER ARNO METRO
ALEK PRESSED
SPADED THINE
AILED RIFT WKS
REAR THULE VIIII
ADS THAT OILED
POACH TWELVE
SPELUNK WIND
HAVOC DALE AMA
APE HOURS ROBES
PAR EATUP SPEAK
ELY DREGS ELLS

Jesus Walks on Water

STAFF THAT HELP
HINDU HATH IDEA
ALTAR ALEE RENT
WEE LANE STINTS
CORK HEN
IALONE CLINGTO
THING SHOP OPR
TINES TIU ASSHE
ORE WIND SPEND
ANCHORS AFRAID
EAR PLOY
DAMASK VEER ERE
ICES INIT ENTER
ARNE NENE SONAR
SEED GOER TRAPS

The Healing of the Boy with Seizures

TARE STALK HAD
STING HEMAN IRE
ATSEA ARAME REM
RYE RADM ERATO
PLIE SOLOMON
SPIRIT HOPED
LILAC USED BRA
ALLY SIMON BRAD
YES NEMO FAITH
SONAR FOAMED
HISBODY DOLL
ASIAN SEED MNO
SAG DIVAN ESAUS
TAN AKISS DOUBT
ECS YEAHE WISE

SCRAMBLED CIRCLES

AH, HINDSIGHT
He should have ducked. Who was he?
GOLIATH
1. GREAT 2. HORSES 3. JEALOUS 4. MIDST 5. JERUSALEM
6. PLUMMET 7. HOSTS

A STORY FOR THE GRANDKIDS
A pile of stones would serve as a way to remember a special event.
MEMORIAL
1. CONSUMED 2. MOCKED 3. MOUNT 4. ALLEGORY 5. TUTORS
6. MANIFEST 7. WEARY 8. FLESH

WOULD *YOU* WANT THIS JOB?
Jesus acted as His disciples' servant.
WASHED THEIR FEET
1. TOWEL 2. GARMENTS 3. HAND 4. HEAD 5. ASIDE 6. WATER
7. HOUR 8. WIPE 9. GIRDED 10. FEAST 11. SUPPER 12. PART

A BIG FISH TALE
Jesus made reference to this slimy story.
JONAH and the WHALE
1. JESUS 2. SWORD 3. NETHER 4. LAMENT 5. PHARAOH 6. DWELT
7. TWELFTH 8. SLAIN 9. FALLEN 10. MULTITUDE

SLAVE LABOR
Who sold Joseph to Potiphar in Egypt?
THE MIDIANITES
1. INFORM 2. FINISH 3. DESTROY 4. BUILT 5. DESOLATE
6. ABOMINATION 7. MIGHTY 8. AGAINST 9. LEASE 10. VISION

LOST AND FOUND
A young boy was found here.
TEMPLE
1. SOUGHT 2. FEAST 3. AMAZED 4. COMPANY 5. KINSFOLK
6. BUSINESS

THE SPACE-TIME CONTINUUM
As their eyes were opened, Jesus did this.
VANISHED
1. BELIEVE 2. TARRY 3. FURLONGS 4. VISION 5. STRANGER
6. SEPULCHRE 7. COMMUNED 8. EXPOUNDED

ORDER UP!
This was found on the ground, but it was good for eating.
MANNA
1. TEMPLES 2. PASTURE 3. GARMENTS 4. NORTHERN 5. VALLEY

SURPRISE VISIT
An angel of the Lord appeared here.
BURNING BUSH
1. JEBUSITES 2. CONSUMED 3. DESERT 4. GROUND 5. PRIEST
6. LAND 7. NIGH 8. JACOB 9. TURNED 10. ASIDE 11. BEHOLD

WATERLOGGED
In the beginning, there was nothing to separate the water, until God
created it. What was it?
EXPANSE
1. CONSUME 2. EXALT 3. PLEASURE 4. SERVANT 5. ANSWER
6. WORSHIP 7. PASTURE

OBEYING JESUS
Jesus rebuked this to come out.
UNCLEAN SPIRIT
1. AUTHORITY 2. QUESTIONED 3. DOCTRINE 4. LOUD 5. OBEY
6. PEACE 7. ASTONISHED 8. SYNAGOGUE 9. SPREAD
10. SCRIBES 11. REGION 12. TORN

KNOWING YOUR BIBLE
What is it that all believers will experience?
RESURRECTION
1. NEAR 2. GREEN 3. SIEGE 4. RULERS 5. GIRDLES 6. SISTER
7. DERISION 8. CONTAIN 9. SCATTER 10. PITY 11. HOUSE
12. HEATHEN

ANAGRAMS

IMPORTANT LOCALES
NINEVEH, MOUNT ARARAT, DAMASCUS

MORE IMPORTANT LOCALES
GARDEN OF EDEN, JERICHO, MOUNT OF OLIVES

SCENES FROM THE EXODUS
PLAGUE OF BLOOD, DEATH OF FIRSTBORN, PARTING OF RED SEA

JESUS WAS HERE
LAST SUPPER, TRANSFIGURATION, ASCENSION

MOSES' STORY
MOUNT SINAI, GOLDEN CALF, BURNING BUSH

ELIJAH'S CHALLENGE
MOUNT CARMEL, PROPHETS OF BAAL, EVENING SACRIFICE

CREATION
DARKNESS, GARDEN OF EDEN, BREATH OF LIFE

AFTER THE RESURRECTION
DOUBTING THOMAS, ROAD TO EMMAUS, THE ASCENSION

MIRACLE TOOLS
HANDKERCHIEFS; FIVE LOAVES, TWO FISH; SIX WATER POTS

HEALED BY JESUS
TEN LEPERS, DAUGHTER OF JAIRUS, CENTURION'S SERVANT

SPOTTY HEADLINES

BATTLE STORIES
JOSHUA, ABSALOM, PHARAOH

GOVERNMENT INTRIGUE
HEROD, PILATE, DANIEL

THEY MET JESUS
SIMEON, ZACCHAEUS, NICODEMUS

RUINED LIVES
ACHAN, ANANIAS, JUDAS

STORIES OF THE MIRACULOUS
SAUL, BARTIMAEUS, PETER

HUSBANDS AND WIVES
JOSEPH, PILATE, LOT

DISCIPLES AND THE MIRACULOUS
SIMON PETER, THOMAS, ANDREW

MEDICAL MIRACLES
PAUL, TABITHA, LAZARUS

MIRACULOUS LEPROSY
NAAMAN, MIRIAM, UZZIAH

MIRACLE MISCELLANY
ELISHA, ISAIAH, ELIJAH

OLD TESTAMENT MIRACLE MEN
JONAH, GIDEON, BALAAM

MISSIONARY MIRACLES
SILAS, PUBLIUS, ELYMAS

TELEPHONE SCRAMBLES

CONVERSIONS
PAUL, RUTH, SAMUEL, CENTURION, PUBLICAN, ABRAHAM, CANAANITE

THANKS FOR YOUR HELP
TYRANNUS, SAMARITAN, CYRUS, JONATHAN, OBADIAH, SHOBI, ABINADAB

SOUND THE TRUMPETS
PRAISE, JERICHO, WARNING, ZION, ANGELS, JUBILEE, EPHRAIM, GATHER

CURSED
CAIN, CANAAN, GROUND, NATURE, SERPENT, JUDAH

ALLEGORIES
HAGAR, LIONESS, SARAH, VINE, VINEYARD, GOMER

IN THE LAND OF PHARAOH
NILE, FAMINE, RED SEA, SLAVERY, SARAI, JOSEPH, MIRIAM, DREAMS

DIVINE REPORTS OF CHRIST'S BIRTH
ANNA, ELIZABETH, JOSEPH, MARY, SHEPHERDS, SIMEON, ZACHARIAS

HEALINGS
SILOAM, ROOFTOP, BLIND, LEPERS, DEMONIC, NAAMAN, SERVANT

MIRACLES CONCERNING ELIJAH
RAVENS, WHIRLWIND, CLOAK, RAIN, DEAD, CHARIOT, BAAL

MISCELLANEOUS MIRACLES
EUTYCHUS, JAIRUS, LOAVES, FLEECE, ENOCH, FURNACE, DONKEY

MIRACLES CONCERNING WATER
ROCK, WINE, PARTED, WALKING, STORM, JORDAN, NETS

MIRACULOUS EVENTS
BABEL, PENTECOST, JERICHO, PROPHETIC, PLAGUES, RAPTURE, MARY

BIBLE QUOTATIONS

TESTED BY FIRE

"He answered and said, Lo, I see four men loose, walking in the midst of the fire, and they have no hurt; and the form of the fourth is like the Son of God." Daniel 3:25

AN EVEN EXCHANGE

"Behold behind him a ram caught in a thicket by his horns: and Abraham went and took the ram, and offered him up for a burnt offering in the stead of his son." Genesis 22:13

DON'T LOOK BACK!

"But his wife looked back from behind him, and she became a pillar of salt." Genesis 19:26

THE BEST BIRTHDAY EVER

"For unto you is born this day in the city of David a Saviour, which is Christ the Lord." Luke 2:11

ANSWERED PRAYER

"Wherefore it came to pass, when the time was come about after Hannah had conceived, that she bare a son, and called his name Samuel, saying, Because I have asked him of the LORD." 1 Samuel 1:20

A MEMORABLE MEAL

"This is my body which is given for you: this do in remembrance of me. Likewise also the cup after supper, saying, This cup is the new testament in my blood, which is shed for you." Luke 22:19–20

A MIRACLE ON A MOUNTAIN

"Jesus taketh with him Peter, and James, and John, and leadeth them up into an high mountain apart by themselves: and he was transfigured before them." Mark 9:2

A SON RETURNED TO HIS MOTHER

"He came and touched the bier: and they that bare him stood still. And he said, Young man, I say unto thee, Arise. And he that was dead sat up, and began to speak." Luke 7:14–15

HIS GOD PROTECTED HIM

"Said Daniel unto the king, O king, live for ever. My God hath sent his angel, and hath shut the lions' mouths, that they have not hurt me." Daniel 6:21–22

SUDDENLY FREE!

"The angel of the Lord came upon him, and a light shined in the prison: and he smote Peter on the side, and raised him up, saying, Arise up quickly. And his chains fell off from his hands." Acts 12:7

TAKING A LAST LOOK

"Men of Galilee, why stand ye gazing up into heaven? this same Jesus, which is taken up from you into heaven, shall so come in like manner as ye have seen him go into heaven." Acts 1:11

THE LORD LEADS HIS PEOPLE

"The LORD went before them by day in a pillar of a cloud, to lead them the way; and by night in a pillar of fire, to give them light; to go by day and night." Exodus 13:21

MORE GREAT BIBLE PUZZLES!

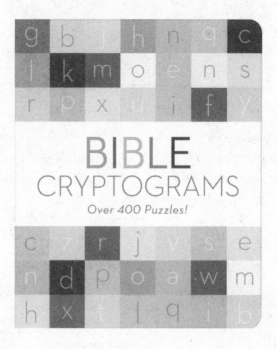

Drawn from the King James Version, these 404 cryptograms each provide a brief passage featuring substituted letters that you'll need to decode to solve the verse. Covering the people, places, things, and ideas of scripture, Bible Cryptograms will entertain and educate you, delivering important Bible truths in an enjoyable puzzle package.

Paperback / 978-1-64352-733-8 / $12.99